The Defence of Worcestershire

and the southern approaches to Birmingham

in World War II

The Defence of Worcestershire

and the southern approaches to Birmingham

in World War II

by

Mick Wilks

Logaston Press

LOGASTON PRESS
Little Logaston Woonton Almeley
Herefordshire HR3 6QH
logastonpress.co.uk

First published by Logaston Press 2007

ISBN 978 1904396 80 2

Typeset by Logaston Press
and printed in Great Britain by
Bell and Bain Ltd., Glasgow

Contents

Acknowledgements

Much credit is due to the Worcestershire Historic Environment and Archaeology Service (WHEAS), and particularly Malcolm Atkin, the County Archaeology Officer, who provided the initial impetus for recording modern defence sites in the county and the administrative backing for it. There is no doubt that the success of the project locally has been due in no small measure to his support and that of his staff, together with the provision of working space by the Archaeology Service that has became a focus for contributors to the study.

Particular thanks are due to Colin Jones, a fellow volunteer in Worcestershire who, in addition to recording many of the sites, is the County Coordinator for the Defence of Worcestershire Project and has created the local computerised database and paper files of defence information for the Historic Environment Record, as well as keeping I and the other volunteers informed and coordinated.

Bernard Lowry who was the Midlands Region Coordinator for the Defence of Britain Project, has been especially helpful and supportive since the beginning of my involvement in defence site recording, and continues still to provide both Colin and I with great friendship, much support and good advice. I must also acknowledge the contributions of Jim Earle, William Foot, John Hellis, Dr Mike Osborne and Dr William Ward, all stalwarts of the original Defence of Britain Project who, over the years, have given me, and my colleagues in Worcestershire, much help and guidance on the subject of military defences.

Thanks are also due to the other local volunteer researchers and contributors who either provided information for the project or pointed us to many of the sites, most notably: the late Ivor Ashman, Michael Barnard, Alan Bassett, Sam Beard, Hal Bethall, Brian Boulby, Brian Brazier, Clive Brooks, Ron Bubb, Les Budd, Pat Burrage, the late Sandy Clarke, Sandy Coates, John Collett, the late Bob Cross, Ken Davis, Pat Dunn, Sheila Edmunds, Gill Edwards, Sam Eedle, Gerry Evans, Graham Evans, Huby Fairhead, Marion Freeman, Philida Gardner, David Guyatt, Stuart Hadaway, Janet Hames, John Hancox, Keith Hartwell, Jack Hawks, Brian Heatley, Ray Holden, Joy Ingram, Mary Jakeman, the late Maurice Jones, Mike Johnson, Bill Kings, Peter Knight, John Lane, Peter Lippett, the late Maurice Loynes, Wilf Mound, the late Howard Miller, Margaret Must, Geoff Neil, Kirsty Nichol, Jack Oliver, Brian Orme, Tom Padgett, Brian Parker, John Percer, Bernard and Olive Poultney, Vernon Pratt, Angela and Charles Purcell, Dr Ernest Putley, Gordon Rae, Mick Ricketts, Jo Roche, the late John Sanders (of Ombersley), John V. Sanders (of Stourbridge), the late Leyland Shawe, the late Derek Smith, Don Southall, the late Peter Skidmore, Paul Stokes, Steve Southwick, Neville Taylor, Steve Taylor, Don Tomlin, Peter Trevett, Alan Turner, Rudy Vitkovskis, Major Ward RE, Marie-Louise Wardle, Mike Watkins, Mike Webster, Bill Weston, Simon Wilkinson, Bettie Williams, Dr Dennis Williams and David

Wynn, together with many other local people, too numerous to list, who have provided small but nevertheless important clues on defence sites in the county.

I should also like to thank the staffs of the County Record Office, the Almonry Museum at Evesham, Bewdley Museum, Malvern Museum, Pershore Heritage Centre, Tenbury Museum, Worcester City Museums Service, as well as the various branches of the County Library in Worcestershire, for their help and guidance in tracking down local defence information. In addition, the local history societies of Alvechurch, Bewdley, Cookley and Wolverley, Crowle, Feckenham, Hagley, together with the Black Country Society and the Kidderminster and Stourport Civic Societies, have given much assistance. The successive Regimental Secretaries and their staff, both full time and voluntary, at the Worcestershire and Sherwood Foresters Regimental Headquarters, Norton Barracks, together with the Chairman and Trustees of the Worcestershire Regiment Museum, have been particularly welcoming and helpful over a long period of time. Latterly, the staff at the former Army Medal Office at Droitwich, were most helpful in allowing me to consult Home Guard personnel files then held by them.

Further afield, I must also acknowledge the help given to me by the staff at the Imperial War Museum, Lambeth, the staff at the National Archive (formerly the Public Record Office) at Kew, the RAF Museum at Hendon, the Dudley Records Centre, as well as the volunteer staff at the Museum of British Resistance at Parham, most notably John Warwicker.

The local media have from time to time provided much needed publicity for the project which, in turn, led to contact with other contributors to the study. These include the BBC Hereford and Worcester Radio, *Black Country Bugle*, *Evesham Journal*, *Malvern Gazette*, *Redditch Advertiser* the *Wolverhampton Express and Star*, and the *Worcester News*. Special thanks are due to the late John Yates, of BBC Midlands Today who, in making a short news programme about our work, enabled some key contacts to be made with members of the British Resistance Organisation.

The following Home Guardsmen and women, and members of the British resistance, or relatives of such men and women, have all shared with me their memories of wartime Worcestershire and I hope more will come forward with information, while there is time. Sadly, some of the people listed have passed away, since I met them, and so I am very pleased to have recorded at least a part of their life experiences for posterity.

Bill Alliband, Bill Allington, Jack Ankers, the late John Annis, Don Archer, David and Judith Ashcroft, Mary Ashfield, Ivor Atkinson, Major John Bailey, Eric Barber, the late John Barker, the late Dr Tony Barling, David Barton, the late Chris Bayliss, Sam Beard, Gordon Bennett, John Bennett, Michael Bingham, John Boaz, the late John Bone, Mr J.M. Bowden, George Briney, Robert Brown, Mary Bulgin, the late Chris Bullock, Dennis Burrows, Edwina Burton, Dennis Chance, John Chater, Jack Clements, Jim Colebrook, Frank Cox, the late Colin Curnock, Roger Curtiss, Bert Davies, Norman Davies, Geoff Devereux, Eric Doughty, Sheila Edmunds, Norman Fairfax, John Fernihough, Harry Fisher, Wilf Gamble, Egbert Ganderton, Mrs Andrew Green, Jim Griffin, Geoff Gurney, Vera Hale, Doug Harries, Keith Hartwell, Gwen Harvey, Tom Harwood, Bill Hay, Les Haynes, Tom Healey, June Hebden, Ron and Jan Henshall, Stuart Hill, Vic Holloway, Jim Holt, Horace Hooper, Llyn James, Desmond Jasper, Bill Jauncey, Lavender and Michael Jones, Lt Colonel Pat Love, Joe Kennedy, Joe King, Bill Kings, Sir Reginald Lechmere, the late Jack Leighton, Richard Mills, Shirley Marler (née van Moppes), George Marshman, the late Fred

Mayo, Ted McGee, Mrs Angus McGregor (née Ashton, via Jo Roche), Margaret Merrick, Jack Miles, Richard Mills, Arthur Minett, Les Moore, Pamela Van Moppes, Mrs C. Morris, Robin Moram, Wilf Mound, Geoff Neil, Tom Padgett, Derrick Pearson, the late Dick Philips, Horace Phillips, Keith Porter, George Pitman, Bill Preece, Toby Preston, Jack Pritchard, Dr Ernest Putley, Stan Ratcliffe, Maurice Reynolds, John Rowberry, the late John Sanders, Ron Seymour, the late Leyland Shawe, John Smith, the late Harvey Southall, the late Charles Stallard, John Stephens, Pam Stubbs, Marion Szczesniak, the late Basil and Ruth Tadman, Jim Terry, the late John Thornton, Albert Tolley, the late Albert Toon, the late Gerry Tysoe, the late George Vater, the late Mr Waldron, Joan Warren, David Westley-Smith, Albert Wharrad (via Mike Johnson), Tim White, Joseph Whitehead, Robin Whittaker, Wilfred Widdows, Harold Wilkins, the family of Reg Wilkinson, David Williams, Reg Wiltshire, Tim and Mrs Wood, Peter Wright, J. Wyle, and John Wythes.

My late uncle, Howard Inight, has unknowingly contributed a great deal to this account from beyond the grave. After serving in tanks at the beginning of the war, he became a member of IS9, a branch of MI9, who were responsible for helping allied aircrew who were evading the Germans and escaped POWs return to Britain. His operational involvement with the organisation was during the period immediately after the D-Day landings and then during the rest of the campaign in North-West Europe. He and his colleagues were sometimes operating behind the enemy lines to rescue evaders. He did much to stimulate my interest in military matters, long before my involvement in the Defence of Britain Project, by providing me with many captured German photographs.

I must sincerely thank the remainder of my close family and friends for enduring the long silences while I was working on the project, and the absences while researching local defences or interviewing contributors. My son and probably many others too circumspect to say, consider that my interest in old concrete to be a little strange, but I think its harmless fun and it gives me immense pleasure! I hope you, the reader, find it of interest too.

Finally, I thank Andy Johnson of Logaston Press for turning my grossly over-long draft into a more readable account and publishing the results.

If I have left anyone out, I apologise. This account has been a long time coming and my memory is not what it was!

Foreword

The author has been researching defence sites in Worcestershire for a number of years, most notably those defences put in place to resist a threatened German invasion from the summer of 1940 onwards. This work came about following early retirement and, as a volunteer researcher with the County Archaeological Service, becoming involved in the Defence of Britain Project. This national project relied on local volunteers to research and record 20th-century defence sites in each county.

The Project was established in 1995 by the Council for British Archaeology, with support from a number of government heritage agencies and was a response to widespread concern that the tangible remains of the sites used for defence during some of our most momentous days were fast disappearing. The original intention was to record all forms of civil and military defence sites but subsequently the effort of the volunteers was directed to recording anti-invasion defences in order to achieve as comprehensive a survey as possible of this one aspect before the project came to an end in March 2002. There was still much to record in the county at that time and so the project was re-launched as a local initiative by the County Archaeology Service, but now called the Defence of Worcestershire Project. The scope has been widened again to record all forms of defence site and the time scale extended to include the 18th and 19th centuries, although most sites relate to World War II. It is this latter period that I find most interesting, and in order to better understand the significance of local sites, my own research was widened to include national defence strategies and the wider European armed conflict that influenced them.

In Worcestershire, defence sites are recorded both electronically and in paper form on the Historic Environment Record (HER) held by the Archaeology Service. At the time of writing there are some 2,000 individual defence sites recorded for Worcestershire. When the project to record them started in 1995, a significant number of the defence sites had already disappeared but, to create as complete a survey as possible, lost sites are being recorded to give an indication of what could once be seen in the county. This process of clearance still continues, indeed national and local planning policies encourage the re-use of so-called 'brown-field sites' for new development and redundant defence sites are targeted for new development. In the following account and in order to illustrate certain aspects of defence, now gone, it has been considered appropriate to include photographs from elsewhere. I hope the preceding acknowledgements adequately reflect the contributions of memories and historic photographs of many people to the project.

Before becoming involved in the Defence of Britain Project I, like probably many others, thought that Worcestershire was something of a military backwater, with little happening other than the various battalions of The Worcestershire Regiment training in the area or going off to garrison duty in the empire, or to fight abroad. At the same time the popular *Dads Army* television series colours the impression most people have of what the Home Guard might have done during World War II. I now know that Worcestershire was the scene of much military activity and complex preparations for defence should a German invasion have occurred, and included the recruitment and training of a resistance organisation. This intriguing aspect of the defence has already been the subject of a book published in 2002 by Logaston Press and entitled *The Mercian Maquis*. This present volume provides the opportunity to bring up to date that particular aspect of defence research, as well as to set out what has been recorded of the more conventional military defences in the county during the period 1940 to 1944. This date range has been deliberately chosen to reflect the start of the main period of anti-invasion defence development in Worcestershire during the summer of 1940, enhancement in 1941, maintenance in 1942, and the start of dismantling in 1943 and 1944.

During World War II, the county was geographically considerably larger than it is now and included the boroughs of Dudley, Halesowen, Oldbury and Stourbridge. For the sake of historic completeness therefore I have included such information on defences in those areas that I have been able to glean from my research. I will be the first to say that there is much more to find out about that part of the historic county.

Investigating defence sites for the project has brought me into contact with a significant number of former Home Guardsmen and women in the county. It has been a privilege to have spoken to this dwindling group of men, and smaller number of women, who gave up so much of their spare time to train and ready themselves for the expected invasion, or to protect key facilities against enemy 'spoiling' attacks. It has become fashionable to denigrate the efforts of the Home Guard, so this account provides the opportunity to put the record straight and to properly reflect the effort put into their preparations for battle and describe their place in the defence of Worcestershire. A brief summary of the history and role of the Home Guard in the county is included in Chapter 11, but it is intended to produce a much fuller history of the force, as a further volume, in due course.

In the course of researching the role of the Home Guard, I have become aware that there is a very limited number of their official documents still surviving. In the Worcestershire area particularly, there seems to have been a wholesale destruction of military orders and defence schemes at the end of the war that has made the task of researching the defence of the county more challenging. Where defence plans have survived they are reproduced in the following account. However, it is likely that a vitally important documentary resource relating to the defence of the county is still held by former Home Guards, or their families. These documents may include photographs, notebooks, papers on the organisation of the Home Guard and sometimes the defence plans for specific localities. These are now precious and irreplaceable and sadly many have already been thrown away as being thought to be of little interest or importance. On the contrary, they are of great interest and value to researchers, and I would urge anyone considering disposing of such documents to deposit them with the County Record Office at County Hall or at least allow them to be copied by the Defence of Worcestershire Project team.

What you will read on the subsequent pages is therefore not the whole account by any means, but is an attempt to set out what has been discovered so far, and will hopefully act to tease out more of the story. Anyone with information on individual sites or memories of the war years is encour-

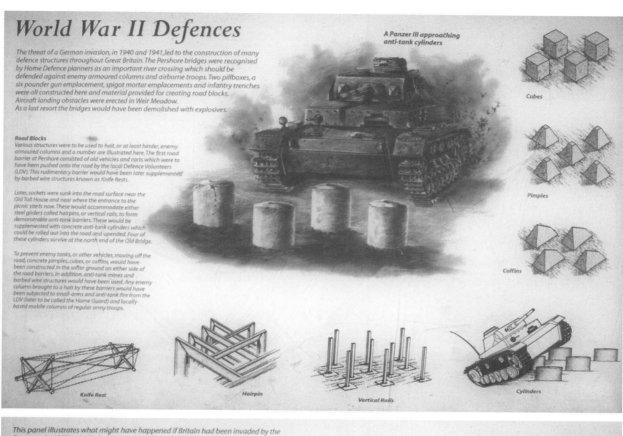

World War II Defences

The threat of a German invasion, in 1940 and 1941, led to the construction of many defence structures throughout Great Britain. The Pershore bridges were recognised by Home Defence planners as an important river crossing which should be defended against enemy armoured columns and airborne troops. Two pillboxes, a six pounder gun emplacement, spigot mortar emplacements and infantry trenches were all constructed here and material provided for creating road blocks. Aircraft landing obstacles were erected in Weir Meadow. As a last resort the bridges would have been demolished with explosives.

Road Blocks

Various structures were to be used to halt, or at least hinder, enemy armoured columns and a number are illustrated here. The first road barrier at Pershore consisted of old vehicles and carts which were to have been pushed onto the road by the local Defence Volunteers (LDV). This rudimentary barrier would have been later supplemented by barbed wire structures known as Knife Rests.

Later, sockets were sunk into the road surface near the Old Toll House and near where the entrance to the picnic site is now. These would accommodate either steel girders called hairpins, or vertical rails, to form demonstrable anti-tank barriers. These would be supplemented with concrete anti-tank cylinders which could be rolled out into the road and upended. Four of these cylinders survive at the north end of the Old Bridge.

To prevent enemy tanks, or other vehicles, moving off the road, concrete pimples, cubes, or coffins, would have been constructed in the softer ground on either side of the road barriers. In addition, anti-tank mines and barbed wire structures would have been used. Any enemy column brought to a halt by these barriers would have been subjected to small-arms and anti-tank fire from the LDV (later to be called the Home Guard) and locally based mobile columns of regular army troops.

A Panzer III approaching anti-tank cylinders

Cubes

Pimples

Coffins

Knife Rest

Hairpin

Vertical Rails

Cylinders

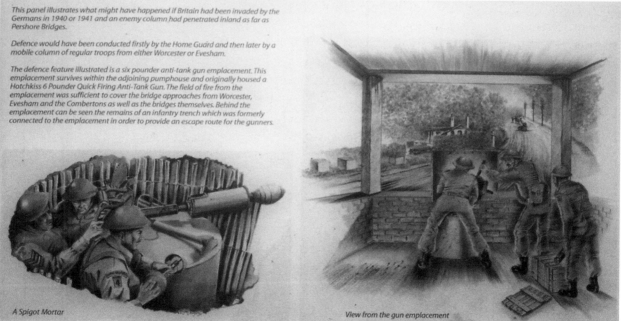

This panel illustrates what might have happened if Britain had been invaded by the Germans in 1940 or 1941 and an enemy column had penetrated inland as far as Pershore Bridges.

Defence would have been conducted firstly by the Home Guard and then later by a mobile column of regular troops from either Worcester or Evesham.

The defence feature illustrated is a six pounder anti-tank gun emplacement. This emplacement survives within the adjoining pumphouse and originally housed a Hotchkiss 6 Pounder Quick Firing Anti-Tank Gun. The field of fire from the emplacement was sufficient to cover the bridge approaches from Worcester, Evesham and the Combertons as well as the bridges themselves. Behind the emplacement can be seen the remains of an infantry trench which was formerly connected to the emplacement in order to provide an escape route for the gunners.

A Spigot Mortar

View from the gun emplacement

Worcestershire County Council have provided interpretation boards at the Pershore Bridges Picnic Place to help visitors understand the significance of the surviving defence structures

aged to contact myself via the publisher or the Defence of Worcestershire Project, Worcestershire Historic Environment and Archaeology Service, Woodbury, University of Worcester, Henwick Grove, Worcester. WR2 6AJ, telephone 01905 855455.

Worcestershire County Council has drawn attention to the importance of the surviving World War II defences at the Pershore Bridges picnic place by providing information panels describing them for the benefit of the visiting public. There is growing evidence in the county of local people preserving the modern defence heritage. If the information collected by the volunteer researchers in Worcestershire result in more of the local defence sites being preserved for future generations to see, understand and appreciate, then our efforts in recording them will have been rewarded.

In the succeeding pages I have identified a number of specific defence structures that remain. Many are on private land, and these should not be viewed from close-quarters without first obtaining permission from the owners to enter the property. In fact, some are still operational and 'sensitive' sites that cannot be visited on a casual basis anyway. Other structures are now in a dangerous condition and so there is also an element of risk in exploring them. Therefore, if you feel the need to look at surviving defence structures, I urge you to be courteous to landowners and careful in your exploration. Many of the sites can, however, be viewed from public roads or rights of way and to help the reader locate sites, I have provided 6 figure Ordnance Survey grid references based on the OS Landranger Series of 1:50,000 scale maps.

CHAPTER 1

Lessons from war on the Continent

The rebuilding of the German armed forces and, in particular, the creation of a large air force by the Nazis in defiance of the Versailles Treaty that had ended World War I, alerted British defence planners to the risk of air attack. The destruction of Guernica in April 1937, by German 'Condor Legion' aircraft, during the Spanish Civil War, seemed to confirm the power of the bomber. The limited British defence expenditure was consequently skewed in favour of the Royal Air Force and the need for parity in the air began the so-called expansion period for the RAF with the development of many new airfields and other support and training establishments. This resulted in a significant increase in both bomber and fighter squadrons as well as, crucially, the development of an early warning system based on the use of the volunteer Observer Corps and radar. Evacuation schemes, particularly of children from major urban areas, the creation of a civil defence organisation and casualty treatment facilities, the issue of gas masks, provision of gas decontamination centres, construction of air raid shelters were all planned for in anticipation of an air attack and the use of poison gas. The relocation of key armaments industries to the relative safety of the West Midlands was started under the shadow factory scheme.

Meanwhile the British Army, strapped for cash, doubled the number of Territorial units in 1939 and was reluctantly prepared to repeat the 1914 model, by becoming once again primarily a continental Expeditionary Force to join the French in resisting any German expansion plans.

Up until September 1939, Hitler's territorial gains had been largely achieved by diplomacy, backed by the threat of force, and policies of appeasement by the other major European powers, but the direct attack on Poland at the beginning of the month introduced to Europe new techniques of warfare that superseded all that had gone before and created an impression of invincibility.

Restricted in size by the Versailles Treaty, the German General Staff had studied very closely advanced warfare theory, including that, ironically, propounded in Britain by Captain Liddell Hart and General Fuller. While arch-conservatism in the British Army, and financial stringency, had prevented the ideas being adopted here, the Germans recognised the value of concentrated offensive action with highly mobile armoured columns, preceded by dive-bombing aircraft used as close support artillery, to provide deep penetration to the rear of any front or defence line. To surprise and speed of operation the Germans added noise and extreme violence to terrorise and demoralise both opposition troops and the civilian population. The bombing of towns and villages

1

in advance of the armoured columns, the Germans had predicted, would cause refugees to flock onto the roads and obstruct the movements of the defending army. Aircraft machine-gunning the columns of refugees added to the confusion.

As well as these direct forms of warfare, the Germans were also to exploit Nazi-sympathisers within the nations being attacked to form what became known as the 'Fifth Column'. This term was first used by the Nationalist General Mola during the Spanish Civil War. Mola had boasted that, in his attack on the Republican held Madrid, he had four columns marching on the capital and a fifth column within the city. Prior to the attack on Poland on 1 September 1939, the Germans had used radio to incite the German-speaking Poles within the areas ceded to Poland following the Versailles Treaty to help the advancing troops by clearing obstructions, reporting on Polish ambush preparations, cutting Polish communications, carrying out guerrilla operations and spreading defeatist propaganda. Arms had been smuggled onto Poland from Rumania by the Abwehr, the German military intelligence organisation, for use by these '*Volksdeutsche*'.

The Polish Army was poorly equipped to withstand the German attack on 1 September, had only a small air force and was severely disadvantaged by its geography. Yet the Germans did not have success everywhere. Once the initial shock of the German tactics had been absorbed, the Poles managed to inflict some significant losses on the advancing German columns using local defence units, while the attack on Warsaw was successfully halted for a while with severe losses to the Germans. During this campaign tanks appeared to be especially vulnerable and of limited effect in well defended urban areas, a factor that would influence the future plans for the defence of Britain.

After the Polish campaign, Britain continued to expand the Royal Air Force in anticipation of an air attack and blockaded Germany with its superior naval forces, while France preferred to continue its primarily defensive strategy, sit behind the Maginot Line, and await an attack. In this the French were aided by the newly formed British Expeditionary Force, that had taken up positions along part of the French border with Belgium and was digging trenches and building pillboxes to belatedly extend the Maginot defences westwards and create again the Western Front of the previous war. These and subsequent actions of the BEF were to be largely controlled by the French General Staff.

The German attack on Denmark and the occupation of the key ports of Norway in the early hours of 9 April 1940 came without any formal declaration of war. Both of these countries had previously announced their neutrality, and were consequently almost totally unprepared for war and certainly not in the form that they now faced. Denmark offered no resistance and was over-run by the Germans within 24 hours by just two motorised brigades. Meanwhile troops hidden on five separate groups of German warships and merchant vessels sailed into Norwegian harbours and achieved almost complete surprise. Oslo was the key objective where, using landings from the sea coordinated with parachute attacks and airborne troop landings, the Germans hoped to capture King Haaken and the Norwegian parliament and bring about a quick capitulation. The Norwegian radio station in Oslo was used by Vidkun Quisling, a Norwegian collaborator and leader of the Norwegian National Socialist Party, to announce that he had now formed the responsible government, and to order that the mobilisation of Norwegian forces be stopped. Ever-after Quisling became the generic term for a collaborator.

Anglo-French landings were belatedly made on the Norwegian coast with forces too weak and poorly armed to resist the German forces advancing northwards. The Allied forces were then evacuated from Norway in early June when disaster overtook the French in their own country and Britain too was threatened with a direct attack. King Haaken and his ministers left Narvik with the British forces and the Norwegian capitulation followed soon afterwards.

The disastrous handling of the Norwegian campaign did much to undermine the authority of Neville Chamberlain and was to lead to his resignation and replacement by Winston Churchill on 10 May. A number of lessons would, however, be learnt from the Norwegian debacle and would influence the defence of Britain:

- the possibility of separate but coordinated attacks from both sea and air;
- the need to defend airfields against airborne attack;
- the need to defend radio stations to prevent their use by the enemy;
- an earlier scheme for evacuating both government and Royal family from London became more relevant.

The attack by Germany on Holland, Belgium and France on 10 May found the allied forces wanting again. The German attacks were cleverly coordinated to disguise the main strategy and having out-manoeuvred the major allied forces, the campaign was quickly concluded.

The invasion of Holland was launched at 3 am. One hour after conventional ground troops had crossed the frontier, paratroops were dropped in large numbers in the west of the country, while the majority of the Dutch Army held the forward defence lines to the east. German para-troops also succeeded in capturing bridges, including those over the River Maas where they were

In any airborne attack, Junkers Ju 52 aircraft, as illustrated here, delivered the first enemy parachutists, quickly followed by more of these aircraft bringing air landed troops onto any captured landing ground. (Courtesy of the late Howard Inight)

aided by troops brought in by floatplanes that had landed on the river. The attack on the Hague was intended to capture Queen Wilhelmina and her government and so hasten a Dutch capitulation. Here, as in Oslo, the German plans were not successful.

The initial landings in Holland by Junkers Ju 52 aircraft had been a costly operation for the Luftwaffe, with two-thirds of the 430 aircraft used being written off or at least not returning to Germany. The Dutch airfields were littered with the wreckage of these aircraft leading to an assumption in Britain that German pilots were deliberately reckless when it came to landing troops and would crash land rather than find somewhere else more suitable to put down.

The capture of one of the Dutch bridges, at Gennep, was achieved by men of the Brandenburg Regiment dressed as Dutch policemen who were able to surprise and overpower the guard before the bridge could be destroyed. This was one of 40 successful operations by this regiment on the Belgian/Dutch border. Subterfuge was clearly another element of German warfare. However, it was the bombardment from the air and destruction of the centre of Rotterdam, on 14 May, together with the threat of similar action at The Hague and Amsterdam that persuaded the Commander in Chief of the Dutch forces to capitulate that day. Queen Wilhelmina and the Dutch government and much of the Dutch Navy were evacuated to Britain in order to carry on the fight.

The simultaneous attack on Belgium was prefaced by dawn bombing raids on the Belgian airfields that destroyed about 30% of their air force on the ground. No attempt had been made to disperse their aircraft. At the same time some of the bridges on the Albert Canal, Belgium's primary defence line, were captured intact and their supposedly impregnable fort at Eban Emael, occupied by glider-borne troops. Hitler wasted no time in broadcasting to the Belgium people that their key fort had been captured. This announcement and the arrival of German troops from the skies, as in Holland, came as a complete surprise and had a devastating effect on the morale of the Belgian people. This was not helped by public warnings of infiltration by Fifth Columnists. Priests and nuns were arrested and much effort was wasted by the military authorities searching for a largely imaginary enemy. The effect was to induce panic in the population, and many of the Belgian troops, with the result that main roads became clogged with civilian refugees, interfering with essential troop movements and their ability to manoeuvre. Much affected by the problem of Belgian refugees thronging the roads, were the British Expeditionary Force and a major element of the French Army. These had been requested at the last moment by the Belgian government to help defend their country and were advancing through Belgium, having left their prepared defences along the Franco-Belgian border.

A crisis in the south had then compelled a withdrawal of the Franco-British force from Belgium. German armoured columns had broken through in the area of Sedan, where relatively weak French and Belgian troops had been unable to prevent the Germans from passing through the heavily wooded Ardennes area and crossing the River Meuse. It soon became clear that the German attacks on Holland and Belgium was a 'Matadors Cloak', as Captain Liddell Hart described it, to tempt the powerful Franco-British forces in northern France to advance into Belgium to meet what the allied command expected to be a repeat of the World War I Schlieffen Plan. Instead, the main thrust had come further to the south, where a combination of air superiority and massed armoured divisions overcame firstly the Belgians and then the French forces in the Ardennes. Over a thousand aircraft were used by the Luftwaffe in support of this advance, including Stuka

As part of their Blitzkrieg all-arms techniques, the Germans used the Junkers Ju 87 `Stuka' in the role of heavy artillery to intimidate opposition troops and civilians during their continental campaigns. Against the RAF in the later air Battle of Britain, the Stuka was shown to be slow and vulnerable, and the type was withdrawn from the battle. Those illustrated here are the later D Model, but display the same angular and intimidating lines as their 1940 predecessor. (Courtesy of the late Howard Inight)

(Sturzkampfbombers) dive bombers, this aircraft type being a feature of the German Blitzkrieg technique. The Stukas were used as ultra mobile, close-support, heavy artillery, destroying many of the defences along the River Meuse and terrorising the opposition.

By 14 May, the Germans had established three bridgeheads across the River Meuse, though not without difficulty. In fact three out of six crossing attempts had failed. A weakly defended weir, at Houx, was one of the first crossing points to be captured. The protection of weirs would consequently feature strongly in the defences of Worcestershire. Twenty-four hours later the German armoured columns had advanced 50 miles into the French interior and in ten days over 200 miles, helped on their way firstly by a lack of any strategic reserve of troops to resist in the French interior, and secondly by the ability of the Germans to replenish their fuel tanks from French roadside filling stations!

Having been cut off from the French army in the south of the country, the Franco-British and Belgian troops trapped in Belgium now retreated to the coast around the port of Dunkirk. The retreat was hastened on 28 May by the capitulation of Belgium and 20,000 of their troops laying down their arms. During the manoeuvres by the British to close the gap created in the perimeter caused by the Belgian collapse, Generals Sir Alan Brooke and Montgomery, and the troops under them, were receiving first hand experience of the Germans in battle, and the need for speed of decision making and action. This was to be of immense value to these officers who were both destined to take leading roles in the defence of Britain against an invasion and later in the prosecution of the war against Germany.

Operation Dynamo, the British plan to evacuate the encircled allied forces had already begun on 25 May, when base personnel and non-combatants were brought away from Dunkirk. By 5 June, when the last ship had left, some 338,000 men, British, French and some Belgians, had been brought to England. This evacuation was a masterpiece of organisation and it should be acknowledged that the senior British naval officer at Dunkirk, who was responsible for controlling the allied shipping there, was the then Captain Tennant, later Admiral, of Upton upon Severn.

The fighting in France continued for another three weeks after the Dunkirk evacuation, when the Germans turned their forces southwards to deal with what remained of the French Army and a reconstituted BEF to the south of the Rivers Somme and Aisne. It is sometimes thought, in the English speaking world particularly, that Dunkirk more or less marked the end of the serious fighting in France. In fact the Germans

The bust of Admiral Sir William Tennant stands in the former churchyard at the entrance to High Street, Upton upon Severn. In May and June 1940 Captain `Bill' Tennant was Senior Naval Officer at Dunkirk, organising the shipping evacuating the British Expeditionary Force from The Mole and the beaches

were to sustain more than 50% of their casualties after Dunkirk, But by 21 June, France had signed surrender documents and the Germans controlled the whole of the French Atlantic coastline.

Many reasons have been put forward for the rapid collapse of France in May and June 1940, but key amongst them must be a failure to recognise from the Polish campaign the German methods of waging war, most notably in the concentrated and coordinated use of armour and aircraft. The lack of coordination between the French Air Force and the Army meant that the latter were often exposed to air attack by the Germans. Air reconnaissance, that should have warned the French of the large numbers of German tanks in the region of the Ardennes was apparently ignored, the General Staff being convinced that the main attack was coming through Holland and Belgium! Another reason for failure was the emphasis by the French High Command on holding lines of defence. This often resulted in units fighting successful holding actions in one place being prematurely withdrawn to create a line elsewhere and any advantage that had been gained, lost. There was also a failure to recognise that while the enemy armoured columns forged ahead,

The Matilda II tank was shown to be markedly superior to the majority of German tanks in 1940 but had been used in 'penny packets' in support of infantry during the campaign in France and so, apart from the counter-attack at Arras, its potential impact had been wasted. (Courtesy of the late Howard Inight)

their main supplies and the bulk of the German army followed at a much slower marching pace and should have been interdicted, consequently isolating the tanks. Even the communications systems between the French General Staff and their armies were not adequate to deal the speed of change that they were experiencing during the Battle for France. The insistence of some French commanders on having written orders before making any move resulted in delays of days, when hours or even minutes were critical in responding to the fast moving form of warfare that the Germans had developed.

In a counter-attack at Arras, the British Matilda II tanks were shown to be markedly superior in both armour and armaments to the majority of German tanks. Elsewhere, many of the French tanks too were shown to be superior to the generally light tanks being used by the Germans, but they had been used in penny-packets as support to infantry instead of being used en-masse.

The British, and some of the better led French infantry, also fought some telling holding battles during the German attacks against the Dunkirk perimeter. One example was at Cassel. This was designated as a 'Nodal Point', a term given by the military to a location where a number of principal roads or railways meet. While in theory an army should be able to traverse open country-side, in practise a highly mobile force, such as that developed by the Germans, needed good roads and communications. By holding a vital communications point for only a short time an enemy advance could be disrupted and delayed. Other holding battles, that had delayed the Germans on their advance to Dunkirk, were those for the towns of Boulogne and Calais, where casualties were again high amongst the mainly lightly armed allied infantrymen who were attacked by tanks, artillery and dive bombers. Nevertheless valuable time was bought in these urban areas.

Of the many lessons learnt from the experience of the BEF in France and Belgium in 1940, the value of slit trenches against dive bombing and gunfire was an important one. A divisional commander reported that his division had made a point of digging slit trenches at once, at any point that they might be attacked by the enemy. They had found that the slit trench was the complete answer to dive bombing, losing not a single man if they were in narrow trenches, and giving great confidence against this type of attack. It was essential to construct as many alternative posts as possible during the night and occupy them before dawn. The importance of having slit trenches available at billets, camps, and barracks in Britain was therefore emphasised, and to construct alternative defence posts in each of their defended localities. Infantry trenches and weapons pits were consequently dug in vast numbers in Britain for anti-invasion defence purposes during 1940/41, though few remain in recognisable form today.

CHAPTER 2

The Defence of Britain — 'The Finest Hour'

The appointment of Winston Churchill as Prime Minister on 10 May 1940 brought a flurry of activity and action to prepare the nation for direct or indirect attack by Germany. That same day the Home Defence Executive was established under the chairmanship of the Commander-in-Chief Home Forces to consider every aspect of Home Defence. The following day Churchill set up his War Cabinet of five members and started appointing new ministers. Moves had already began the day before Churchill was appointed to deal with a potential Fifth Column with the internment of all male aliens between the ages of 16 and 60 living on the east and south coasts as far west as the Isle of Wight. The reports from Holland intensified the xenophobia and by 20 May aliens of all nationalities in Britain were forbidden to possess firearms, ammunition or explosives without a permit and soon afterwards were deprived of bicycles and motor vehicles. Many Italians and Germans would later be shipped from Britain to internment camps on the Isle of Man, and in Canada and Australia.

The government also reacted quickly to the widespread use of parachutists in Holland by calling, on 14 May, for volunteers between the ages of 17 and 65 to join the Local Defence Volunteers (LDV). Their main purpose was to keep watch throughout Britain for enemy parachutists and for collaborators, report them to local Regular Forces, or apprehend and disable them with whatever weapons were available. The signal that more than half a dozen enemy parachutists had actually been seen by the LDV was to be the ringing of the local church bells, although the bells were not intended to be a general signal that an invasion had begun.

Such was the tempo of the time that an extension of the Emergency Powers Act, giving the government wide powers over both people and property for the duration of the war, was passed by Parliament in three hours on 23 May. This legislation was to be used extensively to requisition land and buildings for defence purposes without the normal consultative processes of a democracy and to put individuals at the disposal of His Majesty. To help ensure civilians stayed out of the way of manoeuvring troops and avoid the chaotic road conditions seen in France and Belgium, leaflets were distributed to householders requiring them, in the event of an invasion, to 'stay put', not spread rumours and to immobilise any cars or motorcycles during the period dusk to dawn.

As part of the preparations for an invasion, direction signs were removed from roads and railways to make road navigation difficult for the invading forces. Even references to the locality in shop signs and on the sides of delivery vehicles were to be painted out. A legacy of this policy can still be seen in the countryside, where some ancient milestones are still missing their cast iron direction and distance plates.

General Ironside, then Chief of the Imperial General Staff, offered to take command of Home Forces in order to ready the country for the anticipated German invasion. The offer was accepted by Churchill and he took up the post on 27 May, the very day that the evacuation began in earnest of the British Expeditionary Force from Dunkirk. Ironside was considerably constrained in the task of preparing the country for an invasion by a lack of manpower and materiel resources. Mobility of troops would also be hampered by a lack of transport. Most of the troop-carrying lorries possessed by the British Army were, at that time, being deliberately destroyed in and around Dunkirk.

Issued by the Ministry of Information on behalf of the War Office and the Ministry of Home Security

STAY WHERE YOU ARE

IF this island is invaded by sea or air everyone who is not under orders must stay where he or she is. This is not simply advice : it is an order from the Government, and you must obey it just as soldiers obey their orders. Your order is "Stay Put", but remember that this does not apply until invasion comes.

Why must I stay put?

Because in France, Holland and Belgium, the Germans were helped by the people who took flight before them. Great crowds of refugees blocked all roads. The soldiers who could have defended them could not get at the enemy. The enemy used the refugees as a human shield. These refugees were got out on to the roads by rumour and false orders. Do not be caught out in this way. Do not take any notice of any story telling what the enemy has done or where he is. Do not take orders except from the Military, the Police, the Home Guard (L.D.V.) and the A.R.P. authorities or wardens.

What will happen to me if I don't stay put?

If you do not stay put you will stand a very good chance of being killed. The enemy may machine-gun you from the air in order to increase panic, or you may run into enemy forces which have landed behind you. An official German message was captured in Belgium which ran :

"Watch for civilian refugees on the roads. Harass them as much as possible."

Our soldiers will be hurrying to drive back the invader and will not be able to stop and help you. On the contrary, they will have to turn *you* off the roads so that they can get at the enemy. You will not have reached safety and you will have done just what the enemy wanted you to do.

How shall I prepare to stay put?

Make ready your air-raid shelter; if you have no shelter prepare one. Advice can be obtained from your local Air Raid Warden or in "Your Home as an Air-raid Shelter", the Government booklet which tells you how to prepare a shelter in your house that will be strong enough to protect you against stray shots and falling metal. If you can have a trench ready in your garden or field, so much the better, especially if you live where there is likely to be danger from shell-fire.

How can I help?

You can help by setting a good example to others. Civilians who try to join in the fight are more likely to get in the way than to help. The defeat of an enemy attack is the task of the armed forces which include the Home Guard, so if you wish to fight enrol in the Home Guard. If there is no vacancy for you at the moment register your name for enrolment and you will be called upon as soon as the Army is ready to employ you. For those who cannot join there are many ways in which the Military and Home Guard may need your help in their preparations. Find out what you can do to help in any local defence work that is going on, and be ready to turn your hand to anything if asked by the Military or Home Guard to do so.

If you are responsible for the safety of a factory or some other important building, get in touch with the nearest military authority. You will then be told how your defence should fit in with the military organisation and plans.

What shall I do if the Invader comes my way?

If fighting by organised forces is going on in your district and you have no special duties elsewhere, go to your shelter and stay there till the battle is past. Do not attempt to join in the fight. Behave as if an air-raid were going on. The enemy will seldom turn aside to attack separate houses.

But if small parties are going about threatening persons and property in an area not under enemy control and come your way, you have the right of every man and woman to do what you can to protect yourself, your family and your home.

Stay put.

It's easy to say. When the time comes it may be hard to do. But you have got to do it; and in doing it you will be fighting Britain's battle as bravely as a soldier.

This is one of the leaflets issued to every householder in Britain in an attempt to prevent the problem of refugees thronging the roads, should the country be invaded, and interfering with troop movements as had happened in Belgium and France.
(Image: Worcestershire Regiment Museum)

The return of over 300,000 British troops from Dunkirk, and more later from the south of France, increased Ironside's defence force but the greater problem was that the expanded force was desperately short of heavy weapons. The French campaign had cost the British Army 850 field guns, 310 heavier artillery pieces, 5,000 anti-aircraft guns, 650 anti-tank guns, 6,400 anti-tank rifles, 11,000 machine guns and nearly 700 tanks (98% of the total in France), besides many thousands of tons of ammunition. Since most stocks of equipment had been sent to France, the reserves available were limited and much emphasis was to be put on improvisation, while the armaments industries were busily making up for the losses. Engineers, machinists and other skilled men were quickly released from military service to return to their previous posts in industry in order to speed up the manufacture of armaments.

German propaganda at work. The photograph implies that parachute troops could go into action with small arms and a heavy machine gun immediately on landing.
In fact weapons and ammunition were landed separately, in containers that then had to be found, broken open and the contents distributed before the men could go into action — a delay that could be exploited by an alert defence force. (Courtesy of the late Howard Inight)

General Ironside reported on his plans for defence against an invasion to the Joint Chiefs of Staff meeting on 25 June. He considered that with the then naval and air forces at Britain's disposal, immunity from invasion could not be guaranteed, but that once the Germans had committed themselves, those forces should be able to seriously interrupt the enemy lines of communication. He thought that to achieve the greatest measure of surprise and the greatest concentration of force, the Germans were likely to use the shortest sea and air route for the main effort of invasion but that the possibility of diversionary attacks against the Shetlands, Ireland or the north of Scotland should not be disregarded. Simultaneous attacks at numerous widely scattered points were probable, including ports, the capture of which could allow the rapid unloading of armoured fighting vehicles (AFVs), transport and troops, since speed was considered to be an essential factor. At or near each point of attack, the enemy was likely to use parachute troops to capture landing grounds for use by troop carrying aircraft and to disorganise communications. It was thought that 10 to 15,000 men could be landed in one day in the south-east provided local air superiority could be gained.

General Ironside considered that the tactics used by the Germans on land would not differ materially from those used in France, with widely scattered columns being pushed on without support or protection of the flanks. He thought that, properly equipped and organised, these could be dealt with in detail. It was assumed that while AFVs in considerable numbers could be landed

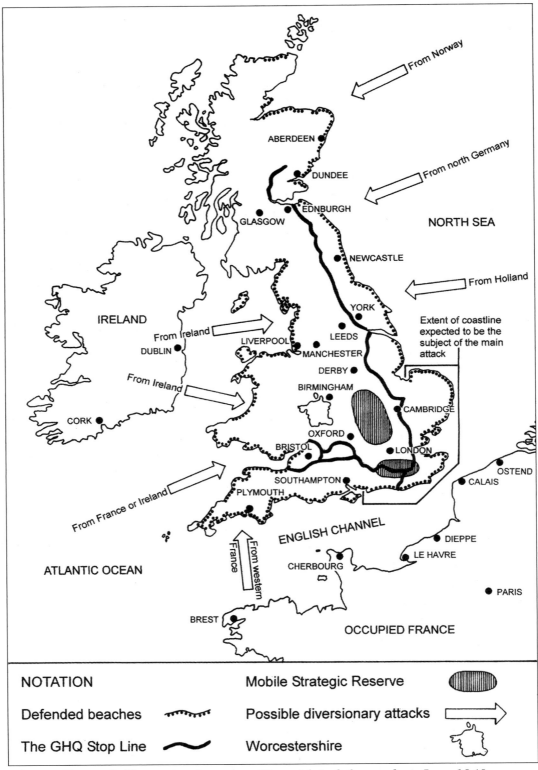

Figure 1. The main elements of Ironside's defence plan, June 1940

12

on open beaches, it was unlikely that sufficient transport for the mobility of infantry and guns would be available until a port with sufficient off-loading facilities had been captured. It was reckoned that the likely area of attack would be dictated by the operational area of enemy fighters and bombers and to which a sea-borne invasion could cross from the continent in the hours of darkness. Initially this was considered to be the area extending from the Wash to Newhaven. He thought at a later date that the possibility of an attack from Ireland on the west coast of England and Wales might have to be considered. This possibility was to have a marked influence on the form of defences in Worcestershire, as shall be seen later.

Ironside recognised that it would be impossible to provide a strong defence at all of the suitable landing beaches on the south and east coasts and that the possibility of an unopposed landing had to be accepted. Also, that there were a large number of ports and airfields close to the coast that would need protecting. The use of gliders that could be pancaked in very small spaces was also to be taken into account as well as the possibility of floatplanes being landed on stretches of water, including reservoirs.

The best method for dealing with enemy parachutists and troops landed from aircraft was considered to be by immediate offensive action to prevent assembly and execution of their plans. It was made clear that unless a specific notification had been received to the contrary, it was to be assumed that troops being landed from aircraft on the ground, whether in British uniform or that of an ally, were hostile. Later an instruction was issued that if eight or more parachutists were seen landing at any one time, it was to be assumed that they were enemy troops, rather than downed aircrew.

To achieve the primary objective of defeating Britain, General Ironside considered that the Germans would attempt to capture the centre of government and the centres of production and supply. Therefore it was necessary to protect London, the industrial areas of the Midlands and the North and the main ports. This would be achieved by both active and passive defences. The former would involve the use of offensive mobile columns, to deal quickly with widely scattered enemy forces before these had time to establish themselves, and a static defence of strong points and stops. He recognised that a static defence only provides limited protection of the most vulnerable points and must be supplemented by the action of mobile columns. However, because mobile counter-attack columns could not be expected to operate immediately over the whole area in which it was possible for the enemy to attack, it was necessary to adopt measures for confining enemy action and delaying their forces until the columns could arrive to deal with them. He considered that: 'stops and strong points would prevent the enemy from running riot and tearing the guts out of the country as had happened in France and Belgium'.

There were consequently three principal elements to Ironside's plans that stemmed from this appreciation of the threats to Britain:

1) Defence in strength of the potential landing beaches around Britain by means of anti-tank obstacles, fortifications, including many thousands of pillboxes and gun emplacements, earthworks, barbed wire barriers and minefields. Figure 1 shows the extent of the beaches to be defended, the idea being to stop as many of the attacking force from gaining a foothold or at least to slow them up and make time for counter-attack forces to be assembled and brought into action.

Evidence of General Ironside's 'Coastal Crust' can be seen on many parts of the British coastline. This double row of anti-tank cubes adjoins the causeway to Lindisfarne, and stretches away to the horizon to both the north, as here, and to the south

The defended beaches stretched for about 2,000 miles; called the 'Coastal Crust' it was to be manned by Regular troops, in some strength. They were expected to fight where they stood. There would be no retreat as had occurred too often in France.

2) A second major line of defence was to be constructed broadly parallel to the south and east coasts, about 50 miles inland and stretching from Bristol to London, around the capital and then northwards to Edinburgh. The purpose of this defence line was to protect London and the country's major industrial areas in the Midlands and the North, that were now busily producing armaments of all kinds to make up for the losses sustained at Dunkirk. Known as the 'GHQ Line', this stop line was intended to protect the industrial areas from armoured columns that may have broken through the beach defences and was to be in the form of a continuous anti-tank ditch, with pillboxes and gun emplacements at close intervals in order to provide overlapping fields of fire. It was not proposed to dig all of this feature anew but to utilise existing rivers, canals, steep inclines and embankments wherever possible, digging new ditches only where necessary to connect these existing natural or man-made features, to create a continuous line of obstacles. The GHQ Line was to be manned primarily by the Local Defence Volunteers who were again expected to stay put and not retreat.

3) A strategic reserve of the Field Army that would be expected to manoeuvre and counter-attack, once the main thrust of the German attack had been recognised. The major part of this reserve was to be stationed to the north of the Thames. It was to be as mobile as possible and was not to be used for manning static defences. In order to counter a possible attack from Wales or the south-west into the Midlands, the headquarters of the 2nd London Division moved on 24 June from Cambridgeshire to Ribbesford House (SO 787 738), near Bewdley, with its brigades located

as follows: the 4th London Infantry Brigade at Saundersfoot, near Tenby; the 5th London Infantry Brigade at Rugeley, near Stafford; the 25th Infantry Brigade at Kington in Herefordshire; and the 36th Independent Infantry Brigade in Malvern. During July, III Corps established its headquarters in Whitchurch, Shropshire, and the 38th Division moved into north Wales. Clearly the French experience had been taken into account.

In addition to these three primary elements of Ironside's defence, there were subsidiary stop lines both in front and behind the GHQ Line, together with defended nodal points or anti-tank islands, all intended to obstruct or delay enemy armoured columns probing inland and help prevent the rapid movement of these columns that had been experienced in France. These delaying tactics would, it was envisaged, allow sufficient time for the strategic reserve to be formed up and directed to the area of the breakthrough. The subsidiary stop lines would again be based upon suitable existing physical features, digging new ditches only where necessary. Road and rail blocks, pillboxes, gun emplacements, barbed wire and minefields were also to be features of these stop lines and it was largely the role of the Local Defence Volunteers to hold these fixed defences.

The generally 'close' countryside of wartime Britain, with many small fields surrounded by thick hedgerows and lines of hedgerow trees, especially in the Midlands, would have forced the Germans to use the main roads that, in those days before motorways and bypasses, generally passed through the centre of towns. The designation of the main towns and cities as 'anti-tank islands', or 'nodal points', and their preparation for all-round defence, would have imposed further delay on the Germans, forcing them to either fight their way through the urban areas, where tanks are vulnerable, or attempt to force their way through the close countryside surrounding the towns.

To disrupt an attack by enemy air landed troops using powered aircraft, typically the Junkers 52, or glider-borne troops, all potential landing grounds were to be obstructed and airfields

One of the many pillboxes and gun emplacements of the GHQ Stop Line that can still be found along the Kennet and Avon Canal. This Type FW3/28a, twin 2 pounder Anti-Tank Gun emplacement is located at SU 351 682, to the east of Hungerford, and still guards a road bridge over the railway, adjoining the canal

defended and garrisoned with regular troops. In order to deal with enemy paratroops who might be landed near to vulnerable points with the intention of capturing them quickly, the LDV were expected to report on their presence and contain the threat with whatever means at their disposal, until Regular Army mobile columns arrived.

The coordination of communications was also addressed during the summer of 1940, by the development of an inter-service wireless system, codenamed 'Beetle'. This had been organised to disseminate information on enemy landings by sea or by air, when the normal means of communications did not meet the necessary requirements. The 'Beetle' system included a wireless transmission network, centring on Fighter Command (Army Intelligence staff attached to Fighter Command would decide what to disseminate to the lower commands); a wireless transmission network centring on the Admiralty; and a broadcasting system in each Army Command with a transmitter in each headquarters. The scale of issue of receivers was to be down to regiments of Royal Artillery and battalions of infantry.

With the 'Beetle' system in place, information would flow from GHQ, Fighter Command, and the Admiralty downwards, while from the anti-aircraft gun sites and searchlights, the LDV, the Observer Corps, Civil Defence services, the police and the railway companies, detailed information on the movement of enemy units would flow back up. It was considered imperative that more than one channel of communication was provided between all headquarters and that telephone, wireless and dispatch riders should be used. In addition, specialised reconnaissance units codenamed 'Phantom' were formed to operate close to the fighting and report up to date intelligence by radio or specialist despatch riders to GHQ and the area commands. Phantom was organised into a number of squadrons that would be expected to continue operating, but in civilian clothing, when their particular area of responsibility was over-run. Clearly the problem of a lack of up-to-date intelligence experienced by the BEF in France was being very seriously addressed by GHQ with the creation of these multiple layers of communication.

It was inevitable that with so many fixed defences to be constructed, the task would be beyond the capacity of the Army's own engineers and while they would plan and direct the construction work, much of it was carried out civilian contractors and local authorities. Bearing in mind the amount of new construction also demanded by the civil defence agencies for, amongst other things, thousands of air raid shelters, it is perhaps not surprising that some strategic materials would run short during the summer of 1940. So much concrete was being poured that shuttering timber and corrugated iron ran out, followed by a cement shortage and that of reinforcing steel. Shortages of excavating machines and wooden poles for obstructing landing grounds were also felt during the summer of 1940.

Besides these largely static and overt defences, a covert guerrilla force began to be organised whose role would be to operate behind enemy lines after an invasion. These unconventional forces had the full support of Winston Churchill, who expected that by their acts of sabotage on the enemy's supply lines and communications, and by spreading terror, would strike some telling blows against the enemy before they were caught and killed as terrorists. Resembling Home Guards in appearance, and officially known as GHQ Auxiliary Units to hide their true character, this secret organisation was recruited primarily from the farming community, who would know their locality intimately, and be able to move around the countryside at night without difficulty. At the time, Britain was unique in being the first country to have recruited and trained a resistance organisation *before* an invasion.

On 19 July 1940, and as part of a speech of triumph to the Reichstag meeting in the Kroll Opera House, Hitler made an offer of peace to Britain, 'not as a vanquished foe begging favours but as a victor, speaking in the name of reason', suggesting that he could see no reason for the war to go on. This gesture was dismissed in a broadcast by the Foreign Secretary, Lord Halifax, on the basis that the British would not capitulate to his will, that our vision of Europe contrasted with that of his and 'that we shall not stop fighting until freedom is secure'.

The stage was now set and increased air attacks upon British shipping by the Luftwaffe presaged the Battle of Britain to be fought in the air that Churchill had predicted. Air superiority by the Germans was an essential pre-requisite for a sea crossing and invasion of Britain, but in the summer of 1940 the policy of expanding the Royal Air Force and the provision of an efficient early warning system, at the expense of the other services in the 1930s, was to pay dividends. Adlertag or Eagle Day, 13 August, was intended to mark the start of the German bombing attacks on British airfields in an attempt to quickly destroy the RAF, but the air battle was to go on throughout the summer, reaching a crescendo in September, before degenerating into attacks on the civilian population and the night blitz of the winter of 1940-41. A significant change of Luftwaffe tactics on 7 September, when the attacks moved from the airfields to the City of London, together with a movement of landing barges to the Channel ports

```
The Fuhrer and Supreme Commander of the Armed Forces.
Fuhrer Headquarters.
16th July 1940.

                        Directive No. 16.
   On preparations for a landing operation against England.

   Since England, in spite of her hopeless military
situation, shows no sign of being ready to come to an
understanding, I have decided to prepare a landing operation
against England and, if necessary carry it out.
   The aim of this operation will be to eliminate the English
homeland as a base for the prosecution of the war against
Germany and if necessary, to occupy it completely.
   I therefore order as follows:

1.   The landing will be in the form of a surprise crossing
on a wide front from about Ramsgate to the area west of the
Isle of Wight. Units of the Air Force will act as artillery
and units of the Navy as engineers.
   The possible advantages of limited operations before the
general crossing (e.g. the occupation of the Isle of Wight
or of the county of Cornwall) are to be considered from the
point of view of each branch of the Armed Forces and the
results reported to me. I reserve the decision to myself.
   Preparations for the entire operation must be completed by
the middle of August.

2.   These preparations must also create such conditions as
will make the landings in England possible, vis:
      a)   The English Air Force must be reduced morally and
      physically that it is unable to deliver any significant
      attack against the German crossing.
      b)   Mine-free channels must be cleared.
      c)   The Straights of Dover must be closely sealed off
      with minefields on both flanks; also the western
      entrance to the Channel approximately on a line
      Alderney - Portland.
      d)   Strong forces of coastal artillery must command and
      Protect the forward coastal area.
      e)   It is desirable that the English Navy be tied down
      before the crossing, both in the North Sea and in the
      Mediterranean (by the Italians). For this purpose we
      must attempt even now to damage English home-based naval
      forces by air and torpedo attack as far as possible ..
   .. The invasion will bear the cover name 'Seelowe'
(Sealion)..

Signed ADOLF HITLER.
```

Hitler's Directive No.16

closest to Britain, and decrypts of coded enemy signals by British Intelligence, were taken as a sign by GHQ that an invasion was imminent. The Home Defence forces were put on full alert, with 24 hour manning of the ground defences for several days. History tells us that the invasion did not take place and Fighter Command were able to continue to deny the Germans the air superiority they had sought, helped enormously by the radar and fighter control system that enabled the RAF to bring their fighters to more or less the right place at more or less the right time.

Anti-aircraft defences proved to be woefully inadequate against the night bombing campaign against Britain during the winter of 1940-41 and the Air Defence Great Britain (ADGB) defences were expanded considerably in and around the vulnerable points and industrial areas to include, not only more and bigger anti-aircraft guns and expanded searchlights belts, but bombing decoy sites, radio counter-measures and radar controlled night-fighters.

It is interesting now to consider the timing and content of Hitler's Directive 16: 'on preparations for a landing against England', codenamed 'Operation Sealion'. This directive was actually issued to his General Staff on 16 July, three days before his 'appeal to reason'. The timing of the Directive and the use of the phrase that the landings would only be carried out 'if necessary' suggest that the preparations for an invasion were perhaps an elaborate bluff to encourage the British to accept his appeal to reason and condone his continued occupation of continental Europe. The fact that preparations for a landing continued through the winter of 1940-41, and well into 1941, after the Battle of Britain had been lost by the Germans, adds weight to this view. Postwar interviews with senior German officers of the Wehrmacht indicate that Hitler was turning his attention to attacking Russia as early as July 1940.

Despite the earlier agreement by the Joint Chiefs of Staff meeting, attended by Winston Churchill, growing criticism of General Ironside's plans, in particular against his reliance so much on fixed lines of defence, led to his replacement, on 21 July 1940, by General Sir Alan Brooke, later Field Marshal Lord Alanbrooke. When relieved of his command by Anthony Eden, Ironside was informed that he was to be replaced by a man with more recent experience of active operations. Brooke had the view that the effort being expended on the construction of the GHQ Line was not the correct way to approach the problem of defending the country. In his opinion, the defence should be far more mobile and offensive in nature. Another form of defence with which he was in disagreement were the massive concrete road blocks at the entry and exit of towns and villages. He had realised in France how much these could hinder the defender's mobility and took steps to stop further constructions and remove some existing ones. He visualised a light defence along the beaches, to hamper and delay landings to a maximum and, in the rear, highly mobile forces trained for aggressive action against any landings, before the Germans had time to become too well established. Heavy air attacks and the use of sprayed mustard gas would have been part of his response to an enemy attack.

Another concern of Brooke, at this time, was that Lord Beaverbrooke, the Minister of Aircraft Production, was forming his own army to protect aircraft factories and had acquired large quantities of armour plating for the production of 'Beaverettes', small armoured vehicles based on the Humber car, to be used by factory Home Guard units. This at a time when armoured vehicles for the Army were in short supply! Beaverbrooke's policy of strongly protecting MAP factories was to have an impact on the defences organised in Worcestershire.

Work on the GHQ Line, subsidiary stop lines and pillbox construction was slowed and eventually stopped. Roads to remain open for use by the Home Defence forces in order to facilitate their rapid movement would be identified and designated either 'Red' or 'Blue' routes according to their importance and orientation. The concept of nodal points or anti-tank islands for all round defence was retained, however, and expanded to include more towns, or parts of towns, villages and river crossing points. These additional, and generally smaller areas, were to be designated 'defended localities' or 'areas of resistance', and would also be prepared for all-round defence. From the larger defended localities counter-attack forces were to sally forth at the appropriate time. In due time, the role of the Home Guard would change too, from simply holding a position to taking on more and more of the counter-attack role.

During Brooke's period of command at GHQ, the Auxiliary Units continued to be recruited and in 1941 were to be supplemented by another secret organisation, called Special Duties Section, that comprised civilian spies and radio operators whose role was to gather intelligence on occupying enemy troops and communicate this by written messages and also transmit from behind enemy lines to hidden Royal Signals radios and thence to the nearest British Army command. This would further enhance the 'Beetle' system.

The German occupation of the French Atlantic coastline during July, and the consequent greater possibility of an attack on the South Wales coast, from Ireland, seems to have influenced General Sir Alan Brooke's redisposition of the Field Force. The 2nd London Division moved its headquarters from Ribbesford House to Whitney Court (SO 270 477), overlooking the Wye valley in west Herefordshire, and the 5th London Infantry Brigade moved from Staffordshire to the Cowbridge/Llantwit area. This seems to reflect Brooke's intention of counter-attacking the enemy nearer the coast. However, the 36th Independent Infantry Brigade remained in Malvern until the following spring.

General Sir Alan Brooke visited the 2nd London Division on 30 August, by flying into Worcester (Perdiswell), and motoring to its headquarters at Whitney on Wye. From here he was able to follow a signals exercise that took him along the Usk valley and on to Pembroke. He apparently 'had a lovely fly back' to Hendon from Pembrey airfield which suggests that he was in a reasonably happy frame of mind. Signs of the 2nd London Division can still be seen at Whitney Court in the form of tunnel entrances in the wooded hillside that gave access to the underground Battle Headquarters beneath the court.

The criticism of General Ironside's approach to defending Britain during 1940 is, in hindsight, largely unjustified. His assessment of the nature of the threat to Britain was not far from what the German staff had been planning. His reliance on static or passive defences as part of the solution was a direct result of a lack of anti-tank weapons and the need to slow up the armoured columns by any available means. By the time General Sir Alan Brooke took command of Home Forces, the losses of these weapons were being made up and a more active form of defence could be considered. It seems often to be forgotten that Ironside did actually lay emphasis on having mobile counter-attack columns as a corollary to the provision of static defences. Brooke had the opportunity to change the emphasis.

The German invasion of Russia, in June 1941, codenamed 'Operation Barbarossa' marked the end of any serious invasion threat to Britain, although it was thought at the time that if Russia quickly collapsed militarily, preparations for an invasion would be renewed and so defence works continued to be constructed until September of that year. Thereafter the defences were to be maintained against the possibility of nuisance raids on Britain by German forces. The arrival of American forces in 1942, as part of the build-up to the D-Day landings in Normandy, finally precluded any serious attempt at a landing in Britain by the Germans.

CHAPTER 3

The Defence of Worcestershire — An Overview

The county of Worcestershire is almost as far from the sea as it is possible to be in Britain, yet from 1940 onwards it was to be heavily defended against German forces that might have broken through the coastal defences and the various stop lines, and were probing inland, or enemy parachutists and air landed troops being transported directly to key objectives. There are several reasons for this.

Worcestershire occupies a key area to the south and south-west of Birmingham and the Black Country and in 1940 these major industrial areas, together with Coventry, contained many strategically important armaments industries. A number of these had resulted from the government's 'shadow factory' scheme of dispersal in the 1930s, when the skills of the West Midlands car assembly workers and engine builders were recognised as being appropriate for military aircraft manufacture and extensive new plant for this purpose was built in the area. As a result the Austin Aero Works at Cofton and Elmdon, the Nuffield Aero factory at Castle Bromwich, the Boulton and Paul Aircraft factory at Pendeford, near Wolverhampton, and the Rover Aero Engine factories at Acocks Green and Solihull had been established. Former car component manufacturers now turned their hands to making aircraft components, such as the SU Carburettor Company which, during the Battle of Britain, was apparently the only factory producing aircraft carburettors, and Serck Radiators who were producing all the radiators and oil coolers for the Spitfires and Hurricanes. Some car companies in the Midlands took on the manufacture of lorries, Bren gun carriers, tank components and a host of other war materials. The Birmingham Small Arms (BSA) Company with their factories at Small Heath and Tyseley had a long tradition of producing armaments, while Dunlop and Goodyear were now producing tyres for the military. Even firms not normally associated with armaments, such as Cadbury's, began to manufacture military hardware. In the 1930s it was thought that the West Midlands was beyond the range of German aircraft but this was to be revised in the light of Germany's occupation of most of continental Europe and her use of paratroops, and so all of these armament factories would need protection.

Worcestershire too was thought to be well placed to accept some of the relocated factories under the 'shadow factory' policy. Under the auspices of the Ministry of Aircraft Production (MAP), companies such as High Duty Alloys (HDA) at Redditch, who were producing forgings and castings for the military aircraft industries, were moved up from the south of England. As part of the policy of dispersal, the Ministry of Supply also moved production facilities into Worcestershire like ICI (Metals) at Summerfield, near Kidderminster, to manufacture small arms ammunition. Later, when the bombing of Birmingham and Coventry disrupted the work of some of the companies there, a second phase of dispersals was carried out and factories moved out into the surrounding counties. One of the more interesting examples was the Rover works that was then manufacturing Bristol aircraft engines, which built an entirely underground factory, with four miles of tunnels, at Drakelow, to the north of Kidderminster. Like Cadbury's at Bournville, many of the established Worcestershire firms changed production entirely to armaments, none more dramatically than the carpet manufacturers at Kidderminster and Stourport who, almost without exception, turned their hand to such work. Even small motor repair garages in Worcestershire began operating under the auspices of the MAP.

The need to store war materials in relatively secure locations resulted in Worcestershire being chosen to accommodate key storage facilities. The most extensive of these was No.25 Maintenance Unit RAF that occupied seven dispersed sites in the countryside to the east of Hartlebury. The Royal Engineers also constructed a major storage facility straddling the county boundary to the north-east of Evesham. Elsewhere stores were established for aviation fuel at Ripple, Worcester (Timberdine), Stourport and Hinton on the Green, and more general fuel and oil stores at Diglis Docks and Stourport, while the Admiralty took over the abandoned GWR tunnel through the Malvern Hills and used it to store bombs, mines and shells. As part of the policy of dispersing storage facilities, an airfield was established at Berrow, one of a number in Britain hidden in deep countryside, to be used primarily for the storage of completed aircraft during the period between leaving the factories and being delivered to the squadrons. On a smaller scale, the newly completed Odeon Cinema, in Worcester, was requisitioned for the storage of aircraft components, while ammunition stores were created in the carpet factories at Foley Mill and the Lowland Works at Kidderminster. Some of these storage facilities were of national importance but all would need to be protected.

The county had also been chosen to accommodate the government, and other key institutions, should London have become untenable through bombing or if an enemy invasion successfully occupied the south-east of Britain. It was also intended that both the British and Dutch royal families should be accommodated in Worcestershire. No doubt the attempts by German paratroops to capture King Haaken and his government in Norway and Queen Wilhelmina and her government in Holland, added urgency to this scheme but in fact plans had been secretly worked out and preparations made for just this eventuality before 1940. As early as the summer of 1938 and before the Munich Agreement had been signed by Neville Chamberlain, representatives of the Office of Works, who had a presence in Worcester, had surveyed the whole of the West Midlands for suitable accommodation. Worcestershire appears to have become a focus for this activity and a number of schools, most of the large hotels and many of the large country houses were in due course requisitioned.

Plans were made for a two-stage move: 'Yellow Move' entailed moving 44,000 staff out of London to the provinces and then, when the capital became untenable, 'Black Move', which involved 16,000 staff from the remaining key ministries, the Cabinet, Prime Minister and the

In the summer of 1940 Madresfield Court, seen here as a backdrop to a parade of M (Malvern) Company of the 7th Worcestershire (Malvern) Battalion Home Guard, was prepared to receive the Royal Family as part of the 'Black Move' evacuation from London.
(Courtesy of Sheila Edmunds)

British and Dutch Royal families moving to Worcestershire. Madresfield Court was provisioned in readiness for the King and his family, Croome Court for the Dutch Royal family, Spetchley Court earmarked for Winston Churchill, and Hindlip Hall and Bevere House for the Cabinet.

Malvern Boys College was one of the properties surveyed in 1939 and requisitioned for use in Black Move, in this case, by the Admiralty. In addition a camp was built off St Andrew's Road in Malvern, in early 1940, as alternative emergency accommodation for the Admiralty.

This case highlights a two-stage process: firstly, the requisitioning of existing buildings at the outbreak of war in anticipation of the move and, secondly, the construction of alternative accommodation on a number of sites in early 1940 of what became known as 'Temporary Office Buildings' (TOBs). These flat-roofed H Block style TOBs can still be seen in the county and were, until recently, largely occupied by government departments. Sites include those at St Andrew's Road, Malvern, now occupied by QinetiQ; Comer Road, Worcester, now occupied by the University of Worcester; Whittington Road, Worcester, occupied by the Department of Environment, Food and Rural Affairs (DEFRA) and the Inland Revenue; at Witton, Droitwich, occupied by The Army Medal Office until recently, and the VAT Office. A small number of TOBs, to the north of Bromsgrove, suggest that this was an incomplete site and may have been part of a larger complex being prepared for occupation by the Foreign and Commonwealth Office which had been planned to come to the town. Other TOB's could be seen at Pale Manor, Malvern, but have recently been demolished to make way for new housing.

Maintaining the ability of the evacuated central government and its ministries to communicate with regional governors, the armed forces and the civil population would have been an important element of Black Move and so, besides the broadcasting facilities provided by the BBC at Wychbold and Wood Norton, wireless stations were established at Pulley Lane, to the south of Droitwich, for the War Office and codenamed 'Chaucer'; at Tallow Hill in Worcester for the Air Ministry and codenamed 'Longfellow' and in the Abbey Hotel Malvern for the Admiralty and codenamed 'Duke'. This last facility was later replaced by a purpose-built wireless station

Temporary Office Buildings (TOBs) at Witton, Droitwich, at SO 894 619. Originally intended for occupation by the 'War Office' as part of the Government evacuation scheme to Worcestershire, they were indeed occupied by Government departments including the Army Medal Office, until recently. Rapidly erected in 1940, examples of these buildings can also be seen in Worcester, Malvern and Bromsgrove

The ends of some of the TOBs on Government evacuation sites were strengthened to form air raid shelters and the photo above shows the ventilators provided for the occupants, while the photo to the right indicates the emergency breakout panel in the end wall, together with the removable steel covering plate

24

off Pickersleigh Avenue in Malvern. This building still exists at SO 788 474 and is now the Civil Service Social Club. Other military wireless facilities were established at Hoo Farm, to the south of Kidderminster, and at Wribbenhall. These two wireless stations were later combined and moved to Park Attwood, near Blakeshall, at SO 797 796. All of these establishments would need to be defended too and the range of defences provided around the government sites suggest that it was in Worcestershire that the last stand around the central government machine would be made, by which time it is likely that the Royal families and the key members of the government would have been evacuated to Canada, via Liverpool, to continue the fight from there. It is interesting to note that another safe house for the British Royal family had been earmarked at Pitchford Hall, in Shropshire, but it seems likely that the remainder, and majority, of the government officials would have to remain in Worcestershire until the end.

Some elements of Yellow Move were in fact carried out and parts of the Air Ministry did move to Worcester, bringing with them numerous RAF training and administrative groups to the area, including No.24 (T) Group to Hindlip Hall and No.81 (Op Trg) Group to the Kings School and later Hillborough; some departments of the War Office and OCTUs came to Droitwich, but the Admiralty sent only a naval basic training unit which occupied the newly-built TOBs off St Andrew's Road in Malvern, to become *HMS Duke*. Some staff from the Bank of England occupied Overbury Court for a short while and others from the India Office came to Bromsgrove School.

Worcestershire came under the military control of Western Command, which stretched from the Severn Estuary to the Scottish borders and included the whole of Wales and western England. For administrative purposes and defence planning, the Western Command area was divided into the East and West Lancashire Areas, the North and South Wales Areas, and the Central Midland Area. Responsibility for coordinating the defence of Worcestershire rested with Central Midland Area Command, whose headquarters was located firstly in Leamington, but during 1940 moved to Orchard Lea in Droitwich and remained there for most of the war. Orchard Lea, a large house, used to stand at the southern end of The Holloway, but the site was redeveloped for housing.

The Central Midland Area comprised the counties of Warwickshire, including Birmingham, Worcestershire, which then incorporated parts of the Black Country including Dudley, Herefordshire and that part of Staffordshire to the south of Watling Street, now the A5. The Central Midlands Area was further sub-divided for defence planning purposes into the Warwickshire and Worcestershire Sub Areas. The former was made up of all of Warwickshire and Birmingham, that part of Staffordshire south of the A5, the County Borough of Dudley and that part of Worcestershire bordering the City of Birmingham. This latter inclusion comprised Oldbury, Warley and the northern part of what is now Bromsgrove District. The reasons for this will become clearer later. The Worcestershire Sub-Area comprised the remainder and major part of Worcestershire and the whole of Herefordshire.

Plans for the defence of the Midlands cascaded down from GHQ Home Forces (HOFOR), from Southern Command in Salisbury and from Western Command at its partially underground headquarters in Chester. The surviving files from those days are, however, not comprehensive and much weeding of information seems to have occurred post-war, particularly for the more detailed aspects of local defence. Nevertheless, it is has been possible to piece together much of the picture of how the county was to have been defended.

Western Command instructions for the defence of the west of Britain and Wales, issued on 9 June 1940, pre-empted General Ironside's more comprehensive plans. Key elements of these instructions were to be carried through into later policy for the defence of Worcestershire and are therefore relevant to this analysis of local defences. These early instructions envisaged that whilst any invasion would probably fall on the east or south coast, there was the possibility of diversionary or subsidiary operations in the Western Command area. It was also considered probable that the enemy would be prepared to accept very high losses. The general policy was that there would be no withdrawal and, should the enemy gain a foothold anywhere, he was to be driven out with the minimum of delay. This was an amazing display of optimism for the summer of 1940, but there was clearly to be no repeat of the French withdrawals in May.

Blocks on road and rail communications were to be designed to prevent or delay the extension of an enemy foothold without prejudicing offensive operations by Home Defence forces. Road blocks were to be constructed in mutual consultation with the civil road authorities and would consist of a slowing down element and a blocking element. A minimum width of roadway was to be left to block with a moveable obstacle. These road blocks were also to be defensible.

Defences in the form of field works (trenches and weapons pits) were envisaged in the first instance, to be replaced as soon as possible by concrete construction, with overhead cover in reinforced concrete. All defences were to be wired with a fence at least 40 yards from the defended points with a second fence at 60 yards to prevent the approach of flame throwers.

At this stage, the Air Ministry was responsible for the destruction or obstruction of landing grounds not required by the RAF and all spaces fit for landing within a five mile radius of landing grounds that were required by the RAF, on a priority basis. However crops were not to be disturbed. In addition to the obstruction of open spaces, straight roads within those areas were also to be obstructed by wire ropes suspended between poles 20 feet from the ground and at 300 yard intervals.

On receipt of the codeword 'Cromwell', denoting that an invasion was *imminent*, troops were to take up battle stations and telegraph wires essential for operational purposes were to be taken over. All troops including Local Defence Volunteers, ADGB (Air Defence Great

This restored Westland Lysander was seen some years ago at Old Warden in Bedfordshire, but in the summer of 1940 a flight of these aircraft was held by 13 Squadron RAF, bombed-up in readiness for an enemy invasion through South Wales. Both Pembridge Landing Ground (later Shobdon Airfield) in Herefordshire and Perdiswell at Worcester were earmarked by 13 Squadron as advanced landing grounds should an enemy attack develop

Britain) troops manning anti-aircraft gun and searchlight positions, and RAF Balloon Barrage personnel were to inflict the maximum number of casualties on the enemy while he was landing, but should the enemy succeed in establishing himself, the area to be held was to be surrounded by a cordon of troops to give time for stronger forces to arrive and act.

No.13 Army Cooperation Squadron RAF was under the direct control of Western Command but in the event of a surprise invasion, Western Command could also call on No.2 Bomber Group to provide one squadron of aircraft. Otherwise all RAF bomber effort against an invasion was to be centralised under the control of GHQ Home Forces. No.13 Squadron operated Westland Lysander aircraft and five of their aircraft were kept 'bombed up' at night and were immediately available to deter an attack at first light. Aircraft from 13 Squadron also carried out dawn reconnaissance of the South Wales Coast and the west coast of England when the state of the tide was suitable for dawn landings. Should an invasion have occurred in South Wales and major operations developed, then a flight of these aircraft would have operated from advanced landing grounds including Pembridge (later to be called RAF Shobdon) in Herefordshire and Perdiswell (later RAF Worcester).

Southern Command was particularly productive with their paperwork and instructions, and some of it survives. A memorandum of 22 June, copied to the Central Midland Area, explains that the purpose of 'stops' may not have been made clear and that they were designed to counteract two threats: an armoured fighting vehicle (AFV) attack which may have broken through the beach defences to a considerable depth and found its way well inland; and a large scale air-borne attack.

It was envisaged that these lines of 'stops' would be based on anti-tank obstacles with wire and fields of fire from a concrete pillbox system distributed in depth, covering those obstacles. Although it was said this state of affairs would not arise in the immediate future, the object was to divide England into several 'fields' surrounded by a hedge of anti-tank obstacles which was strong defensively and would use natural features where possible. Should AFVs or airborne attacks break into the enclo-

The purpose of stop lines was to counteract an armoured fighting vehicle attack that had broken through the beach defences and made its way inland. The picture depicts German armoured vehicles held up at a border crossing. Before the breakthrough at Sedan, a massive traffic jam of armoured vehicles 150 kilometres long was created back into Germany! It should have been seen by air reconnaissance and attacked, but the French High Command, who were convinced that the main attack was coming through Holland and Belgium, ignored the threat until too late. (Courtesy of the late Howard Inight)

sure, the policy was to 'let in the dogs in the shape of armoured formations, or other troops, to round up the cattle'. 'Fields' in this context could represent quite large areas of countryside and at this stage, in Worcestershire, the major 'field' comprised a large proportion of the county area.

This colourfully phrased memorandum was followed up the very next day with yet more advice by proposing a stop line to completely enclose Birmingham, Nuneaton and Coventry and another stop line to divide the Central Midland Area from the South Midland Area (essentially Gloucestershire, Oxfordshire and Berkshire) into small enclosures within which would be scattered, at focal points of communications, 'anti-tank islands' through which AFVs could not pass and around which they could only go with difficulty. A very generalised plan, with little geographical detail, and issued the same day, indicates that in Worcestershire, Kidderminster, Worcester and Redditch were shown as anti-tank islands and that the stop line to surround Birmingham, Nuneaton and Coventry was drawn along the River Severn, west of Kidderminster, down to a position north of Worcester. Here it went eastwards through the Droitwich area, presumably following the Droitwich Junction Canal, then north-eastwards to the north of Redditch, presumably following the Worcester–Birmingham Canal, before turning south-eastwards towards Stratford, again presumably along the Stratford Canal. See Figure 16 for a deduced route of this stop line through Worcestershire.

A Western Command instruction dated 5 July 1940 refined the previous instructions and appears to have incorporated at least some of Southern Command's ideas. The general policy was rephrased as:

a) To prevent any hostile attempts at invasion either by air-borne or sea-borne troops by the defence of all beaches affording facilities for landing; by the defence of aerodromes and by the creation of obstacles on other areas suitable for air-borne landings.

b) To extend through all vulnerable parts of the Command a number of lines, in which an enemy, advancing with tanks, from east and west, will find no gaps or weak places whatever and up against which he will be held firm until mobile troops can attack and destroy him.

Some 28 stop lines were now proposed in the Command area, along which defence posts, road blocks and anti-tank obstacles were to be constructed under the direction of the Area Commander. In nearly all cases it was stated that those lines would have to be manned by LDVs (Local Defence Volunteers) who would be drawn from villages or portions of towns as close as possible to the parts for which these men would be responsible. As a rule, the instruction goes on, while establishing all-round defence at each post, they should first prepare against advances from the east and secondly from the west.

Of the 28 stop lines envisaged in these instructions, three affected Worcestershire:

1) The line of the River Severn, from Tewkesbury to Shrewsbury and onto Llandrinio, just over the Welsh border. This was the re-use of an ancient defence boundary which had served to restrict Welsh incursions throughout history.

2) The line of the River Avon, from Tewkesbury to the neighbourhood of Coventry.

3) The line of the River Teme from its junction with the River Severn to Ludlow.

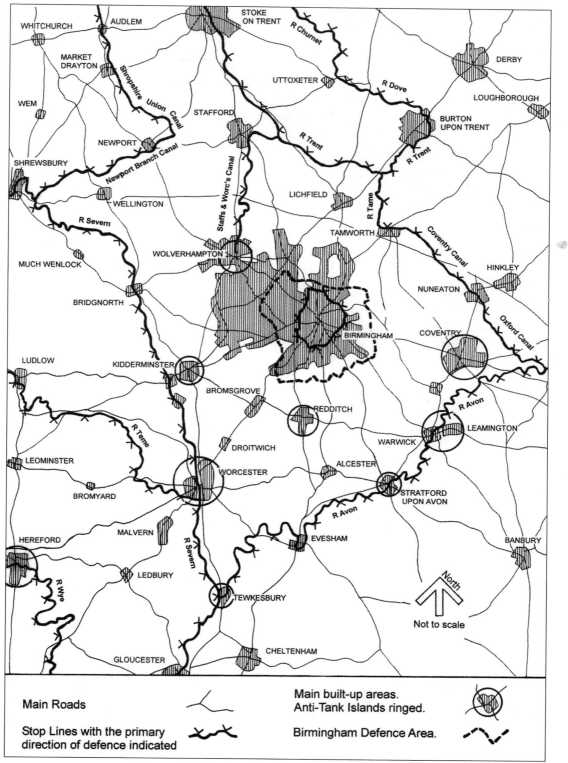

Figure 2. The Midlands Defences, 1940/41

Further afield, stop lines were also planned along the Rivers Wye and Usk to provide a succession of linear defence features between the South Wales ports and the Midlands. It was noted that neither of these rivers were good anti-tank barriers because when water levels were low, they could be easily forded.

From the full list of 28 Stop Lines it is clear that a number of them formed a complete defence ring around the vulnerable West Midlands (see Figure 2). This provides confirmation of the earlier premise that many of the defences established in Worcestershire were to provide protection for Birmingham, the Black Country and Coventry. Although the Southern Command idea of a stop line from the River Severn through Droitwich and then to the north of Redditch had not been included in the list of 28 now proposed, field work for the earlier Defence of Britain Project does indicate that at least some work was carried out on such a stop line. It is also clear that the Avon Stop Line would satisfy the other Southern Command idea, to divide the Central Midland Area from the South Midland Area and create the 'fields' envisaged earlier.

Another Western Command instruction issued in August 1940 developed the policy further, envisaging a sufficient static defence force utilising Regular troops based in the area and the Home Guard (by this time the LDV had been renamed) to hold the enemy, supported by a very active offensive by Field Force formations and other mobile forces. A summary of these forces is provided below. This instruction also reflected the shortage of labour and materials for the construction of defence works by proposing that the stop lines would now be completed on a priority basis. The Avon Stop Line was placed in Category One, the Severn Stop Line in Category Three and the Teme Stop Line in Category Four of five categories. Work was to be carried out as economically as possible in accordance with these priorities. Attention was drawn to the need for the construction of Company defended areas, with all-round defence to cover main lines of communication; the preparation of anti-tank obstacles and traps to enable the Home Guard to deal effectively with any unexpected breakthrough by hostile tanks; and all-round defence of towns and villages to forbid entry to the enemy, to force him aside and to break up his cohesion so as to make him easier prey to the mobile troops.

To summarise the various instructions, the defences to be put in place in Worcestershire to deal with the perceived threats in the summer of 1940 were a combination of stop lines along the rivers Severn, Avon and Teme; anti-tank islands based on the nodal points of Worcester, Kidderminster and Redditch prepared for all-round defence; and road blocks and associated defence posts, constructed primarily on the road crossings over rivers and streams and the approaches to them; as well as on the road approaches to, and within, the anti-tank islands and other settlements, including the smallest of villages in the county. Road blocks were also to be constructed where a road cutting might be conducive to trapping enemy vehicles or tanks. Blocks were also to be formed on rail crossings of watercourses or approaches to defended settlements, since it had become apparent that the Germans would move armoured columns along rail track-beds where necessary.

The system of defences included the obstruction of potential landing grounds; protection of vulnerable points (VPs) — the key infrastructure, war production and storage facilities referred to earlier; and the defence of airfields.

Other defence measures included the protection of petrol supplies and their obstruction or destruction to prevent the enemy using them; disposal of unexploded bombs, shells and mines;

assistance to civil authorities, and road control. A so-called 'Battle Dump' of defence materials was established at the Southfield Street Drill Hall, in Worcester, for issue after 'Action Stations' had been called. The reference to action stations here is presumed to mean when 'Cromwell' was broadcast.

Observer Corps and Anti-Aircraft personnel were already reporting any parachute descents using civil communications but these were to be supplemented by wireless (W/T) or dispatch riders (DR) in case of breakdown. Instructions say that on receipt of a codeword — it was not given but presumed to be 'Cromwell' — from Western Command, the GPO were intending to cut off all civil subscribers during the emergency. Western Command added another layer of communications to those arrangements under 'Beetle', described in the last chapter. This was considered necessary in case the normal lines of communication were put out of action by enemy air activity. During August 1940, the Chief Signals Officer of the Command organised a number wireless sets that were to be made available, with signallers, to provide an additional means of communication between all Area and Sub Area headquarters in the Command area. A high powered set was to be supplied to the Central Midlands Headquarters, with subsidiary sets supplied to the Worcester Sub Area Headquarters at Droitwich, the Coventry Sub Area Headquarters and the Birmingham Garrison. Pigeon services were also developed, with a main loft at Norton Barracks and with some Home Guard units. The pigeon service was maintained until April 1943.

A defence scheme prepared in May 1941 for the Birmingham Garrison acknowledged that Birmingham and the Black Country would almost certainly be the ultimate objective of any hostile troops that may have gained entry by whatever means, into the Central Midland Area. The outer defences were the stop lines and anti-tank islands and the nodal points or anti-tank islands in the surrounding counties.

The next line of defence was established immediately around the city and was called The Birmingham Defence Area. This incorporated parts of Worcestershire, including Oldbury, Warley, part of Halesowen, the northern part of what is now Bromsgrove District, as well as a part of Staffordshire. The third line of defence was in the form of a stop line, incorporating canals and railway cuttings within the built-up area of the city, and the fourth, and final, defence area in the city centre, designated as 'the keep'.

Although General Sir Alan Brooke replaced General Ironside as Commander in Chief, Home Forces on 20 July 1940, it was some time before Brooke's dislike of linear defences was felt in Western Command. Western Command's view was that there was really no difference of doctrine: that its use of the term 'stop line' was for the sake of brevity, to describe a series of localities prepared for all-round defence, sited to deter the enemy, especially armoured columns, at the crossings over otherwise natural obstacles. As late as 22 February 1942, the term stop line was used in Western Command's 'Exercise Avon', organised to test the defences along that river. It is significant that the use of the term 'stop line' was eventually abolished, *by order*, in the Central Midlands District in April 1942. Defences were henceforth to be based on a framework of anti-tank islands and centres of resistance. These were to be held to 'the last man and the last round' in an effort to exert maximum delay on invading columns.

Birmingham itself became an anti-tank island and lost its inner and outer defence lines. These were replaced by a series of closely spaced defended localities that were largely concen-

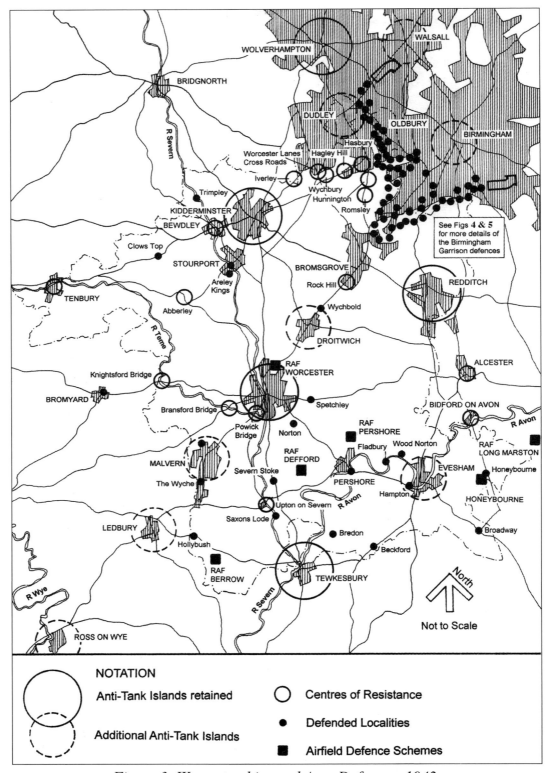

Figure 3. Worcestershire and Area Defences, 1942

32

trated around the outskirts of the city, some of them being located in Worcestershire (see Figures 3 and 4). These defended locations are sometimes referred to in Birmingham Zone defence schemes as 'studs', possibly to obscure their purpose to any casual observer. Fortunately, a defence scheme for three of Birmingham's defended localities has survived, two of which are in the extreme northeast corner of Worcestershire. Such plans are now a rarity and so this defence scheme is reproduced in Figure 5. It gives a good indication of the number of individual defence features constructed in just one small part of the county. Berry Mound, near Majors Green, at SP 095 780 is one of three Iron Age forts in Worcestershire known to have be re-used for defence purposes in 1940, the others being Bredon Hill and Wychbury, to the north of Hagley.

As a result of the orders from higher authority, Droitwich, Malvern and Evesham were designated as anti-tank islands in 1942, while Worcester, Kidderminster and Redditch retained that status. However, like Birmingham, Worcester city would lose its concentric linear defences to be replaced by a series of centres of resistance adjoining the main accesses (see Chapter 6). Elsewhere in the county, it is apparent that specific localities already provided with all-round defences under the older defence schemes were simply re-designated as either centres of resistance or defended locali-

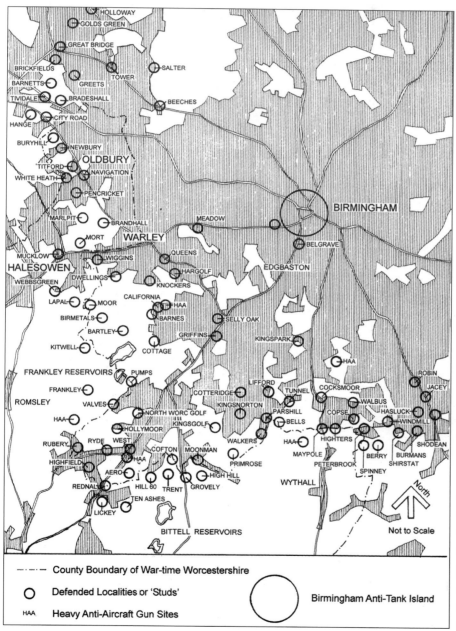

Figure 4. Defended localities of the Birmingham garrison within and adjacent to Worcestershire

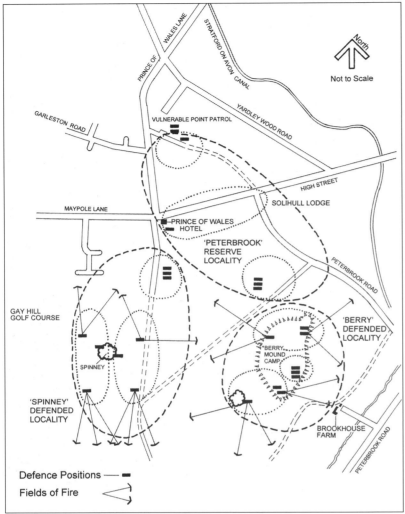

Defence Positions ———— ▬
Fields of Fire ⟨—

*Figure 5. Defence schemes for the 'Peterbrook', 'Berry'
and 'Spinney' defended localities of the Birmingham Garrison*

ties, including a number of well defended river crossings on the former stop lines. A hierarchy of stand-alone defence features was now established in Worcestershire and this is illustrated on Figure 3. The redesignation of river crossings and some of the settlements already defended illustrates, perhaps, that an evolution of defences came under General Sir Alan Brooke's influence, rather than wholesale change.

It is significant, too, that by 1942 a bridge demolition strategy had been included in local defence instructions. These instructions made it clear that demolition of bridges was not to be planned for nor prepared without instructions from the Sub District HQ with the exception of the following bridges across the River Severn for which plans for demolition were already in being: the road bridges at Stourport, Holt Fleet and Upton on Severn, and the Worcester railway bridge. Hitherto, it is assumed that all threatened bridges in the county would have been demolished if the positions around them had became untenable while under attack, but in the 1942 strategy, the retention of the road bridges over the River Severn at Bewdley and Worcester suggests that any enemy attack from the west was being encouraged to head for the anti-tank islands of Kidderminster and Worcester. Here enemy armoured columns would have been most vulnerable and would have become enmeshed in these urban areas which had been specifically prepared for causing maximum delay to the enemy. Surviving details of the defences around Worcester Bridge suggest that a major action would have to take place before the enemy could get near or over the bridge. Keeping the bridges intact at Bewdley and Worcester would also allow counter-attack forces from these areas to meet and deal with any enemy attack from the west.

Troops available for defence in Worcestershire in the summer of 1940, and afterwards, included those of No.23 Infantry Training Centre at Norton Barracks (SO 869 518), Worcester.

After the Dunkirk evacuation, this former depot of the Worcestershire Regiment had expanded considerably to accommodate a large increase of recruits and conscripts from South Staffordshire as well as Worcestershire. In addition to defending the depot and manning some of the defences in Worcester, the Commanding Officer, Colonel Melville Lee, organised a mobile column that had special responsibility for dealing with any parachute attacks on the airfields at Worcester and Pershore, as well as Brockworth (Gloucester) and Staverton (Cheltenham). Later, after their construction, the airfields at Defford and Honeybourne would be added to the task list of No.23 ITC mobile column. This counter-attack force was available before any elements of the Field Force made their appearance in Worcestershire and it could be fairly claimed that Norton Barracks, in addition to its training role, provided a defence force for the county that outlasted all the others, being available at both the beginning and the end of the war.

There was one infamous operation by No.23 ITC in June 1940, when word was received at the barracks that German parachutists had been spotted in the vicinity of Bewdley. The LDV had been called out over a wide rural area, church bells had been rung, road barriers erected and the locality combed for parachutists. The excitement lasted all day and brought out crowds of spectators from the town bent on

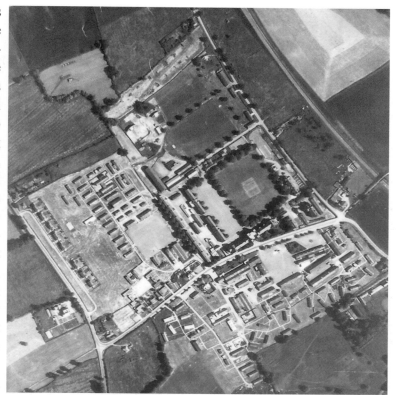

Top: This 1960s air photograph shows the wartime extensions to Norton Barracks, mainly to the south of Crookbarrow Road. The Keep can be seen between the cricket ground and this road. The site has been largely redeveloped for housing. (Courtesy of WHEAS)
Lower: In the recent redevelopment of Norton Barracks, the historic 19th-century Keep has been converted to luxury apartments. During World War II a light anti-aircraft Bren gun was mounted on the taller of the towers

The Depot Training Staff officers of No.23 Infantry Training Centre, Norton Barracks, during the first years of the war. From left to right on the front row are: unknown, Captain Jarrett (R Company Cdr), Major Moss (Training Officer), unknown ATS Cdr, Major de Courcy Ireland, Lt Col R.H. Melville Lee, Major Keir-Molliet (Adjutant), unknown ATS, Major Scott, Captain J.W. Tingey (Depot QM), unknown. None are known in the second row. In the back row only two are known: Captain Rollestone, second from the left, and 2nd Lt Michael Ratcliffe, second from the right. (Photo: The Worcestershire Regiment Museum)

watching the action, completely ignoring the advice from the government to 'stay put' and remain indoors if the invasion should come! While the mobile column from Norton Barracks headed towards Bewdley in their miscellaneous collection of vehicles, headed by a Bren Gun Carrier, a second marching column followed at a much slower pace with a young lieutenant leading. Sam Beard, the Depot Runner, marched alongside pushing his bicycle, since he had been told in no uncertain terms that he would not be riding it until ordered to do so in his message carrying capacity. Until then he was to have no advantages over his marching colleagues, but during the march some of the men prevailed upon him to sling their rifles on his bike which became heavier and heavier. The lieutenant was unfamiliar with the county and took the right, instead of the left, fork at Barbourne and was heading towards Droitwich, when Major Moss in his car caught up with the column and told the embarrassed lieutenant in no uncertain terms that he was going in the wrong direction. Forthwith, the column left the road and headed for Bewdley across country, with Sam having to lift his bike over the various obstacles on the way and becoming an increasing encumbrance. Eventually, the column reached Bewdley where they were set the task of scouring Ribbesford Woods for the supposed enemy parachutists. None were found and at the end of a long day it was concluded that the parachutists were in fact hay cocks which had been whipped up by a low-flying British aircraft.

Amongst its many other functions, Norton Barracks was to become a storage depot for up to 19 Midland Red buses for use in moving troops around the country and, as far as can be ascertained, these vehicles remained in their original bright red colouring! Another function of

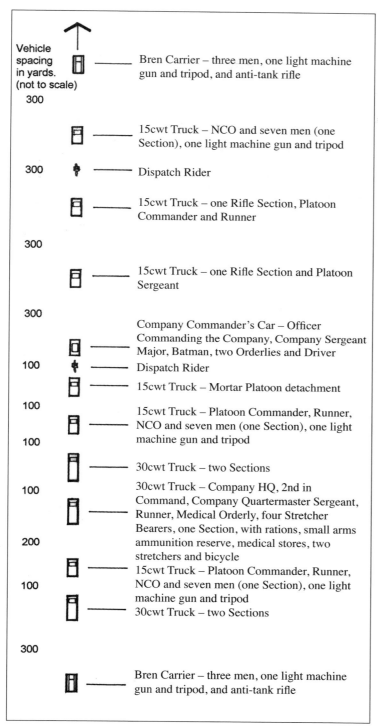

Vehicle spacing in yards. (not to scale)

300 — Bren Carrier – three men, one light machine gun and tripod, and anti-tank rifle

300 — 15cwt Truck – NCO and seven men (one Section), one light machine gun and tripod

300 — Dispatch Rider

— 15cwt Truck – one Rifle Section, Platoon Commander and Runner

300 — 15cwt Truck – one Rifle Section and Platoon Sergeant

300 — Company Commander's Car – Officer Commanding the Company, Company Sergeant Major, Batman, two Orderlies and Driver

100 — Dispatch Rider

— 15cwt Truck – Mortar Platoon detachment

100 — 15cwt Truck – Platoon Commander, Runner, NCO and seven men (one Section), one light machine gun and tripod

100 — 30cwt Truck – two Sections

100 — 30cwt Truck – Company HQ, 2nd in Command, Company Quartermaster Sergeant, Runner, Medical Orderly, four Stretcher Bearers, one Section, with rations, small arms ammunition reserve, medical stores, two stretchers and bicycle

200 — 15cwt Truck – Platoon Commander, Runner, NCO and seven men (one Section), one light machine gun and tripod

100 — 30cwt Truck – two Sections

300 — Bren Carrier – three men, one light machine gun and tripod, and anti-tank rifle

Figure 6. Organisation of the 7th Battalion, The Queen's Own Royal West Kent Regiment mobile column, July 1940, HQ, Oriel Villa, Worcester Road, Great Malvern

the barracks was to provide a prisoner of war compound, and presumably the associated guard in the event of its use for the incarceration of German troops captured during any invasion of this corner of Britain.

Other mobile counter-attack columns were formed by three infantry battalions of the 36th Independent Infantry Brigade of the 2nd London Division, whose headquarters was at Crown Lea (SO 792 455), Barnards Green, Malvern. Details of the mobile column organised by one of those battalions, the 7th Battalion, Queen's Own Royal West Kent Regiment have survived and are illustrated in Figure 6. It was intended that all personnel, arms, ammunition and stores were to be ready at two hours notice by day, and half an hour by night. The Motor Transport Officer was to have transport, including Bren Carriers, parked ready to move off whilst dispatch riders were to be on duty round the clock. These arrangements must reflect reasonably closely those of other columns.

Attached to the 36th Brigade in Malvern during 1940 were the 149th Field Regiment Royal Artillery, accommodated in a tented camp in Blackmore Park and mobile troops of the 62nd Anti-Tank Regiment operating 6 pdr Hotchkiss Mk II quick firing guns. A further three batteries from the 62nd A/T Regiment were detached from their headquarters in Stoneleigh Park, Warwickshire, to man a total of 16 6 pdr guns in fixed emplacements in the Central Midland Area. Seven of these emplacements have been identified in Worcestershire and will be referred to later. While in Malvern, this unit trained local units of the Home Guard in the use of the Hotchkiss at a temporary range established at British Camp reservoir (SO 764 398), prior to handing over the guns in the spring of 1941.

Elements of the 210th Infantry Brigade including the 8th Battalion, The Essex Regiment, with their HQ at Bentley Manor (SO 999 663) and The Sillins (SP 013 696), near Redditch; the 9th Battalion of the same Regiment at Park Attwood and the 9th Battalion Royal West Kents at unidentified billets in Malvern also organised mobile columns, as did the 11th and 12th Battalions, The Royal Fusiliers, and the 2nd Battalion, The London Rifles, of the 40th London Infantry Brigade, all being billeted in the county for a few months during 1940/41.

Ribbesford House, in the background of this photograph, was the headquarters of the 2nd London Division for a short time in the summer of 1940, and was in continuous military occupation by a number of units until late 1944, when the Free French left. The cadet in the foreground wears the distinctive floppy beret of the 'Cadets de la France Libre'. (Courtesy of Bewdley Museum)

After these elements of the Field Force in Worcestershire moved off in 1941, being replaced in quick succession by the 18th Infantry Division and then the 53rd Welsh Division, both establishing their headquarters at Ribbesford House. From 1942, when all units of the Field Force had left the county, the sailors at *HMS Duke*, in Malvern, formed a mobile column and, by 1943, three anti-parachute platoons that were to operate within a five-mile radius of Malvern, including a counter-attack role at Berrow airfield should it be threatened. The Cadets de la France Libre or 'Fighting Free French' also formed a mobile column that was to be used to good effect in local Home Guard exercises. This Free French officer training unit had arrived in 1940 and had occupied No.5 House at Malvern College until 1942 when it moved to Ribbesford House, where the cadets stayed until 1944. Elements of the Belgian Army in Britain, including an armoured car battalion, were also based in Malvern for a short period during 1941-42 before moving to South Wales and would have contributed to the mobile forces.

With manpower numbers of around 19,000 men, the largest single static force in the county was the LDV/Home Guard that would garrison the majority of the fixed defences. However, the Royal Artillery troops of the Air Defence Great Britain (ADGB) of the numerous searchlights and anti-aircraft guns would take on any enemy troops in the vicinity of their sites, whilst the guards on vulnerable points, including men of the 11th Battalion, The Royal Warwickshire Regiment and Military Police, would contribute to the static force by manning the defences around their sites. Other units contributing to the county's defence were Numbers 167 and 168 Officer Cadet Training Units (OCTU) that came into the county during 1940 and stayed until 1941, initially occupying some of the TOBs at Droitwich and later moving to those at Pale Manor in Malvern, that were then temporarily named the Alma Barracks. The 12th Battalion, The Worcestershire Regiment, also spent a few months in the county at Dudley, during 1940, before moving off to South Wales for coastal defence duties, as did the 70th Battalion, The Royal Warwickshire Regiment, which was billeted in Malvern Link from December 1940 to June 1941. Another static unit was the Royal Army Pay Corps based at Pike Mills in Kidderminster for most of the war. At the majority of airfields in the county, the RAF would provide their own defence.

The self-styled 'Dodford Killing Machine' was to become part of the 2nd Worcestershire (Bromsgrove) Battalion Home Guard. The miscellany of equipment and uniform and lack of insignia identifies this as an early photograph of the LDV/Home Guard, taken in the summer of 1940 but, as the text explains, the unit would not have been alone in defending their part of Worcestershire. (Courtesy of Bill Kings who appears in the front row, fourth from the left)

This is not a comprehensive list of units that were based in the county but serves to indicate that the LDV/Home Guard would not have been alone in providing defence but would, in the critical 1940-41 period, share the responsibility with Regular troops that in total probably matched them in numbers.

The civilian police were not deemed to be part of the armed forces of the crown, nevertheless, they had arms available for use against saboteurs, raiding parties or small enemy forces that were likely to use firearms. Should enemy forces occupy a district or a town, even if temporarily, selected police personnel with their arms were to be withdrawn for use elsewhere, leaving sufficient personnel without firearms to assist in the control of the population in the area occupied.

None of the defence schemes or operational instructions issued in the Worcestershire Sub Area refer to the GHQ Auxiliary Units, or indeed any of the covert forces referred to earlier. Nevertheless, analysis of the disposition of these resistance forces does indicate that they were planned to be an integral part of the overall scheme of defence for the county, rather than as a separate entity.

Work on new defences in Worcestershire seems to have come to an end in August 1942 as an order from the Battalion Commander of the 12th Worcestershire (Warley) Battalion Home Guard made it clear that *no* new defence work would be started in that area, unless of such a minor nature that it could be completed by 29 August that year. It is likely that other commanders were issuing similar instructions to their units.

Local consideration was being given to dismantling unwanted defences as early as April 1943, when the Battalion Commander of the 2nd Worcestershire (Bromsgrove) Battalion Home Guard issued orders to his unit commanders to undertake a survey of slit trenches, weapons pits and barbed wire and to consider which of them no longer served any useful purpose and could be dispensed with. Such trenches and weapons pits were to be filled in and wire collected and stored at their headquarters. Again it is likely that this action was not confined to one battalion.

CHAPTER 4

Defence of Airfields
and the Obstruction of Landing Grounds

It was expected that a German bombing campaign would be aimed at the destruction of our air power, as well as civilian and industrial targets. New RAF establishments were therefore located and designed to minimise the effect of bombing and airfields provided with a widely dispersed layout of aircraft hard-standings. However, it was not until the spring of 1940 that it was fully realised by Home Defence planners that the airfields and other potential landing grounds could also be a target for capture and utilisation by invading airborne troops.

Initially, the British response was to increase airfield ground defences throughout the country, primarily with rudimentary infantry trench works and Lewis gun positions, and to obstruct other potential landing grounds around London and within five miles of operational airfields. Towards the end of May, the policy of obstructing landing grounds was extended to all areas within five miles of vulnerable locations.

Winston Churchill took a keen interest in airfield defences and declared that 'each airman should have his place in the defence scheme. It must be understood by all ranks that they are expected to fight and die in the defence of their airfields. Every building which fits in with the scheme of defence should be prepared so that each has to be conquered one by one by the enemy's parachute or glider troops. In two or three hours the Army will arrive ...'. He wanted every airfield to be a stronghold of fighting airmen and every man in the RAF to be armed with something, even a pike or mace, and that they should do at least an hour's drill and practice every day. In due time, the RAF Regiment would be formed.

In the September of 1940, the Taylor Report provided a more systematic basis for airfield defence, with the scale of defences on each airfield being related to the location of the facility. Those within 20 miles of a port would be Class I; those within five miles of an inland vulnerable point, such as an armaments production or storage facility would be Class II, while those with low risk would be Class III. The Central Midland Defence Scheme of December 1940 categorised airfields in Worcestershire as follows: Worcester (Perdiswell), Category II; Pershore, then under construction and nearing completion, also as Category II; while Honeybourne, under construction and some way off completion, was Category III. Defford Airfield was not listed.

Taylor envisaged that a typical attack on an airfield would have three phases: a heavy opening bombing and machine gun attack to create confusion, send some of the defenders to their air raid shelters and destroy some of their defences. This would be followed by the dropping of parachutists, equipped with automatic weapons, grenades and probably mortars and flamethrowers to seize the airfield. Gas might be used. Finally, large numbers of infantry would then arrive in transport aircraft, supported by covering fire from the paratroops already on the ground, and landing either directly on the airfield or in the surrounding area. Throughout, it was anticipated that Luftwaffe fighters would provide a screen around the operations to fend off British ground or air attacks. It was expected that the attack would come at dawn.

The successful capture of Crete, in May 1941, solely by airborne troops, both parachute and air-landed, arriving on and around Maleme Airfield itself, albeit with heavy casualties, forced a

This air photograph, taken in the late 1960s, shows a number of the 'frying pan' aircraft hard standings on the north side of Honeybourne airfield and illustrates well the RAF policy of dispersing aircraft away from the main airfield in order to reduce losses through bombing or strafing attacks. Cow Honeybourne village is to the top right of the photograph.
(Courtesy of WHEAS)

Right: Bernard Lowry and Mike Osborne inspect a light anti-aircraft position formed from two sunken pre-cast concrete sewer pipes at Long Marston airfield, a feature that would have been seen around the perimeter of most wartime airfields. A pair of Lewis guns would probably have occupied this position. The building in the background is a transformer plinth

re-assessment of airfield defences in Britain. Instead of isolated defence posts and pillboxes, it was decided that henceforth defended localities should be formed within the airfield perimeter and that a mobile reserve should be formed to counter attack any enemy that penetrated the defences. The means of transporting the mobile defence reserve on airfields led to some interesting improvised armoured vehicles being created, including the Armadillo. This was basically a pillbox mounted on a heavy lorry. There is evidence of at least one of these being provided in Worcestershire, as well as Humber Beaverettes (see Figure 7). The influence of the airborne attack on Crete can be seen by comparing the defences of the airfields in Worcestershire. Honeybourne, the last airfield to be constructed in the county had numerous defended localities provided mainly within its perimeter track, whereas Pershore, completed earlier, had pillboxes built on the approaches to the airfield.

Right: Figure 7. Rapid Reaction, 1940: The Armadillo and Beaverette

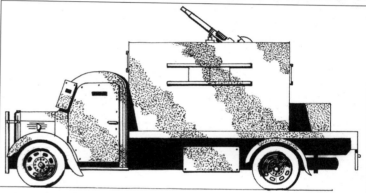

The Armadillo
This was a mobile pillbox based on any available commercial flat-bed vehicle and quickly constructed for use by the RAF in 1940, primarily for airfield defence and rapid deployment against enemy parachute troops. The pillbox was a simple wooden structure with double-skin plywood facing. The gravel infill between the two skins apparently provided adequate protection against small arms fire for the riflemen and Lewis gun crew. There appears also to have been an all-metal version of the Armadillo. Loopholes were provided on each face of the pillbox with sliding steel shutters. Bolt-on armour plate would provided protection for the driver, engine and radiator. Armadillos were deployed at both Pershore and Defford airfields.

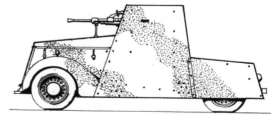

The Beaverette Mk I
Inspired by Lord Beaverbrook, Minister of Aircraft Production, the Beaverette was based on the 14 hp Standard car. The vehicle was intended for protection of MAP factories and airfields, although some were used by Regular Army mobile counter-attack columns for deployment against parachute troops. On the Mk I, mild steel plating and oak planks provided protection for the occupants and the main armament was either a Bren light machine gun or a Boys anti-tank rifle. Improved versions were made available later, based on the Humber Super Snipe car, the final Mk IV version incorporating a small turret. A Beaverette was deployed at Perdiswell airfield and there is evidence of their use in mobile columns in Worcestershire.

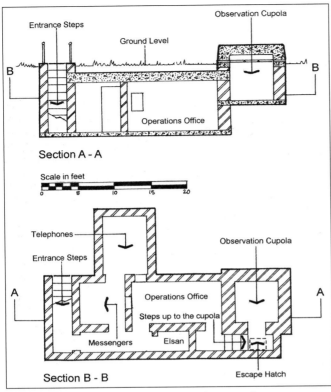

Section A - A

Scale in feet

Section B - B

Figure 8. Type 11008/41 Battle Headquarters as provided at Defford, Honeybourne, Perdiswell and Pershore airfields

To provide a more coordinated defence of airfields, a design for a standard Air Ministry Battle Headquarters was also issued in May 1941. This was a largely underground structure with only a strong, concrete-covered, observation cupola showing above ground. Designated the Air Ministry Type No.11008/41 (see Figure 8), all of the airfields in Worcestershire, with the exception of Berrow, were provided with one. The battle headquarters was normally sited on the highest point on, or adjoining, the airfield and from here the defence forces would be directed by telephone and runners. Also during 1941, the Blacker Bombard or Spigot Mortar became available and this weapon was eventually to provide the basis of anti-tank defence for airfields, although the priorities for issue meant that airfields came after provision had been made for beach defences and nodal points.

1 February 1942 saw the formation of the RAF Regiment. Prior to this date airfield defence had been taken on by the

All that can normally be seen of the RAF Type 41/11008 Battle Headquarters is the heavy concrete observation cupola, the majority of the accommodation being underground. This one survives at Long Marston, Warwickshire, the former satellite airfield for RAF Honeybourne, but another can be visited at the Wellesbourne Air Museum

Men of the 9th Worcestershire (Redditch) Battalion Home Guard practise with their Blacker Bombard or Spigot Mortar on a portable mounting. These weapons were to be used primarily in an anti-tank role at road blocks and at airfields. (Courtesy of Mr E.P. Grace via Mike Johnson)

Administrative and General Duties branch of the airfield establishment and manned by NCOs and aircraftsmen, armed with light weapons. After the RAF Regiment had been formed the standard infantry 3 inch Mortar was supplied. Light anti-aircraft weapons supplied to the RAF Regiment initially included Lewis, Browning and Vickers machine guns on anti-aircraft mountings, but from 1943 Hispano 20 mm ex-aircraft cannon were also used in this role.

In addition to the active military defences put in place to deal with direct enemy attack, passive defences were also provided to protect ground crews working out on the airfield, or aircrews caught out in the open during an air attack. These took the form of trench shelters, or above-ground, but open-topped, brick-built blast shelters, or earth-covered above ground shelters, usually of pre-formed concrete construction produced by the Stanton Company. Stanton shelters were also used extensively on the dispersed RAF domestic sites.

Other passive forms of defence included attempts to camouflage the airfield by various means and where evidence of this policy has been found this is described in the following sections dealing with individual airfields. However, the initial methods of camouflage by painting in hedgerow patterns and spraying grass in irregular patches to simulate fields was found to be wasteful of manpower, and so differential mowing of the airfield grassed areas, or use of fertilisers, or different grass mixes on selected areas provided a lower-cost approach to camouflage. The camouflage of buildings was achieved usually by painting them in irregular patterns of green, brown and black, although hangars tended to be painted a matt bituminous black.

Another form of passive defence was the provision of decoy sites in open countryside and away from the parent airfields. Of the airfields in Worcestershire, only Pershore and Defford were provided with decoys and the details of these can be found in Chapter 10.

In the summer of 1940 there were two extant airfields: Perdiswell, later to become RAF Worcester and the small, former private, airfield at Tilesford, to the north of Pinvin. No records have been found of the defences for Tilesford but by the end of 1940, it was be massively extended to become RAF Pershore, whilst entirely new airfields were being constructed at Defford and Honeybourne, all for training Bomber Command aircrew. Further small grass landing grounds were added at Littleworth and Berrow in 1941. These airfields will now be looked at in the chronological order of their construction and use, and their defences described where known.

Perdiswell Airfield (RAF Worcester)

Sited just to the north of Bilford Road and on former parkland attached to Perdiswell Hall, Worcester City Council chose to establish a municipal airport here in 1931. The limited landing space of just 1,000 yards north to south and 800 yards east to west meant that the airport was really suitable only for light aircraft and not serious airline services. However, the Munich crisis of 1938 resulted in substantially increased flying activity there, primarily by the Austin Aircraft Division using the airfield for the flight testing of Fairy Battle light bombers then being built as part of the shadow factory scheme at Longbridge. After this contract with the Air Ministry had been completed by Austins, the airfield returned to only occasional use during 1940.

Clearly the airfield would have provided a wonderful opportunity for German airborne troops to be landed in some quantity for an attack on Worcester, and to prevent its use by enemy aircraft during the summer of that year, the grass landing strips were obstructed with scrap cars and unwanted agricultural implements. These could be quickly moved to one side should the airfield be required for RAF use, for example, by the No.13 Squadron Westland Lysander aircraft, should they need to be used in an anti-invasion bombing role as mentioned in Chapter 2. When the No.2 Elementary Flying Training School RAF arrived later in 1940 to begin training ab

This painting by the late Maurice Jones captures the character of Perdiswell Airfield during the early part of the war with No.2 EFTS operating their Tiger Moths.
The north-south runway can be seen to the left in this view, looking north from about the centre of the airfield. The outline of the blister hangar in the background can still be discerned in dry weather in the turf of one of the golf fairways.
(Courtesy of the late Maurice Jones)

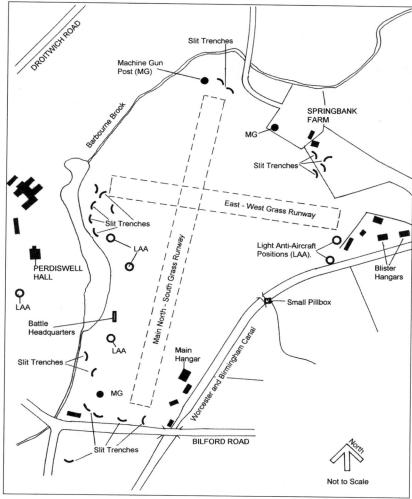

Figure 9. RAF Worcester, Perdiswell, airfield defences, July 1943

initio pilots, the scrap vehicles were stored almost permanently along the western boundary of the airfield and remained there until the end of the war.

Responsibility for the airfield's defence from May 1940 was initially given to the Worcester Local Defence Volunteers, later renamed the 1st Worcestershire (Worcester) Battalion Home Guard, and remained with them until the middle of January 1941 when a platoon of the 11th Battalion, the Royal Warwickshire Regiment arrived to provide a day and night guard. From February 1942, the RAF Regiment provided the defence for the airfield.

One of the few Standing Order papers for the Worcester Local Defence Volunteers that have survived, detailed a minimum of 14 men and a Section Leader for defence of the airfield, with a minimum of seven rifles to be issued. Initially three defence posts were formed on the airfield: Post A (East Trench), near the canal bridge; Post B (West Trench), the location of which has been identified by the late Maurice Jones as west of the centre of the main north-south runway, and Post C (South Trench), located near the then main entrance to the airfield, off Bilford Road. These posts were to be fully manned during stand-to and two men were to patrol. Post B was to have two men on duty throughout the tour of duty from 8.30 pm until 5 am.

An account of these early days of the Worcester LDV duty at Perdiswell has been recorded by the late Peter Whittaker who recalled that protection of the airfield was one of the first tasks of the LDV immediately after their initial parade at Silver Street Drill Hall. The war situation was so tense then that the first men on duty were issued with their few rifles and sent off post-haste to the airfield with the ammunition loose, in bags. There had been no time to make up clips and so the first patrols were conducted with the magazines empty and just 'one up the spout'! He remembered that the slit trenches were dug to provide a cross-fire over the airfield.

The smallest pillbox of them all? This small brick defence post can still be found on the canal bridge at SO 859 574, adjoining the former airfield at Perdiswell

In late 1940, the RAF increased its use of Perdiswell as a satellite landing ground by No.2 Elementary Flying School, then based at Staverton airfield, near Cheltenham. 1941 brought a further increase in flying, with No.2 EFTS moving the whole of its organisation to Perdiswell and then, to cope with the amount of flying training, opening a relief landing ground at Littleworth. The defences for Perdiswell were then considerably expanded and Figure 9 shows the range of defences available in July 1943.

During the early part of the invasion scare period, a Beaverette Armoured Car was observed to be often stationed outside the airfield boundary and alongside the Droitwich Road. Whether this was part of the airfield defences or to help protect the Ministry of Aircraft Production factory run by the Metal Castings is not clear.

Nothing remains above ground of the fixed airfield defences now, apart from a tiny brick-built defence post on the canal bridge at SO 859 574.

None of the passive defence structures of Perdiswell remain, but earth-covered shelters are remembered by the author as being sited in the wide tree-covered grass verge, alongside the A38, opposite where The Perdiswell pub is now. The hummocky nature of the ground here suggests that some of the structures may still be present.

Pershore Airfield

This airfield has its origins in a small pre-war private airfield run by the Worcestershire Flying Club at Tilesford which was requisitioned by the RAF at the outset of the war. It was then considerably expanded to become No.23 Operational Training Unit (OTU) and used to train Bomber Command aircrew using Vickers Wellington aircraft. Rather like Perdiswell Airfield, the layout of Pershore Airfield betrays its early war origins by having almost all the personnel accommodation within the airfield boundary. Only the WAAF site is located away from the airfield, near Pinvin. On the major airfields built later in the county, the domestic sites would be dispersed over a wide rural area in order to minimise the effects of air attacks. Care would be taken of the aircraft at Pershore with 'frying pan' dispersals or hard standings spread out into the countryside surrounding the perimeter track. This is clear from Figure 11. Pershore Airfield was the longest lasting of the wartime airfields in Worcestershire, not closing down for flying until the end of 1978.

In the spring of 1941, when the airfield was reopened as an OTU, the airfield defences must have been extensive. No defence plans have so far been found, apart from an airfield plan showing the location of a Type 11008/41 Battle Headquarters on the east side of the airfield and a number of small arms ammunition stores and 'defence huts', the latter presumably to provide shelter for the airfield defence force when not occupying their defence posts. The defence huts may, therefore, indicate where there were former defence positions or pillboxes.

The location of the battle headquarters and three recorded pillboxes tell us something of the defence layout. The sole remaining pillbox is located on the left-hand side of the airfield approach road from Pinvin, adjoining Piddle Brook on the opposite side to the Willow Bank Nursing Home, at SO 963 501 (see Figure 10). Another pillbox of the same hexagonal type can be seen on recent air photographs, sited in a hedgerow approximately ¼ mile to the north-east of Throckmorton Farm, and appears to have been demolished only in the last two years. Yet another is remembered as being sited on the side of the road just beyond Throckmorton village, to the east of the airfield. These represent just a small proportion of what would have been a continuous ring of such defence posts around the airfield, but the key point is that they were some distance from the airfield and reflected the then current view that any enemy parachute troops were expected to have landed some way from the airfield and then move cross-country or along the local roads to make their attack. This view would change later!

Glyn Warren, in his history of Pershore Airfield, identifies four brick and concrete pillboxes still existing in 1982, but unfortunately not their locations. He also records

The last remaining pillbox protecting Pershore Airfield can be seen at SO 963 501, adjoining Long Lane, Tilesford.
Figure 10 (below). The plan of this Type FW3/22 pillbox

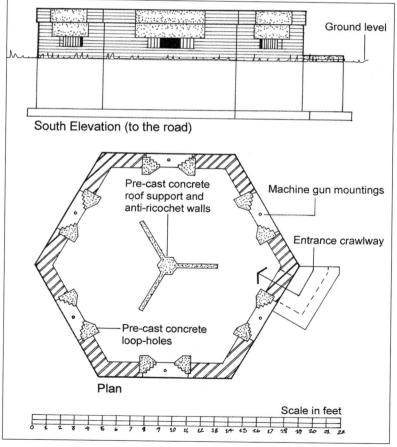

South Elevation (to the road)

Plan

Pre-cast concrete roof support and anti-ricochet walls

Machine gun mountings

Entrance crawlway

Pre-cast concrete loop-holes

Ground level

Scale in feet

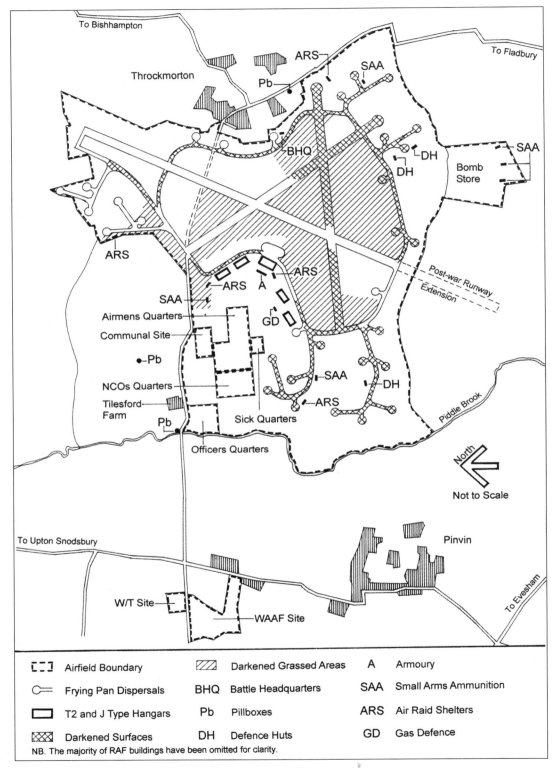

Figure 11. Pershore Airfield defences

50

the availability of two defence vehicles each manned by a driver, three riflemen and armed with a Lewis Gun on a Scarff Ring. These were probably Armadillos. One of these vehicles was posted each night near the control tower, while the other was stationed somewhere on the perimeter track near No.5 Gun Post. The latter was probably a light anti-aircraft position and the numbering suggests at least four others, although where they were will probably remain a mystery.

Figure 11 illustrates what is known about the airfield defences. Initial responsibility for the defence of the airfield was in the hands of Lieutenant Colonel E.D.B. Oxley MC.

From 1942, airfield defence became the responsibility of No.4313 and No.4318 Flights of the RAF Regiment and in an exercise with the Pershore Company of Home Guard, during 1943, these Flights apparently succeeded in capturing Pershore Railway Station and the nearby Atlas Works.

It is significant that Pershore Airfield is the only airfield in the county where a GHQ Auxiliary patrol was specifically recruited to keep it under observation and, should it have been captured and occupied by the Germans, to sabotage their aircraft, fuel and munitions stores (see Chapter 12).

Many methods were tried for reducing the visual impact of concrete and tarmac runways, perimeter tracks and aircraft dispersals on the landscape, in particular the shine from hard surfaces that was apparent during wet weather and when observed from the air. Pershore airfield was used for the first experiments in the use of wood chips as a means of texturing the surfaces to reduce shine. Apparently the experiment was successful and this became the standard method elsewhere. Other than this fact, no details of the wartime camouflage scheme for the airfield have so far been found, but a post-war scheme showing differential colouring for the main runways, and for the grass management, suggests that the wartime scheme may have been perpetuated into the Cold War period and so has been reproduced on Figure 11.

A guard hut, the main hangars and the control tower remain on the airfield but most of the smaller structures have been cleared away. One Stanton air raid shelter remains by the side of the road across the former airfield, from Pinvin to Throckmorton.

Berrow Landing Ground

This grass airfield, at SO 803 340, was created out of a number of fields and taken into use by the RAF in March 1941 as No.5 Satellite Landing Ground. Only the Watch Office, now converted into a bungalow, can be seen from the road at SO 802 345. The airfield was primarily a discrete storage facility, hidden in deep countryside, where newly-built aircraft could be kept under camouflaged dispersals until needed by operational squadrons. It was also used occasionally by gliders from Shobdon, Herefordshire, and aircraft from Defford, landing here in connection with the adjoining Sledge Green radar facility of Telecommunications Research Establishment (TRE). Two runways were provided, one with a north-south orientation being used almost exclusively, but a second, and separate, east-west track along the line of the present M50 Motorway was also available. The airfield was closed in May 1945. None of the airfield defences remain but an aerial photograph of 1942 indicates that there were five circular defence positions in the locations shown on Figure 12. These were almost certainly sandbagged emplacements for light anti-aircraft weapons, probably Lewis guns and would have been used in a ground defence role if needed.

Airfield defence was initially provided by the 11th Battalion, The Royal Warwickshire Regiment, that was billeted in the farm buildings at The Hill, at SO 804 351. Later the task of

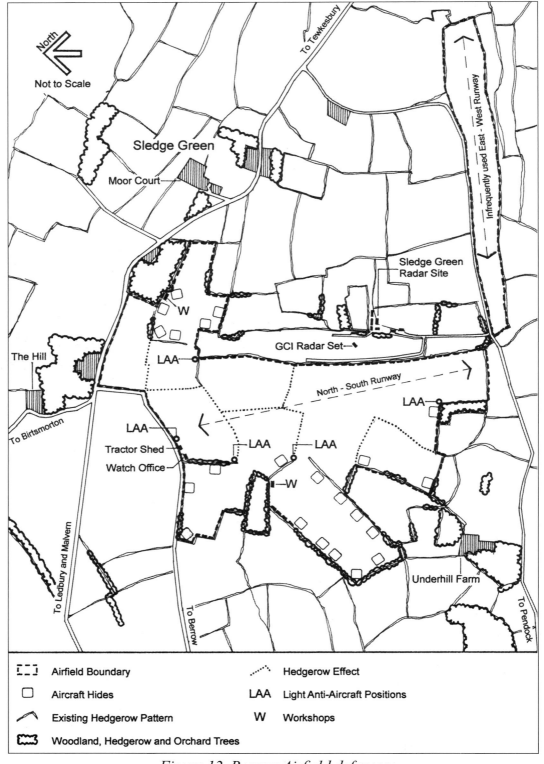

Figure 12. Berrow Airfield defences

defence was taken on by a Home Guard platoon formed at the airfield from civilian staff employed there. This became No.13b Platoon of the 7th Worcestershire (Malvern) Battalion Home Guard, the Platoon Commander being Lieutenant Briden.

Having removed a number of hedgerows to create this grass-covered landing ground, the former location of the hedges was painted back in to disguise the presence of the north-south orientated runway. The material used was a bituminous paint, and the late Derek Smith remembered his father being asked to let his cattle onto the airfield, when there was no flying, in an effort to create the appearance of farmed countryside. Unfortunately, the paint was toxic and he lost some of his cattle as a result of ingesting it!

Littleworth Satellite Landing Ground

Established by No.2 EFTS of RAF Worcester as a relief landing ground for Perdiswell, the only sign that there was an airfield here is the large and derelict, hangar-like building alongside the road to Pershore at SO 896 507. This was in fact an agricultural building but was utilised during the operational use of the landing ground to shelter a fire tender. No defences have so far been identified for the landing ground. However, it seems likely that such a large field, before being used by No.2 EFTS, would have been obstructed in some way to prevent enemy aircraft from landing there. No evidence has come forward for this, however.

This skeletal hangar-like building alongside the Worcester-Pershore road is a reminder that there was once a satellite landing ground at Littleworth. Although of agricultural origins, this building was used by the No.2 Elementary Flying Training School of Perdiswell to accommodate their fire tender

Defford Airfield

Defford was the next major airfield to be constructed in the county, being completed in September 1941 as a satellite for No.23 OTU at Pershore. Its use as a bomber crew training airfield came to an end in May 1942, when it was occupied by the Telecommunications Flying Unit (TFU), attached to the TRE that had then arrived at Malvern. Many additional aircraft hard standings were provided, mainly in the wooded area on the west side of the airfield, for the vastly increased number of aircraft to be operated by the TFU, the pilots and ground crews being provided by both a Naval Air Section of the Fleet Air Arm, as well as the Royal Air Force. The main north-south runway was also extended southwards to accommodate larger aircraft along with many dispersals provided on the south side of the airfield to be used by visiting operational aircraft to have radar equipment fitted by a Special Installations Unit. Defford airfield was unique in Worcestershire in the use of blast pens to protect some of the aircraft hard standings and it is presumed that some of the aircraft used here for experimental purposes were irreplaceable and needed the extra protection these raised earthwork defences provided. It could also be as a result of the close proximity of

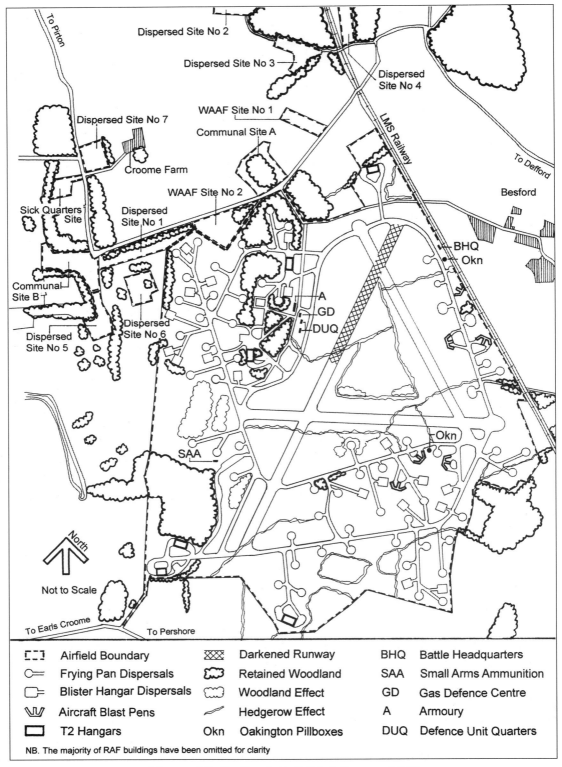

Legend

⊏⊐	Airfield Boundary	⊠⊠⊠	Darkened Runway	BHQ	Battle Headquarters
◠=	Frying Pan Dispersals	◠◠	Retained Woodland	SAA	Small Arms Ammunition
◻=	Blister Hangar Dispersals	◠◠◠	Woodland Effect	GD	Gas Defence Centre
ⱵⱵ	Aircraft Blast Pens	⁓	Hedgerow Effect	A	Armoury
▢	T2 Hangars	Okn	Oakington Pillboxes	DUQ	Defence Unit Quarters

NB. The majority of RAF buildings have been omitted for clarity

Figure 13. Defford Airfield defences, 1942

the LMS railway to the east side of the railway preventing wider dispersal of open hard standings into the surrounding countryside. Figure 13 illustrates these features of the airfield and the greater efforts made to disperse the domestic sites for personnel than at RAF Pershore, to minimise the effects of an enemy air attack.

Nothing appears to remain of the airfield defences, apart from a number of blast and air raid shelters hidden in the woods. One or two Stanton air raid shelters and an emergency water supply tank for fire-fighting purposes survive on one of the former dispersed domestic sites in the woods to the north of the airfield at SO 902 462. As a result of having an airfield sited close-by, and the expectation of air attacks on the airfield affecting the village, Besford was provided with a large civilian style surface air raid shelter. This can still be seen at SO 909 449.

An Air Ministry airfield layout plan indicates that there was a Battle Headquarters sited on the east side of the airfield, near the railway line, with an Oakington pillbox (see Figure 14) immediately to the south of it. Another Oakington pillbox was located to the south of the perimeter track, on the northern edge of the aircraft dispersal area. The Battle Headquarters type is not specified but was most likely to have been a Type 11008/41. No Oakington pillboxes remain in the county now but there are some surviving on Long Marston Airfield, to the north-east of Evesham, but in Warwickshire. They are of a low profile mushroom form and provide 360 degrees field of fire. The location of these defence posts on the airfield itself reflect the experiences of defence forces on Crete, where the enemy parachutists and the follow up air landed troops arrived on the airfield itself.

Glyn Warren notes that even before the airfield was opened for flying by No.23 OTU, an Armadillo was despatched from Pershore, together with an RAF corporal and ten men, to provide some defence for Defford. No details of subsequent ground defence forces have been found so far.

Wartime photographs reveal the methods of camouflaging the airfield by darkening the surface of the northern section of the main runway and the creation of a pattern of false hedgerows and fields running counter to the pattern of the main runways. Existing woodlands were used to provide a degree of camouflage. Remnants of camouflage paint can also be seen on the few remaining technical buildings at SO 896 445.

The airfield ceased to be used for flying by the TFU in 1957, when the runways, despite an extension, were no longer adequate for the faster jets then being used in radar experiments. Part of the airfield is still used for satellite tracking purposes and radar dishes can still be seen. Two of the former hangars have been converted to form the basis of an animal feed mill in the south-west corner of the airfield, while the former bomb store and a few huts remain on the former technical site. Otherwise little can be seen of the former airfield buildings. However, the former Sick Quarters Site is almost complete and can still be seen on the edge of Croome Park, at SO 887 452, and is now owned, and being restored, by the National Trust.

Honeybourne Airfield

Completed in November 1941, this airfield was first occupied by RAF Ferry Training units, until No.24 OTU arrived in March 1942 with their Armstrong Whitworth Whitleys. The airfield would then remain a Bomber Command operational training facility until July 1945, when it was passed to Maintenance Command. Flying ceased in August 1946.

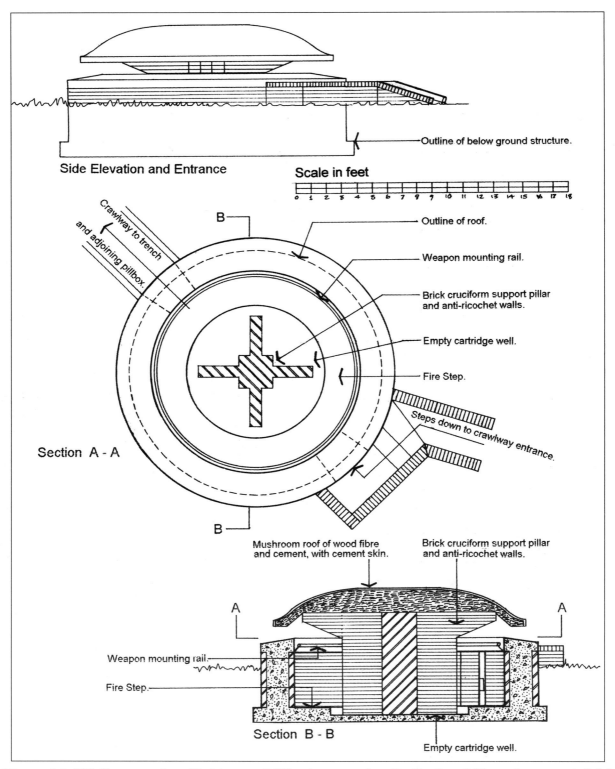

Side Elevation and Entrance

Outline of below ground structure.

Scale in feet

0 1 2 3 4 5 6 7 8 9 10 11 12 13 14 15 16 17 18

Crawlway to trench and adjoining pillbox.

B

Outline of roof.

Weapon mounting rail.

Brick cruciform support pillar and anti-ricochet walls.

Empty cartridge well.

Fire Step.

Section A - A

Steps down to crawlway entrance.

B

Mushroom roof of wood fibre and cement, with cement skin.

Brick cruciform support pillar and anti-ricochet walls.

A

A

Weapon mounting rail.

Fire Step.

Section B - B

Empty cartridge well.

Figure 14. FC Construction (Oakington Pillbox), as used at Defford and Honeybourne airfields

56

*Bernard Lowry admires an FC Construction,
or Oakington Pillbox, at Long Marston Airfield
in Warwickshire. Once numerous in Worcestershire,
there are none now left in the county*

*This 1960s air photograph shows two of the Oakington
Pillbox complexes at Honeybourne, with their distinctive
three-armed connecting trench systems. None remain now.
The airfield Control Tower (now a house) and the ancillary
buildings can be seen in the top left of the photograph, with
Ryknild Street along the bottom. Clearly influenced by the
invasion of Crete and the capture of Maleme Airfield
by German parachute troops, the defence positions at
Honeybourne are within the perimeter track.
(Courtesy of WHEAS)*

None of the airfield ground defences appear to remain now, although an Air Ministry airfield plan indicates that they were extensive. A Type 11008/41 Battle Headquarters was located on the west side of what is now Cow Honeybourne village playing field and six 'defence localities' were spaced around the inside of the airfield perimeter track. Clearly the experiences at Maleme airfield, Crete, had been taken into account here. There is a suspicious bramble thicket on the edge of the village playing field that might hide the remains of the Battle Headquarters, and one of the defence localities recently showed up as a crop mark, which suggests that these largely concrete structures were not totally demolished when the main airfield was cleared for agricultural use. Some of the structures may remain under the ground surface.

Figure 15 indicates that five of the six defence localities were three-armed zig-zag trench systems, with either an arrowhead-shaped firing position — or an Oakington Pillbox — at the end of each arm. The sixth defence location, sited at the north and higher side of the airfield, was a single trench system incorporating four Oakington pillboxes, over 200 yards long and providing a wide field of fire over the

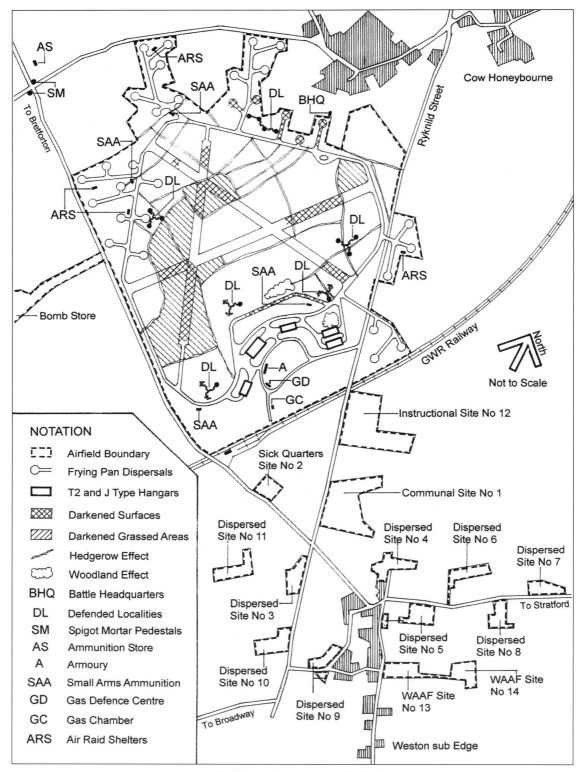

NOTATION

⌐⌐⌐	Airfield Boundary
⊂—	Frying Pan Dispersals
▭	T2 and J Type Hangars
▨	Darkened Surfaces
▧	Darkened Grassed Areas
∿	Hedgerow Effect
☁	Woodland Effect
BHQ	Battle Headquarters
DL	Defended Localities
SM	Spigot Mortar Pedestals
AS	Ammunition Store
A	Armoury
SAA	Small Arms Ammunition
GD	Gas Defence Centre
GC	Gas Chamber
ARS	Air Raid Shelters

Figure 15. Honeybourne Airfield defences

58

airfield. Two of the former small arms ammunition stores can still be seen on the airfield, one near the former control tower and a second at SP 114 417. Defence of the airfield was the responsibility of Lieutenant Colonel C.J.M. Riley MC.

Of the passive defences, there are still a number of blast shelters to be seen near the Technical Site, on the airfield, and at the Instructional and Communal Sites on the east side of the Honeybourne to Weston-sub-Edge road. Stanton surface shelters can also still be seen on some of the former RAF dispersed domestic sites around Weston-sub-Edge. A particularly good collection still remains on the right-hand side of the road out of the village, towards Mickleton, presumably

One of two Small Arms Ammunition Stores that survive on the former Honeybourne Airfield. Of temporary brick and asbestos construction, this example can still be seen near the Bretforton to Weston sub Edge road, in the south-west corner of the airfield

A number of blast shelters survive near Defford and Honeybourne airfields. These were provided for RAF personnel who might be caught out in the open during an enemy air raid on their airfield or dispersed site

kept because they make good animal shelters. Wartime air photographs indicate that attempts to camouflage the airfield were comprehensive and included painting in false hedgerows and differing crop patterns over the runways. These are shown diagrammatically in Figure 15.

It is also clear that the wider dispersal of the domestic sites around and beyond Weston-sub-Edge village was an attempt to 'lose' them amongst the buildings of the village and wider countryside to camouflage their existence. The result was a long hike to and from the airfield by the personnel and, with about 2,000 RAF men and women accommodated in and around a small village, no doubt a massive impact on the social life of the community, if only to drink the Weston Arms pub dry!

Although most of the ground defence structures have now gone, for anyone interested in wartime airfield buildings, Honeybourne has the best preserved collection of any of the former airfields in Worcestershire. A visit to the technical site, now Honeybourne Trading Estate at SP 117 423 and the two former RAF communal sites at SP 121 421 and SP 123 417, would be rewarding. However, all three sites are now used

The distinctive barrel-shaped form of the Stanton air raid shelter can still be found in the vicinity of airfields in Worcestershire, this example being seen on the site of a former dispersed site of Honeybourne Airfield, in Weston-sub-Edge village. It has lost some of its earth covering and the brick entrance way, but is otherwise complete. The shelter had a pre-formed concrete interior

The people of Bretforton have indicated their pride in the two spigot mortar pedestals on the crossroads at SP 099 429 by mounting small plaques on them to explain their purpose. The pedestals were probably part of the Honeybourne airfield defences, the weapon being mounted on the stainless steel pintle

for commercial purposes and it is inevitable that continuing change and redevelopment will lead to a gradual loss of the original buildings. Sadly, one of the last few remaining circular, corrugated metal, emergency fire-fighting water tanks left in Worcestershire, has gone in recent years.

Outside the airfield, two spigot mortar pedestals and a Home Guard ammunition store remain to be seen at the crossroads near the north-west corner of the airfield, at SP 099 429, near Bretforton. These were almost certainly part of the outer defences of the airfield. Local residents have drawn attention to the importance of these defence structures by applying metal plaques to them, but the associated Home Guard ammunition store, in the field to the north, is apparently not the subject of such local interest and has deteriorated badly in recent years.

Obstructing Potential Landing Grounds

Instructions for the obstruction of appropriate areas of open land or stretches of water, as a deterrent against enemy aircraft landing, were sent by the Midland Regional Office in Great Charles Street, Birmingham to Worcestershire County Council on 6 July 1940, with a requirement to start work at once. It was suggested that the services of local town planning officers, who knew the location of such features, and other suitably qualified persons should be called upon to volunteer their services for the task. A broadcast appeal for volunteers to help was also made by the government. The instructions issued required that priority should be given to the obstruction of potential landing grounds in the vicinity of towns, railway junctions and marshalling yards, and trunk roads or factories of importance. These potential landing grounds were level grassed areas, including such facilities as golf courses, parks and sports grounds, measuring more than 300 yards in any direction. Suggested methods of obstruction included: ditches at least 4 feet wide and 3 feet 6 inches deep dug across the land at 200-yard intervals; lines of old vehicles at similar intervals (the value of these obstacles could be increased by loading them with earth); lines of felled trees, stumps etc; fencing of various types, but to be strong and firmly fixed, sufficient to overturn an aircraft; concrete cubes measuring about 3 feet 6 inches, in lines; and low, rough stone walling. Clearly the experiences in Holland, where Junkers Ju 52 aircraft were landed almost anywhere where there was sufficient or, in some cases, insufficient space, had been taken to heart!

There were limitations on the work, however: no crops were to be interfered with at the time as food supply was of paramount importance, nor were communications to be interfered with; and shortages of squared timber or steel meant limitations on their use as obstructions too. It was suggested that timber unusable for other purposes, such as stout poles, sunk into the ground and spaced at intervals could be used. The requirement by the Ministry of Agriculture to avoid interfering with arable land probably accounts for why a number of very large but cultivated fields in the Severn and Teme valleys were not obstructed. The soft nature of cultivated land would be an obstruction in itself, if not to aircraft landing then certainly to their taking off again. On grasslands, however, farmers were urged, via the local press, to cooperate in their obstruction by building their hayricks, where possible, in the middle of the fields which might be used by the enemy as landing grounds. It was put to farmers that it would be useful to build two or more ricks, spaced across the field. On the other hand, the building of hayricks near existing aerodromes was to be avoided if at all possible!

Clearly influenced again by the Dutch experience, the instructions went on to point out that lakes, reservoirs and stretches of river could be used to land troop carrying floatplanes and that it was necessary to guard against this eventuality. It was said that these heavy machines needed a low gliding angle when coming into land, requiring 250 to 300 yards of water in which to pull up. It was suggested that some planes could land in water only 2 feet 6 inches deep. Types of obstruction for these situations included: lines of barrels, sleepers, logs, thick branches of trees etc interconnected with wire and anchored to heavy weights at intervals; boats, barges and rafts similarly connected and anchored (to delay the use of these as ferries by enemy troops, it was suggested that they should be partially filled with water and loaded with ballast to increase their weight); strong wooden fencing stretched between stout posts that was intended to float on the surface and have wire concertinas placed on top; ropes slung between stout poles about two feet above the surface although it was pointed out that the quantity of wire rope available was limited; and piles driven in at 60 feet intervals, rising to at least four feet above the surface of the water. Use of squared timber and steel was again to be kept to a minimum.

The response to these instructions was made by the then County Planning Officer whose staff was detailed to firstly identify areas of land that needed obstructing and then organise the marking out ready for labouring gangs to follow up with the obstructions. Rough hewn strong wooden poles were erected so that about 12 feet of each pole stuck out of the ground and the effect was a small forest of poles. These were thought to have been sufficiently adequate to damage the wings of aircraft attempting to land so as to prevent them taking off again.

This late 1960s air photograph of the partially flooded large ham at Tewkesbury illustrates very well part of the grid pattern of trenches dug in 1940 to obstruct this potential landing ground for enemy aircraft. The trenches can still be discerned on the ground here, as can those on some of the Worcestershire hams, notably at Upton upon Severn. (Courtesy of WHEAS)

Although no contemporary maps have survived indicating which large open spaces were so obstructed have been found, eyewitness accounts have resulted in a good number being identified. These include the large riverside hams and fields at Upton on Severn, Kempsey, Powick, Wyre Piddle and Pershore; Boughton Park Golf Course, Pitchcroft and Perdiswell in Worcester, two large fields near Bransford Bridge, another near New Mill Bridge at Shelsley Beauchamp, two large fields and the golf course at Redditch; one to the west of the area that became Merebrook Camp, and another to the north of the future Blackmore No.1 Camp, both near Malvern, together with a large field to the south of Pershore airfield. This latter area was eventually to be used for a post-war southward runway extension. There will be many other examples of large fields which were obstructed that have yet to come to light and be recorded.

The majority of fields or hams appear to have been obstructed with wooden poles, but lengths of steel tram rail, apparently salvaged from the former Tram Depot in St John's were used at Boughton Park and at Pitchcroft. Steel poles were also used on Kempsey Ham, the stubs of which can still be seen. Concrete blocks were used at Shelsley Beauchamp and at Redditch Golf Course.

Bill Allington recalls that the poles used at his father's farm at Lower Howsen were not very good quality and quickly rotted. At some stage it appears that the poles on the Hams at Upton were replaced by a grid pattern of trenches which can be clearly seen on air photographs taken at the end of the war, and although backfilled at some stage, can still be seen as a green pattern in the parched grass, particularly during periods of dry weather.

Only two instances of water obstruction have been recorded: an eyewitness account of steel cables being stretched across the River Severn to the south of Stourport Bridge (one of the steel tethering stanchions for anchoring one of two cables here still exists at SO 812 708); and a pattern of floating obstructions on the Bartley Reservoir, on the edge of the county near Frankley, at SP 005 811.

It is likely that the Upper and Lower Bittell canal feeder reservoirs at Hopwood (SP 020 750) were obstructed, but no evidence of this has been found so far.

CHAPTER 5

Stop Lines

In Chapter 2, reference is made to four principal stop lines being constructed in Worcestershire; firstly, a Southern Command proposal for a line through the centre and north-east quarter of the county and then the later Western Command lines along the rivers Avon, Severn and Teme (see Figure 16). However, before any construction work could start, recce parties from III Corps, comprising an infantry officer, a Royal Engineer officer, a draughtsman/clerk, and possibly a Royal Armoured Corps officer went out and surveyed the stop lines, and armed with pegs, paint and the requisite 1/25,000 (2½ inches to 1 mile) scale maps, marked out the proposed defences. The recce party indicated the location of defence works on the ground with the pegs and paint, and recorded them on maps. As part of the survey, watercourses were also to be carefully looked at to ensure that their depth and dimensions constituted an adequate anti-tank obstacle. Sadly none of the reconnaissance maps for Worcestershire appear to have survived.

In connection with the point about the adequacy, or otherwise, of the watercourses in Worcestershire, it would be worthwhile looking at the wading and climbing ability of the more common of German tanks available for an invasion in 1940 and 1941 (see Figure 17), and then consider how our local rivers would have matched up to the requirements. The majority of these tanks were perhaps not as capable as the propaganda films would portray and many people would believe. The maximum slope climbing figures indicated relate to dry conditions. These figures would be reduced during wet weather or on muddy river banks, and would have been influenced by the soil conditions too, the wet clay of much of Worcestershire being about as slippery as it gets!

Clearly the Czechoslovakian built PzKw 38(t), requisitioned by the Germans when that country was occupied in 1938, outperformed the German-built machines in both wading and climbing ability. Some 138 PzKw III and 48 of the PzKw IV tanks were converted to become Tauchpanzer, or deep fording tanks, specifically for the invasion of Britain. Being probably the first ashore, they would also be the first to be disabled by the defence, if they had not already foundered off-shore, and so it is unlikely that any would have reached Worcestershire. Therefore, the River Avon would have provided an adequate obstacle to the unmodified tanks, but the River

Severn would have been a quite formidable obstacle to them, certainly up to Bewdley, where the shallows to the south of the bridge there may have been a cause for concern to the defenders. However, the water depth of the Teme, in places, would have been very suspect, although the generally deep, steep, and unstable banks would have compensated to a degree. The canals in the county, with their vertical masonry flanking walls, would have performed well as anti-tank ditches. However, the protection of lock gates was considered to be crucial in order to prevent their use by enemy troops as crossing points.

It was recognised by Royal Engineer recce parties that the construction of the defence lines in Worcestershire would take some time and so priorities for work were to be clearly stated in their reports. Consequently crossings of primary importance were to be put into a state of defence before other less important parts of the line. The final results of the recce parties' work was to be a system of all-round defence at main crossings, linked up to a line of defended localities along the whole front, covering with anti-tank and small arms fire any other possible tank crossing points, and covering with small arms fire the whole of the line of the obstacle. The totality of all these defences was enormous. What has been identified by the Defence of Worcestershire Project and what remains is but a tiny fraction of what was constructed.

There is good documentary evidence that construction work on the three main stop lines in Worcestershire began in August 1940, under the direction of Royal Engineer Field Park Companies attached to III Corps. No documentary details have been found for the construction of the Southern Command stop line from the River Severn, through Droitwich, along the Droitwich Junction Canal and the Birmingham–Worcester Canal to

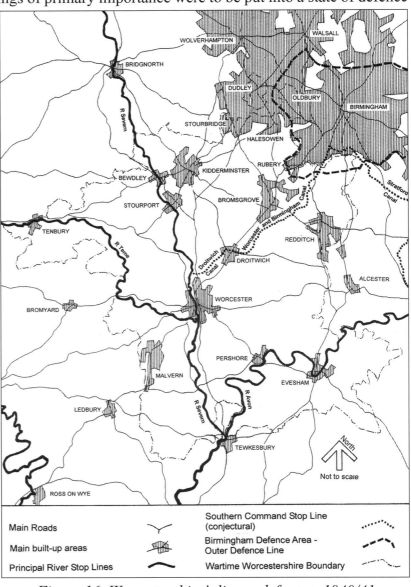

Figure 16. Worcestershire's linear defences, 1940/41

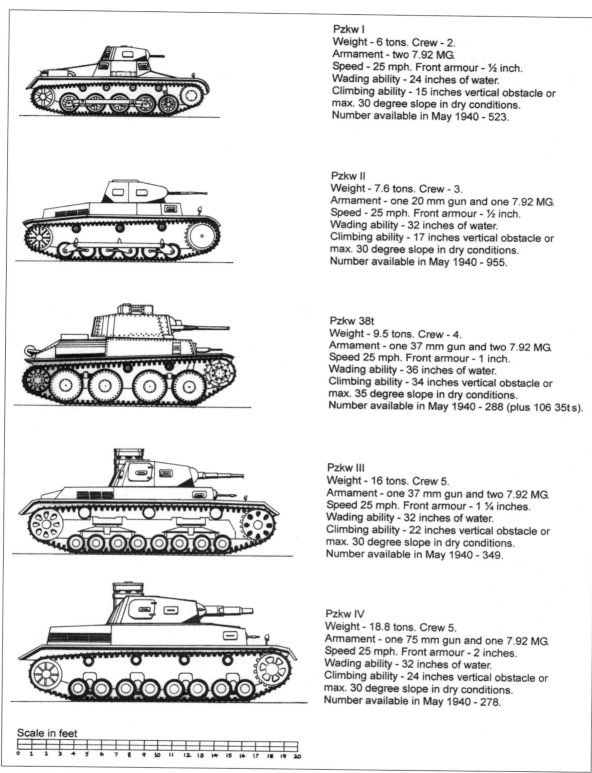

Pzkw I
Weight - 6 tons. Crew - 2.
Armament - two 7.92 MG.
Speed - 25 mph. Front armour - ½ inch.
Wading ability - 24 inches of water.
Climbing ability - 15 inches vertical obstacle or
max. 30 degree slope in dry conditions.
Number available in May 1940 - 523.

Pzkw II
Weight - 7.6 tons. Crew - 3.
Armament - one 20 mm gun and one 7.92 MG.
Speed - 25 mph. Front armour - ½ inch.
Wading ability - 32 inches of water.
Climbing ability - 17 inches vertical obstacle or
max. 30 degree slope in dry conditions.
Number available in May 1940 - 955.

Pzkw 38t
Weight - 9.5 tons. Crew - 4.
Armament - one 37 mm gun and two 7.92 MG.
Speed 25 mph. Front armour - 1 inch.
Wading ability - 36 inches of water.
Climbing ability - 34 inches vertical obstacle or
max. 35 degree slope in dry conditions.
Number available in May 1940 - 288 (plus 106 35t s).

Pzkw III
Weight - 16 tons. Crew 5.
Armament - one 37 mm gun and two 7.92 MG.
Speed 25 mph. Front armour - 1 ¼ inches.
Wading ability - 32 inches of water.
Climbing ability - 22 inches vertical obstacle or
max. 30 degree slope in dry conditions.
Number available in May 1940 - 349.

Pzkw IV
Weight - 18.8 tons. Crew 5.
Armament - one 75 mm gun and one 7.92 MG.
Speed 25 mph. Front armour - 2 inches.
Wading ability - 32 inches of water.
Climbing ability - 24 inches vertical obstacle or
max. 30 degree slope in dry conditions.
Number available in May 1940 - 278.

Scale in feet
0 1 2 3 4 5 6 7 8 9 10 11 12 13 14 15 16 17 18 19 20

Figure 17. Panzer profiles. The essential features of the principal Germans tanks of 1940/41

the north-east corner of the county, yet a few of defence features recorded along that line suggest that at least a start was made on its construction in 1940.

Shortages of various construction materials during August 1940, notably the cement required for mixing concrete and allied shuttering materials, led to demands for careful use of materials and priorities being set for the work on the various stop lines in Western Command. In Worcestershire, this resulted in the Avon line having highest priority, followed by the Severn and then Teme lines. The survival of more structures along the Avon Stop Line suggests the priority system was implemented.

In March 1941, probably due to the realisation that fully manning long defence lines was beyond the capacity of the available Home Guard troops, and probably influenced by the realisation that the German invasion fleet assembled in the Channel ports was not capable of making a successful landing in more than one location, a list of priorities for defending the Midlands stop lines was established as follows:

Priority 1 - The River Avon Stop Line, from the River Severn to Leamington, facing south, and then on to Braunston.

Priority 2 - The River Severn Stop Line, from Tewkesbury to Llandrino; the stop line from Leamington to Coventry and Nuneaton using the Avon and canal; and the River Wye Stop Line, from its mouth to Hay, facing west.

Priority 3 - The River Teme Stop Line from the Severn to Ludlow and the Wolverhampton-Stafford Canal.

Lowest Priority - Maintenance of works along the Stratford-on-Avon to Tamworth Stop Line, facing east.

The main stop line defences were to face the directions from which tank attacks were thought to be most likely. Nevertheless, positions and localities covering blocks or gaps were still to be organised for all-round defence, since enemy parachutists might, it was considered, attempt to assist the forward movement of tanks by attacking from the rear.

What follows is a survey of the defence features along each of the stop lines in Worcestershire drawn from an amalgam of contemporary documentary sources (primarily National Archive files), eyewitness accounts, published accounts, contemporary photographic evidence and, of course, what remains.

The Southern Command Stop Line from the River Severn to the North-East Corner of the County

Figure 16 indicates the deduced route of this stop line. A scatter of surviving defence structures and eyewitness accounts of others provides evidence of at least some work on this stop line.

At the important crossing by the A449 Ross-on-Wye and South Wales to Wolverhampton road, the River Salwarpe and the Droitwich Junction Canal are in a deep cutting and an efficient anti-tank block could be created. Since the war Hawford Bridge has been completely rebuilt and the road widened to dual carriageway standards and so nothing remains of the original wartime crossing, at SO 845 602, or its defences. However, a collection of anti-tank cylinders is recalled

Once intended to stop a German column crossing the Droitwich Junction Canal at Porter's Mill, these anti-tank cylinders are now used to help prevent motorists from driving into the canal at SO 861 601, a short distance to the south of the mill

The Stent pillbox adjoining the signal box at Droitwich Station covers the railway approaches to the town as well as forming part of the Junction Canal Stop Line, while these few cylinders (below) at the end of Vines Lane are all that remain of the Chapel Bridge road block

by one witness as being stored on the side of the road here during the war. It is certain that other forms of anti-tank barrier would have been provided on such an important road.

A few anti-tank cylinders still remain near Porter's Mill, adjoining the canal, to suggest that there was a road block on the canal bridge at SO 862 664 and intimates that other canal crossing points would have been blocked too. A prefabricated Stent pillbox can be seen in the former railway coalyard of Droitwich Station, at SO 894 636, one of only two Stents now left in the county. There is also a small collection of anti-tank cylinders near Chapel Bridge, at SO 902 634. These would have formed part of an important block on the bridge that then carried the A38 over the Droitwich Junction Canal and River Salwarpe. They would probably have supplemented a vertical rail or hairpin block.

A former Home Guard, the late Mr Waldron, remembered a substantial block being created on the canal bridge adjoining the Eagle and Sun public house, at SO 922 629. It comprised two fixed concrete cubes, one on each side of the road, with sockets in the road between to form a vertical rail block (see Figure 18). In addition a collection of anti-tank cylinders was stored on the side of the road. All of these features have now gone. (Two cylinders could be seen until recently, on either side of the entrance to the waste disposal site.)

A couple of earthworks have been discovered in the open field

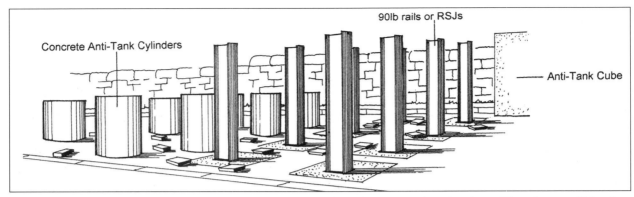

Figure 18. The vertical rail block, supplemented with anti-tank cylinders. This form of block was used extensively on the stop lines and anti-tank islands in Worcestershire, where fixed concrete cubes were often used to block the footpaths and narrow the carriageway. The anti-tank cylinders would be laid out on the expected enemy approach side of the block

immediately to the south-east of the southern Tardebigge Tunnel entrance, at SO 997 694, that may be former Home Guard defence works, but have yet to be proved as such. It is, however, very likely that the canal tunnel would have been defended as a vulnerable point of local importance, whether part of the stop line or not, although no scheme for the defence has been discovered yet.

A collection of large anti-tank cylinders is scattered in the vicinity of a former gravel working and refuse tip at SP 100 778, near Brookhouse Farm, Majors Green. These were almost certainly collected from a road block location on the nearby Stratford upon Avon Canal, to which the Southern Command stop line through Worcestershire was to be linked. Berry Mound, an Iron Age Fort situated close to the canal was re-fortified in 1940, to form one of Birmingham City's outer defences (see Figure 5). The defended locality would have been linked to the stop line defences.

The Avon Stop Line

Contemporary documentary and photographic evidence, a significant amount of eyewitness evidence and a good survival of structures make this the most fully understood of the stop lines in Worcestershire. It also provides an illustration of the amount of work that must have been put into the less well recorded stop lines elsewhere in the county. Nevertheless, the majority of the defences along the Avon Stop Line have already disappeared into obscurity and will probably never now be recorded. As an example of just how much has gone, there are just seven defence features still existing at the Pershore bridges, out of over 30 that have been recorded for that crossing point. The survival rate is much less elsewhere.

Construction of this stop line, from Tewkesbury to Leamington, was the responsibility of the 293rd Field Park Company of III Corps, with the 217th Field Company taking the left side of the river and 216th Field Company, the right. They began work on 1 August 1940, worked through the remainder of that month and the whole of September, before moving off to Halton in Lancashire for training, in early October. In an instruction issued on 10 August 1940 by Lieutenant Colonel W.H. Blagdon, Commander Royal Engineers of III Corps, from his headquarters in the White Lion, overlooking the river bridge, at Bidford on Avon, it was explained that the priority for work should be all the river crossings. Here blocks were to be constructed on or near crossings, with infantry posts covering both the crossings and approaches. The posts were to be well hidden, taking advantage of existing cover such as buildings and hedgerows. These infantry positions were to be designed for the strength of one company (a hundred or so men) for important crossings and for a platoon (thirty or so men) at minor crossings. Apart from bridges, there were a number of locks and weirs to be considered. These were to be reconnoitred and proposals for their defence to be prepared as quickly as possible.

Subsequent work was to be undertaken for the improvement of the river as an obstacle, by deepening any fords and shallow sections, raising banks and the creation of minefields, anti-tank ditches or other works (unspecified). Excavators were to be made available on application to III Corps. Helping the III Corps engineers with the construction of the stop line was the civil engineering company, Wilson Lovell & Company, of Wolverhampton.

Bridges were to be reconnoitred for demolition and reports made on cases where bridges carried essential services that could not be interrupted. The preparation of explosive chambers was not to be carried out until approval had been obtained. It was noted that many bridges and roads carried GPO cables which were important for military communications and reports on potential bridge demolitions were to contain information on what cables would be damaged. Despite these constraints, the bridge at Pershore (presumed to be the modern bridge) and one of the two bridges at Evesham (not specified) were later earmarked for demolition although no evidence of demolition chambers being constructed has been found.

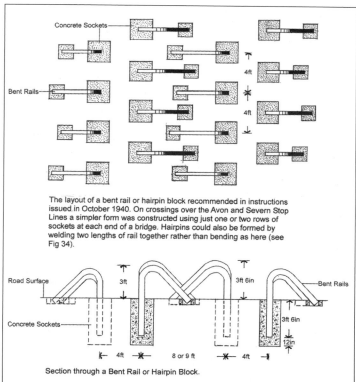

The layout of a bent rail or hairpin block recommended in instructions issued in October 1940. On crossings over the Avon and Severn Stop Lines a simpler form was constructed using just one or two rows of sockets at each end of a bridge. Hairpins could also be formed by welding two lengths of rail together rather than bending as here (see Fig 34).

Section through a Bent Rail or Hairpin Block.

Figure 19. Bent rail (or hairpin) road block

Because this stop line was to deal primarily with an attack from the south, in addition to defence works immediately on the River Avon, it was required that a line of 'company localities' were to be reconnoitred in a zone about 2,000 yards to the north of the river, the defences to be formed in villages, woods and on high ground. Only one or two of these have been recorded but, as a consequence, the numbers of defence posts must have been enormous on so long a stop line.

Lieutenant Colonel Blagden's instructions refer to a number of octagonal concrete blocks having already been provided as a removable element for road blocks in the area but that in future short lengths of rail let into sockets and made by civilian contractors should be used. It was suggested that hairpin blocks 'as used in North Wales might also be used' (see Figure 19). He instructed that for the

Above: Cropthorne Mill at Fladbury was one of several mills along the Avon Stop Line fortified and in this case occupied by troops for a short period during World War II

Lower right: Both of these buildings were prepared for the defence of Workman Bridge at Evesham from the town side, while a 6 pounder Hotchkiss was emplaced in front of the second building on the left

Below: All that remains of the defences at Abbey Road Bridge, Evesham are these concrete cylinders or cheeses, which once supported a pillbox built into the bank here. The sandbags are a post-war form of bank strengthening around the storm water outfall

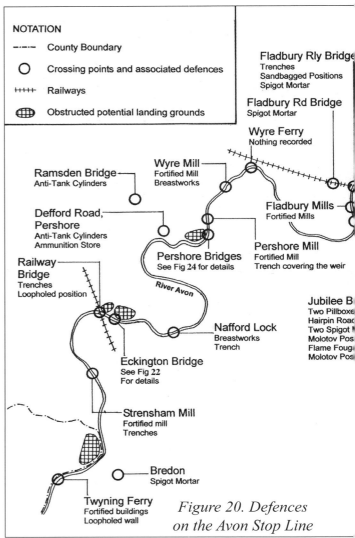

NOTATION

—·—·— County Boundary

◯ Crossing points and associated defences

++++ Railways

⬭ Obstructed potential landing grounds

Fladbury Rly Bridge
Trenches
Sandbagged Positions
Spigot Mortar

Fladbury Rd Bridge
Spigot Mortar

Wyre Ferry
Nothing recorded

Wyre Mill
Fortified Mill
Breastworks

Fladbury Mills
Fortified Mills

Ramsden Bridge
Anti-Tank Cylinders

Defford Road, Pershore
Anti-Tank Cylinders
Ammunition Store

Pershore Bridges
See Fig 24 for details

Pershore Mill
Fortified Mill
Trench covering the weir

River Avon

Railway Bridge
Trenches
Loopholed position

Jubilee B
Two Pillboxe
Hairpin Road
Two Spigot M
Molotov Pos
Flame Foug
Molotov Pos

Nafford Lock
Breastworks
Trench

Eckington Bridge
See Fig 22
For details

Strensham Mill
Fortified mill
Trenches

Bredon
Spigot Mortar

Twyning Ferry
Fortified buildings
Loopholed wall

Figure 20. Defences on the Avon Stop Line

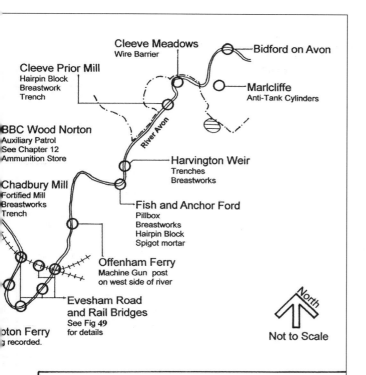

Cleeve Meadows
Wire Barrier

Bidford on Avon

Cleeve Prior Mill
Hairpin Block
Breastwork
Trench

Marlcliffe
Anti-Tank Cylinders

BBC Wood Norton
Auxiliary Patrol
See Chapter 12
Ammunition Store

River Avon

Harvington Weir
Trenches
Breastworks

Chadbury Mill
Fortified Mill
Breastworks
Trench

Fish and Anchor Ford
Pillbox
Breastworks
Hairpin Block
Spigot mortar

Offenham Ferry
Machine Gun post
on west side of river

Evesham Road
and Rail Bridges
See Fig 49
for details

...ton Ferry
...g recorded.

North

Not to Scale

Surviving defence structures can still be seen at:

Bredon - Spigot Mortar mounting at SO 927 368.

Eckington Bridge - Stent Pillbox at SO 923 424, Spigot Mortar mounting at SO 923 422, and defence earthwork at SO 923 423.

Pershore Bridges - 6 pdr Emplacement at SO 953 449, Anti-Tank Cylinders at SO 952 452, Spigot Mortar mounting at SO 950 450, and trench at SO 953 448.

Abbey Road Bridge, Evesham - Anti-Tank Cheeses used as bank strengthening at SP 034 431.

Fish and Anchor Ford - Pillbox at SP 066 471, sockets for a hairpin road block at SP 066 470, and a Spigot Mortar mounting at SP 064 470.

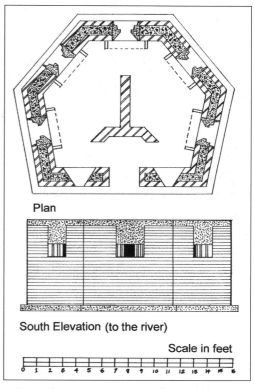

Plan

South Elevation (to the river)

Scale in feet

Figure 21 (above). Type FW3/24 pillbox, Fish and Anchor, Offenham (SP 066 471) This Type FW3/24 or `LDV' pillbox covers the ford near the pub (below right), whilst the interior (below left) reveals the pre-cast standard loopholes of this type, the anti-ricochet wall to the right and the stubs of rail that once supported wooden elbow-rests for the riflemen

present, road blocks were to consist of one row of cubes or blocks with one row of removable blocks (this is presumed to refer to fixed concrete blocks at the side of the road and moveable cylinders and hairpins on the carriageway). The placing of additional rows of blocking materials were to follow later, if required. Unlike any of the other Field Park Companies working on the stop lines in Worcestershire, the 217th Field Park Company did leave a broad list of the works undertaken in their War Diary.

Other defence works would be added to some of the main river crossings in the following year, for example Spigot Mortar positions, while others were adapted to become defended localities in their own right or, in the case of Evesham, become an anti-tank island. A combination of the 217th Field Company's list of works, eyewitness accounts, photographs and recorded surviving defence structures has resulted in the catalogue of defences for the Avon Stop Line set out on Figure 20. Good survivals of structures and eyewitness accounts of others at both Eckington and Pershore Bridges have allowed the defence layouts illustrated in Figures 21 and 23 to be produced. At Pershore Bridges, a number of excavations made by the County Archaeological Service and wartime photographs provided locations for some of the structures. The output from these and some intensive investigations by the Defence of Britain volunteers were incorporated in some interpretation panels that can now be seen around the refurbished picnic place and boat moorings. The picnicking facilities at both Eckington and Pershore Bridges make them good places to visit and view 1940s defences.

The stop line defences at Evesham were later incorporated in the Evesham anti-tank island and are illustrated in the next chapter, specifically Figure 49.

Apparent from the details of this stop line are the number of fortified mills and defences covering the weirs along the river and clearly a response to the use by the Germans of the Houx Weir to cross the River Meuse in May 1940.

In this 1960s air photograph, Home Guard trenches are still apparent on the island nearest Strensham Mill, with one very sinuous trench located adjacent to the weir. (Courtesy of WHEAS)

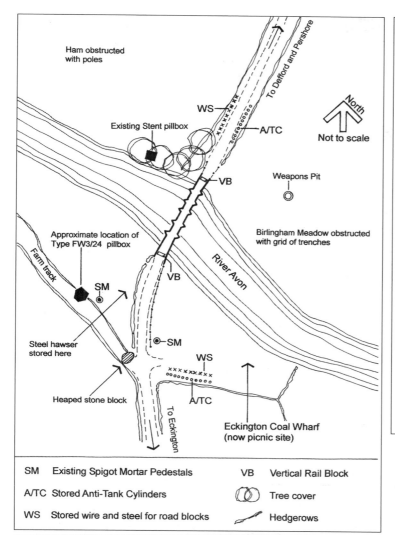

Ham obstructed
with poles

To Defford and Pershore

WS

Existing Stent pillbox

A/TC

North
Not to scale

VB

Weapons Pit

Approximate location of
Type FW3/24 pillbox

Birlingham Meadow obstructed
with grid of trenches

Farm track

River Avon

SM

VB

Steel hawser
stored here

SM

WS

Heaped stone block

A/TC

To Eckington

Eckington Coal Wharf
(now picnic site)

SM	Existing Spigot Mortar Pedestals	VB	Vertical Rail Block
A/TC	Stored Anti-Tank Cylinders		Tree cover
WS	Stored wire and steel for road blocks		Hedgerows

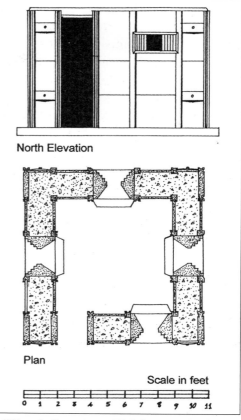

North Elevation

Plan

Scale in feet

0 1 2 3 4 5 6 7 8 9 10 11

The defences at Eckington Bridge on the Avon Stop Line

Left: Figure 22. Plan of the defences
Above: Figure 23. Stent Prefabricated pillbox at Eckington Birdige

The Stent pillbox at Eckington still guards the medieval bridge, but for how long? Successive floods have seriously undermined and weakened the structure, and only the willow tree that once provided camouflage prevents it from falling into the river

The remains of a Home Guard trench system can still be found in the woodland behind the 6 pounder emplacement at Pershore Bridges Picnic Place

This standard Home Guard ammunition store, near Pershore Bridges, was the best example left in the county until it was demolished recently

Pershore Bridges defences on the Avon Stop Line
(this page and opposite)

Right: The former 6 pounder gun emplacement at Pershore Bridges has been converted to become the pumping station for Pershore College of Horticulture

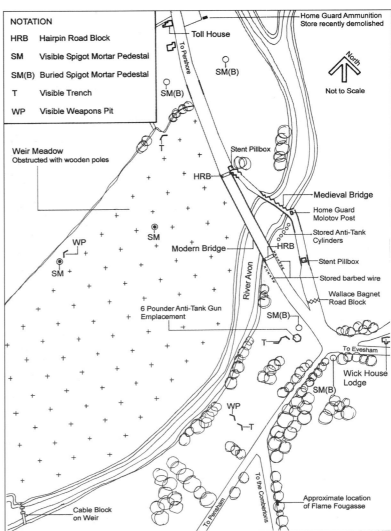

NOTATION

HRB	Hairpin Road Block
SM	Visible Spigot Mortar Pedestal
SM(B)	Buried Spigot Mortar Pedestal
T	Visible Trench
WP	Visible Weapons Pit

Toll House

To Pershore

SM(B)

SM(B)

Home Guard Ammunition Store recently demolished

North
Not to Scale

Weir Meadow
Obstructed with wooden poles

T

Stent Pillbox

HRB

Medieval Bridge

Home Guard Molotov Post

Stored Anti-Tank Cylinders

HRB

Stent Pillbox

Stored barbed wire

Wallace Bagnet Road Block

WP

SM

SM

Modern Bridge

River Avon

6 Pounder Anti-Tank Gun Emplacement

SM(B)

T

To Evesham

Wick House Lodge

SM(B)

WP

T

Cable Block on Weir

To Pensham

To the Combertons

Approximate location of Flame Fougasse

Figure 24. Plan of the defences

Pershore Bridges in the immediate post-war period. The two Stent pillboxes at each end of the medieval bridge still existed and a field of fire has been created by lopping the trees and hedgerow in the foreground. What appears to be a barbed wire barrier can be seen just above the foreground trees, with anti-tank cylinders stored on the river bank, just to the left of the nearest pillbox. (Courtesy of Marion Freeman)

Pershore Mill was destroyed by fire many years ago but was prepared as a defence position in 1940, overlooking the adjoining weir. (Courtesy of Marion Freeman)

These anti-tank cylinders at the town end of the old bridge at Pershore are the most obvious of the surviving World War II defences at the picnic place. Although not in their original location, they do, however, fulfil their original function of blocking this now redundant road to traffic

The Severn Stop Line

No list of proposed defence works by the III Corps Royal Engineers has so far been found and so the following description is based on a combination of recorded surviving structures, eyewitness accounts of what had been seen in the past, and post-war publications that either refer to defences or contain old photographs from which defences can be recognised. Construction of the stop line, initially, was by civil contract under the supervision of Lieutenants Astle and Vimycombe, Field Engineers of the 2nd London Division. The civilian contractors were again Wilson Lovell & Co Ltd of Wolverhampton. Later, the Royal Engineers of the 293rd Field Park Company took on responsibility for the construction of this stop line, although it is not clear whether the civilian contractors continued with this Field Park Company. During the summer and autumn of 1940, the 293rd Field Park Company were based at Ribbesford House, before moving, during October, into winter quarters at The Sillins and Bentley Manor, near Redditch.

Tewkesbury, in Gloucestershire, Worcester and Kidderminster were all designated as anti-tank islands from 1940 onwards and their defences would have contributed to a greater or lesser degree to the Severn Stop Line defences. These anti-tank island defences will be considered in some detail in the next chapter. The recorded defences for the Severn Stop Line are shown in Figure 26 but bearing in mind the extent of the recorded works for the Avon Stop Line, these must be accepted as just a fraction of what was constructed from 1940 onwards.

A number of ferries existed across the River Severn during the war but no details of how they were to defended or their use by invaders prevented, but a surviving defence plan for the locks and weir at Diglis and reproduced in Figure 28 provides a good illustration of the defences that must have existed on the weirs elsewhere in the county. A possibly unique, in Worcestershire, concrete

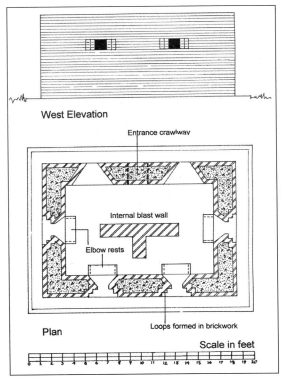

West Elevation

Entrance crawlway

Internal blast wall

Elbow rests

Loops formed in brickwork

Plan

Scale in feet

Above: This rectangular Type FW3/26 pillbox at Saxons Lode covered the former railway crossing of the river at the aviation fuel depot as well as forming part of the Severn Stop Line.
Left: Figure 25. The Type FW3/26 variant pillbox at Ripple Petrol Depot (SO 864 390)

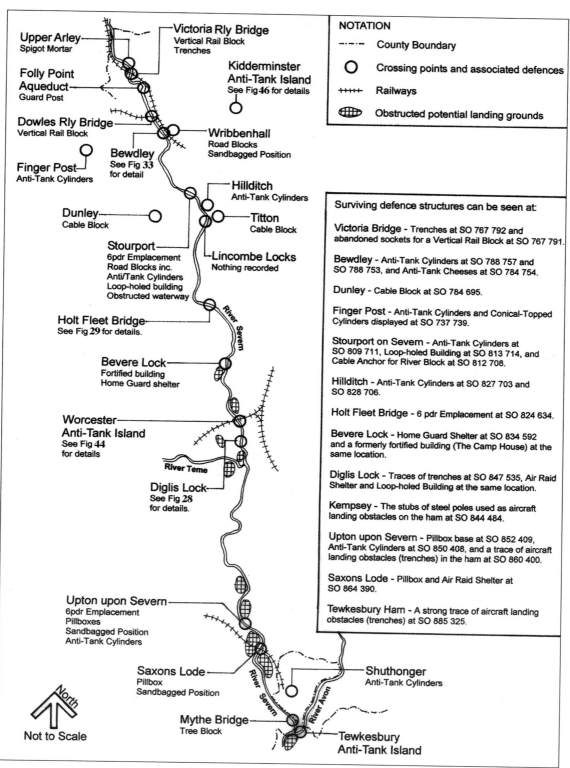

Figure 26. Defences on the Severn Stop Line

air raid shelter still exists on the lock island, at SO 847 535, as does a loophole in the adjoining building. A hollow next to the air raid shelter suggests that this was one of several weapons pits dug in the area. Another hollow of a weapons pit can also be seen in the river bank to the south of the locks.

Figure 27. Conjectural sketch of the pillbox sited in the embankment immediately to the east of the bridge at Upton upon Severn and adjoining Fish Meadow

Jack Miles, a former Home Guard, described for us the defences around Holt Fleet Bridge that are shown in Figure 29, and recent waterproofing work on the bridge by the Highways Authority revealed a second set of sockets under the road surface at the north end of the bridge. It is likely that many other sockets remain beneath the road surface elsewhere

This 1960s air photograph of Upton Bridge and area shows that the 6 pounder Hotchkiss emplacement still remained in Fish Meadow. The hexagonal emplacement is marked with the letter A on the east side of the river, opposite the Hanley Road filling station and a short distance from the river bank. North is to the right of the picture. The location of the pillbox base is indicated by the letter B. (Courtesy of WHEAS)

Fortified in 1940 as a part of the defences around the Diglis Lock and weir area, this workshop building, at SO 847 535, still has a loophole, but it has been glazed to form a small window

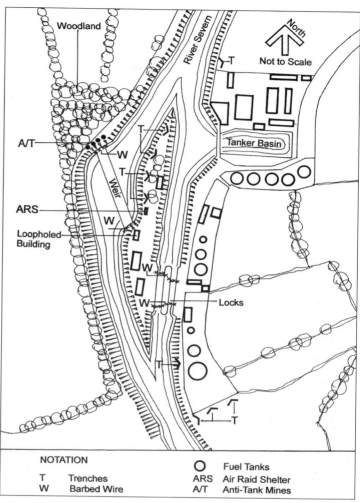

Figure 28. Diglis Dock and Weir defences

waiting to be exposed when resurfacing work is carried out. The combination of defences, including the three-barrel flame fougasse and the road on the west side of the river being in cutting, form a perfect tank trap.

The 6 pdr Hotchkiss emplacement, standing on the east side of the river at SO 824 634 and facing the approach down the hill to the bridge from Holt Heath indicates that it was primarily to deal with an enemy attack from the west. The emplacement is the last surviving, intact emplacement of this type in the West Midlands. It ought to be recognised as such and be given some positive protection. The emplacement was apparently disguised as a café, complete with 'café' sign on top of the concrete roof.

The Camp House pub, near Bevere Island on the Severn, was a Home Guard defence post, with loopholes inserted into the wall of what is now the gents' urinal, below the 'Camp House' sign

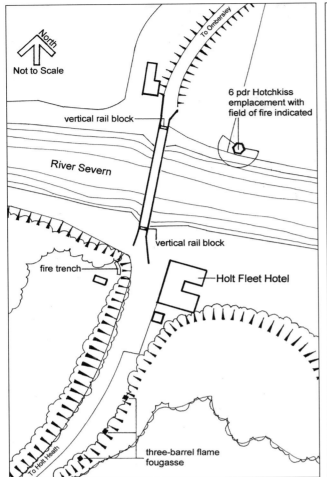

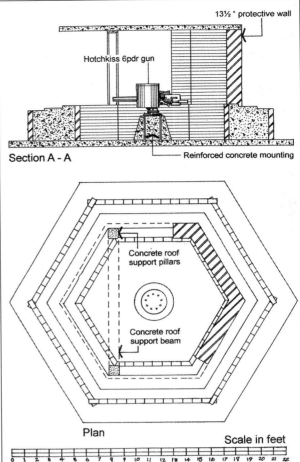

Figure 29. Holt Fleet Bridge defences   *Figure 30. 6 pdr anti-tank gun emplacement*

The last remaining complete 6 pounder Hotchkiss gun emplacement in the West Midlands can be found still covering the western approach to Holt Fleet Bridge over the River Severn. The trees have since been removed

The concrete mounting for the Hotchkiss remains inside the Holt Fleet emplacement, from which the former armament can be deduced

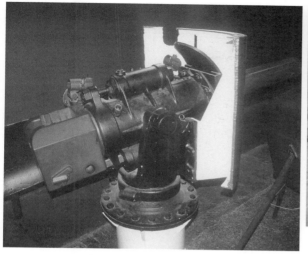

Of late 19th-century naval origin, the Hotchkiss 6 pounder also saw service in the side sponsons of World War I 'Male' tanks before being placed into store. This example can be seen at the Bovington Tank Museum in Dorset

Removal of the road surface at Holt Bridge in 2004 revealed the concrete sockets constructed here in the summer of 1940 to create an anti-tank block. Lengths of steel joists would have been lifted into the sockets to create a small 'thicket' of steel, supplemented with anti-tank cylinders, to create a tank-proof block

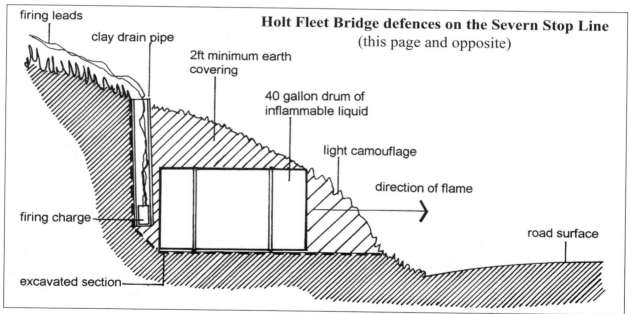

Holt Fleet Bridge defences on the Severn Stop Line
(this page and opposite)

firing leads

clay drain pipe

2ft minimum earth covering

40 gallon drum of inflammable liquid

light camouflage

direction of flame

firing charge

road surface

excavated section

Figure 31. When fired, the Flame Fougasse would project a sheet of flame 10 feet wide and 30 feet long, sufficient to disable a tank and its crew. A similar, but simpler device, was the Flame Trap, where the flammable liquid would be released from the barrel via a tap and hose, using gravity to spread it over the road surface. A Verey Light or Molotov Cocktail would then be used to ignite the fluid. Both means of attacking tanks would require them to have been drawn to a halt by a road block, preferably in a defile

The mounting for the Hotchkiss remains inside the emplacement. Jack Miles confirms that the gun was mounted here in 1940 and was to be operated by the Regular Army — this will have been a detachment of the 62nd Anti-Tank Regiment, who were apparently billeted in the Dorothy

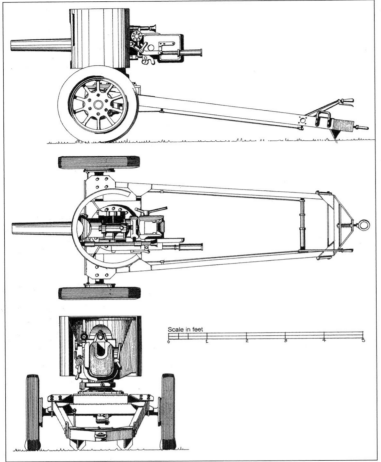

Left: Figure 32. Handed over by the 62nd Anti-Tank Regiment to some of the Worcestershire Home Guard battalions in the spring of 1941, the Hotchkiss 6 pdr guns from the emplacements along the Severn and Avon Stop Lines were mounted on simply constructed trails for mobile operations. The trail utilised easily sourced mild steel sections and plate, welded together and mounted on an Austin 12 car axle and wheels. The design was standardised and could be locally produced. The Hotchkiss depicted, with its rounded steel shield, betrays its World War I tank origins, but for greater protection of the crew, the sides of the shield could be cut off, reversed and re-welded to form a wider shield. Firing solid 6 pound shot, the quick-firing Hotchkiss would have been more than capable of dealing with the generally light German tanks of 1940/41

Scale in feet

Left: The former tourist information point near Stourport Civic Centre was an adapted 6 pounder gun emplacement. Sadly, this last substantive remnant of the Stourport Bridge defences was demolished only a short time ago

Café, now the Spa Store. Later the Ombersley Company Home Guard took over the gun. It was then removed from the emplacement and mounted on a two-wheeled trail to provide the Company with a more mobile field artillery piece (see Figure 32).

A combination of published sources, contemporary photographs and eyewitness accounts provide a comprehensive picture of the defences on and around Bewdley Bridge. These are illustrated on Figure 33 and indicate a number of road blocks, fortified buildings, weapons positions and a pillbox. Even the former riverside bandstand, that was located at SO 787 753, was sandbagged to provide a defence post. The base of this former bandstand survived until recently, at the northern end of Severnside South, adjoining the river, but was recently cleared away as part of a riverside enhancement and flood alleviation scheme. All that remains of Bewdley's defences are a few anti-tank cheeses stacked up on the side of Bank Hill, at SO 784 754, and some anti-tank cylinders on the east side of the river behind the Rowing Club, at SO 788 757. A few more cylinders can be seen in the river at SO 788 753.

The river crossing at Bewdley should have had a 6 pdr Hotchkiss emplacement on the east side of the river,

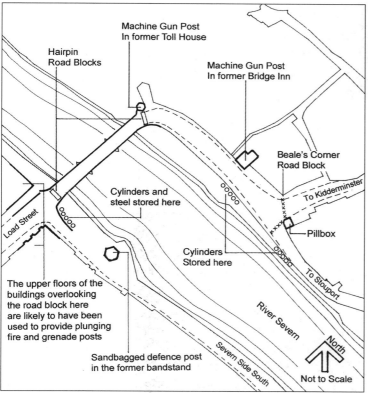

Figure 33. Defences around Bewdley Bridge

Part of the Wribbenhall pillbox can be seen in this photograph of the corner of the Stourport and Kidderminster roads. The pillbox occupied the front garden of the house on the corner and appears to have been a hybrid of Type 25 (circular) and Type 26 (square) designs, the curved section following the lines of the garden's retaining wall, which can still be seen here. The pillbox had loopholes covering the Kidderminster approach to Bewdley, as seen here, the Beale's Corner road block, the bridge approaches from the east, and across the river to Severn Side South

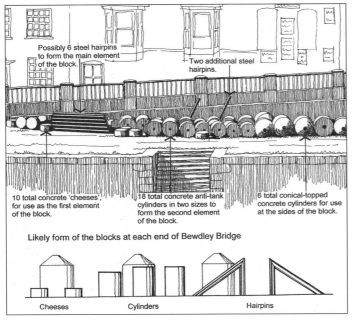

Possibly 6 steel hairpins to form the main element of the block.

Two additional steel hairpins.

10 total concrete 'cheeses', for use as the first element of the block.

18 total concrete anti-tank cylinders in two sizes to form the second element of the block.

6 total conical-topped concrete cylinders for use at the sides of the block.

Likely form of the blocks at each end of Bewdley Bridge

Cheeses   Cylinders   Hairpins

as elsewhere on the Severn Stop Line, but no evidence has been found for this yet. A likely location would have been to the north of the bridge, in the vicinity of the present Rowing Club building, at SO 786 756.

Well to the west of Bewdley, but contributing to the Severn Stop Line defences, road blocks and an anti-tank gun position were provided, covering the junction of the Tenbury and Cleobury Mortimer roads at Finger Post, Callow Hill. The anti-tank gun was located in the front garden of the bungalow, adjoining the motor garage, and two conical topped cylinders can still be seen at the entrance to the sports field opposite at SO 737 739. These appear to be the last of this type still surviving in Worcestershire. In addition, perhaps the most complete and best preserved set of conventional anti-tank cylinders were, until recently, located in the wood at the bottom of this field. They had been rolled down the hill into the wood by the local Home Guard, who by their bit of end-of-war fun has by chance preserved a significant piece of wartime heritage! Their value as historical artefacts has recently been recognised by the local Oak Lands District History Society who have arranged for their rescue, and with the approval of the Far Forest Society, their relocation near to the wartime road block position on the main road, together with an appropriate interpretation board.

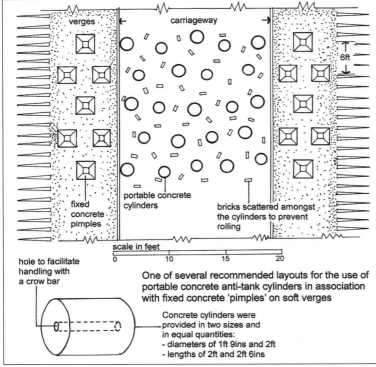

verges   carriageway

6ft

fixed concrete pimples

portable concrete cylinders

bricks scattered amongst the cylinders to prevent rolling

scale in feet

0   10   15   20

hole to facilitate handling with a crow bar

One of several recommended layouts for the use of portable concrete anti-tank cylinders in association with fixed concrete 'pimples' on soft verges

Concrete cylinders were provided in two sizes and in equal quantities:
- diameters of 1ft 9ins and 2ft
- lengths of 2ft and 2ft 6ins

Figures 34 and 35. The top figure shows a complete set of blocking materials that had been stored adjoining the town end of Bewdley Bridge. This diagram illustrates the recommended layout for anti-tank cylinders issued in August 1940, utilising the pyramidal shaped 'pimples' to permanently block the grass verge. The larger conical-topped cylinders at Bewdley seem to have been provided to serve the same purpose

This wartime photograph of a flooded Severn Side South at Bewdley clearly shows the sandbagged defence position built into the former bandstand. The loopholes would have provided an ambush position for local Home Guard riflemen covering the road block on the town end of the bridge, immediately behind the photographer. (Courtesy of Bewdley Museum)

Left: These two conical-topped cylinders at the entrance to the Far Forest Society sports ground are the last of their type in Worcestershire. These, and the complete set of anti-tank cylinders in the background, have been displayed on the initiative of the local Oak Lands District History Society in collaboration with the Far Forest Society, and with financial support from the Local Heritage Initiative fund

Lower left: Colin Jones locates the position of a Home Guard slit trench that was once used to guard the Victoria Bridge carrying the Severn Valley Railway over the River Severn, near Upper Arley

The Teme Stop Line

Work on this stop line seems to have been started concurrently with that on the Severn, by engineers of III Corps, but few official defence proposals have been sourced. The following list of defences is again just a fraction of what must have been, and has been largely compiled from eyewitness accounts or what can still be seen on the ground, together with brief mentions of defences in the History of C Company (Abberley) of the 11th Worcestershire (Stourport) Battalion Home Guard. The River Teme, from its confluence with the River Severn to the Powick bridges, was part of the outer defences for Worcester Anti-Tank Island and will be looked at again in the following chapter. The recorded defence features of this stop line, together with those that remain are shown in Figure 36.

A defence plan and written defence appreciation, or more precisely a critique, of the defences at Bransford Bridge, produced in 1940 by an assistant Platoon Commander, Ashley Break TD, of the 1st Worcestershire (Worcester) Battalion Home Guard has survived, and this not only sets out very clearly the range of defences in this particular vicinity but also provides a good insight into just how extensive the defences must have been on all the other major river crossings on the Teme Stop Line, or indeed the stop lines elsewhere in the county. Ashley Break's critique is reproduced in full below. It should be read in conjunction with the defence plan reproduced as Figure 37.

Most striking are the number of trenches — he refers to them as weapons pits — that were dug around the crossing point and the fact that there were two block houses, or pill-boxes in the lane behind the Fox Inn. One of these existed until very recently, on the north

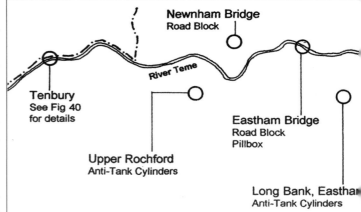

Newnham Bridge
Road Block

River Teme

Tenbury
See Fig 40
for details

Eastham Bridge
Road Block
Pillbox

Upper Rochford
Anti-Tank Cylinders

Long Bank, Eastham
Anti-Tank Cylinders

North

Not to Scale

Surviving defence structures can be seen at :

Collins Green - Anti-Tank Cylinders at SO 737 569.

Hill End - Anti-Tank Cylinders at SO 745 569.

New Mill Bridge - Ammunition Store at SO 728 623.

Stanford Bridge - Pillbox at SO 715 658.

Long Bank, Eastham - Anti-Tank Cylinders at SO 671 675.

Upper Rochford - Anti-Tank Cylinders at SO 641 668.

Tenbury - Home Guard Company HQ (now the Police Station at SO 592 681, formerly loop-holed wall at SO 597 683, Anti-Tank Cylinders at SO 596 679, and Gas Decontamination Facility (Tenbury Pump Rooms) at SO 597 683.

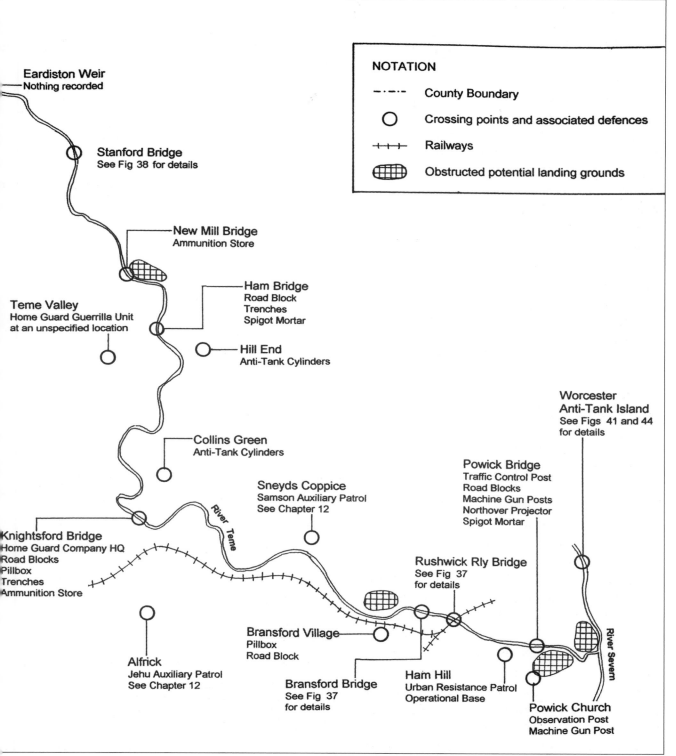

Figure 36. Defences on the Teme Stop Line

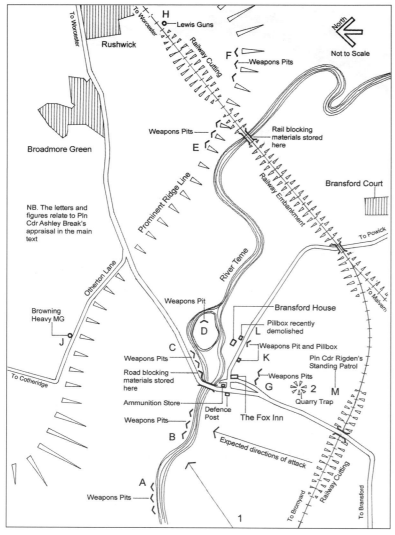

Figure 37. Bransford Bridge defences, based upon an appraisal by Ashley Break (see opposite)

side of the lane, at SO 805 532, and was a brick-built variation on the FW3/26 type, located to blend in with the adjoining garden wall of Bransford House and farm buildings. A heavy machine gun post was sited on the ridge to the north of the bridge, at SO 806 538, from where there are good fields of fire onto the bridge and the approaches to Worcester. Of this and the other defence features there is no sign, but eyewitnesses remember a corrugated iron ammunition store being sited at the south-eastern end of the bridge and anti-tank cylinders stored where the large lay-by is now, to the north of the river, at SO 804 533. Another witness remembers an old lorry being stored on the south-east side of the bridge, ready to be drawn across the side road by the Fox Inn to form a block. A third witness can remember a defence position, possibly a pillbox, being built on the opposite side of the main road, at SO 803 532, but there is no other evidence of this and it may be the bombing post referred to by Ashley Break.

In his report to Colonel Cotton OBE, MC, TD, of the 1st Worcestershire (Worcester) Battalion Home Guard, on 20 December 1940, Ashley Break writes:

Left: This enlarged Type FW3/26 pillbox was built onto the garden wall of Bransford House and was the sole remnant of the extensive defences around Bransford Bridge until demolished only recently

The position on the bridge and the weapons pits A, B and C are dominated from the high ground south of the single line from Bromyard.

Range from cutting to bridge 500 yds.

Range from 1) to bridge 700 yds.

From these positions very heavy casualties could be inflicted on reinforcements proceeding down the road running S W from Worcester to Bransford bridge by MG fire.

Ranges from cuttings 800 yds to 1,000 yds.

From these positions mortars could throw smoke bombs which (with only civilian respirators available) would completely blind the defences at A, B, C, D, G, K, and L.

If the day was windless and the Germans used HE bombs, they might drive the defenders from A, B and G, if the defenders had no mortars with which to retaliate.

Two mortars with an effective range of 1,000 yds, could turn the cuttings on position 1) into shell traps.

Platoon Commander Rigden suggested a standing patrol at position M. His suggested line of retirement is on NW side of double railway, over railway bridge to H.

At position 2) there is a small quarry, with a natural fire step. There is a covered approach through the small wood to the east of it. This quarry should be filled with barbed wire to deny it to the enemy. If the wire was hidden it might prove a very nice trap.

The Teme can be crossed at many points, either by felling trees across it, or by ferrying men over in assault boats, or by using a kapok assault bridge.

Small parties of Germans could be put over with LMGs, take the Browning MG in the flank and the weapon pits A, B and G in reverse.

The same thing could happen on the east of the position. The banks must be patrolled and a reserve kept in hand to deal with such attempted crossings, or the position made capable of all round defence.

Trenches must be drained, men of 50/60 who are not physically hard will lose their efficiency rapidly if they have to stand in wet trenches. The questions of shelter and rationing (with hot meals) must also be considered, if wastage is to be kept down.

Signed Ashley Break - A/Platoon Commander

This report appears to have been made to Colonel Cotton for a meeting at Bransford on Saturday 21 December, for which Ashley Break tendered his apologies due to illness. Was this liaison meeting perhaps an attempt by Colonel Cotton to improve the defences at Bransford Bridge, that was located in the 7th Worcestershire (Malvern) Battalion area of responsibility but on a key approach to Worcester Anti-Tank Island?

Strangely no-one can remember any obstructions in the riverside meadows to prevent airborne troops being landed there, but two large fields a half mile to the north-west of the bridge were obstructed with wooden poles.

Further afield, a pillbox was sited in Leigh Sinton, on the south-east corner of the junction of the main road and the B4503 to Malvern Link, at SO 782 508, and would have covered the approaches to Bransford Bridge from the south-west.

The Bransford Bridge area was later to be designated as a defended locality when the concept of stop lines was abandoned.

K Company (Knightwick) of the 7th Worcestershire (Malvern) Battalion Home Guard with Company Commander Dr R.H. Clarke seated in the centre of the third row. The photograph was taken on the bank of the River Teme, behind Dr Clarke's house, adjoining the present surgery in Knightwick. The Company ammunition store was to the right of the picture. (Courtesy of Mrs Margaret Merrick whose father, Dick James, is in the centre of the back row)

Knightsford Bridge was a key defence position. Here the River Teme has broken through the range of hills that divide Herefordshire from Worcestershire, to form a relatively flat approach to the river crossing and then on to Worcester along the A44. It is likely that any enemy armoured columns coming from the west would have found this the most convenient route into the county, so avoiding the alternative steep and twisting approaches over hills into Worcestershire, that would be both difficult for tanks to negotiate and where they would be most vulnerable to ambush. However, the present road bridge did not exist in 1940, the wartime crossing point being a hundred yards or so upstream, near the Talbot Inn, at SO 732 560. The bridge abutments can still be seen and a foot bridge replaces the former road bridge. Of the defences around this key crossing point, almost nothing exists and no plans have been found so far. However, the defences must have been at least as extensive as those shown on the plan for Bransford Bridge, for this crossing point at Knightwick was also to be designated as a defended locality later. It is also significant that an Auxiliary patrol was formed to operate in this area.

Eyewitnesses remember a pillbox and a trench system being sited on the hill due east of and overlooking the bridge, at SO 736 563, and a set of anti-tank cylinders being stored on the roadside by what is now the Talbot car park, at SO 733 560. It is likely that the Talbot itself would have been fortified and probably some of the other buildings in the vicinity of the bridge. Some of the cylinders survive and have been moved to the side of the road at Collins Green, where they have been used to protect the grass verges on the east side of the road, at SO 738 571.

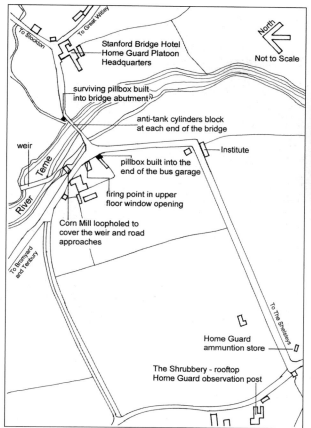

Stanford Bridge Hotel was the HQ of No.11 Platoon (Stanford and Shelsleys) of C Company, 11th Worcestershire (Stourport) Battalion Home Guard, which was responsible for garrisoning the defences around the nearby bridge over the River Teme. It is likely that the hotel itself would have been fortified in the event of an invasion

Left: Figure 38. Stanford Bridge defences

Below: Figure 39. Type FW3/22 variant pillbox at SO 715 658

It is significant that the Headquarters of K Company (Knightwick) of the 7th Worcestershire (Malvern) Battalion Home Guard was located in Dr R.H. Clarke's Surgery, just a short way to the west of the bridge, at SO 731 558. Dr Clarke was the Company Commander and had previously served as a Surgeon Lieutenant in the Royal Navy. The Company ammunition and armaments store was sited close by, behind the present butchers shop, and has only recently been demolished. Former member of the Home Guard, Les Moore, remembers that a Northover Projector and a Spigot Mortar were stored there and that it was the standard form of Home Guard store used else-

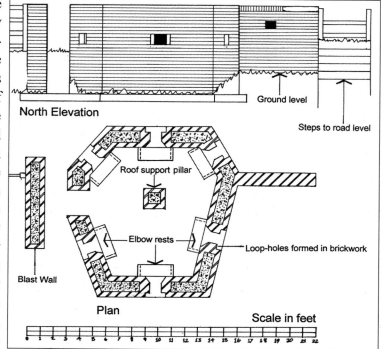

The old bridge at Stanford on Teme still has its pillbox, built into the abutments on the east side of the river. This pillbox appears to be a variant of the Type FW3/22 and still has its blast wall protecting the entrance, although this and some of the loopholes have been blocked up

where in Worcestershire, constructed with corrugated iron Anderson shelter sections.

The last surviving pillbox on the Teme Stop Line can still be seen at Stanford Bridge, built into the old bridge abutment on the north-east side, at SO 715 658. A good eyewitness account from John Lane of the other defences around the bridge has allowed the preparation of Figure 38.

Figure 40 shows the defences for Tenbury, together with the town rifle range. These have been gleaned from contemporary documentary sources and eyewitness accounts. The Tenbury Pump Rooms have recently been restored and their unusual architecture make them worth a visit. The position of the loopholes in the wall adjoining the Kyre Brook can still be discerned.

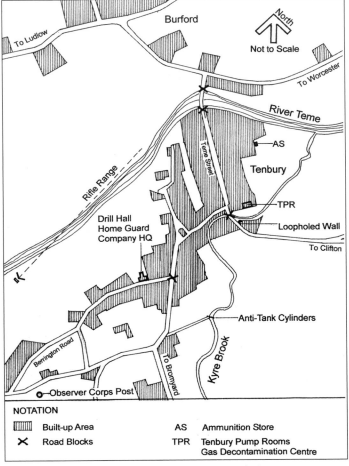

Figure 40. Known Tenbury defences

92

CHAPTER 6

Nodal Points, Anti-Tank Islands, Centres of Resistance and Defended Localities

'Nodal point' was the established military term used to describe an urban area prepared for all-round defence in order to deny the enemy the use of main roads that, in an age before motorways and bypasses, invariably passed through or joined with other main roads in the centre of towns. In the summer of 1940, numerous towns and cities throughout Britain were designated as 'nodal points' as part of General Ironside's plans for defence. Experience gained during the Spanish Civil War, in the Polish campaign, and again in the later stages in the Battle of France, had shown that German armoured columns were particularly vulnerable to overhead attack from buildings in urban areas and could be successfully delayed by determined defence, even with light weapons. This was to be demonstrated again later in the war, at Arnhem, where a small group of lightly armed British paratroops were able to defend the road bridge there over the Neder Rijn against German troops and armoured vehicles for several days, before they were overwhelmed. This was achieved largely by rapidly fortifying the adjacent buildings overlooking the bridge.

The alternative term for a nodal point of 'anti-tank island' appears to have emanated from Southern Command instructions in 1940, probably to reflect the ability of defended towns to successfully counter the threat of enemy armoured columns. Worcester, Kidderminster and Redditch were designated as anti-tank islands following the early influence of Southern Command over defence policy in the county, but later in 1940 the term can be found in defence schemes as far north as Wolverhampton. However, by June 1942, the term anti-tank island had been more widely adopted and many of the towns further north in the Western Command area were given this new designation.

Anti-tank islands were apparently not to be regarded as fortresses to withstand a lengthy siege but were to be capable of holding out against the leading elements of armoured or infantry divisions for several days. The defences of anti-tank islands were initially proposed to include a ring of anti-tank obstacles around the area, consisting of the buildings of the town, together with natural obstacles, such as rivers, streams and woodlands, supplemented by road blocks, rail blocks, short lengths of anti-tank ditches or anti-tank scaffolding. Anti-tank minefields, to be laid when troops were called to 'action stations' or later, according to the situation, were to be authorised to block gaps where other obstacles could not be used. Some of the mines could be located outside the ring of main obstacles.

All anti-tank islands were intended to have at their centre a strong point or 'keep' that was to be so placed, often at the main road junction in the centre of town, that it would continue to deny the road system to the enemy for as long as possible. The keep was to have two other purposes: firstly, to contain the defence commander's headquarters and secondly his main reserve of troops. Once battle was joined, the defence force commander could only influence the progress of the battle by the use of this reserve. The keep was to have its own all-round defences in order to be a secure base for a counter-attack force. It was not intended to be a sort of inner position to which troops from the outer defences could retire: they were to stay put and defend their positions to 'the last man and the last round.' Secondly, it was to be the last place to hold out, when the rest of the town had been over-run.

What of the civilian population in the anti-tank island while the fighting was going on around them? The instruction to the local administrators was that civil preparations should be made to enable the anti-tank island to be self-supporting, not so much against a siege but against the possibility that supplies would be cut off. An Invasion Committee, attended by the local military commander, would consequently be established by the local authority to administer those preparations. Anti-tank islands were to be stocked with food, ammunition, water and medical supplies when operations were imminent in that locality. So far as food and water was concerned, both the garrison and the civil population would go onto short rations immediately it became apparent that the town would be cut off by the enemy. While the general rule was that civilians would stay put, military commanders could make plans for their removal to a short distance away from areas where their presence might endanger defending troops.

The last remaining wartime emergency food store in Worcester City? Provided to feed the city's population during an emergency, this building still stands at the corner of York Place and Albany Terrace.
(Courtesy of Colin Jones)

'Centres of resistance' were to developed on certain routes likely to be used by the enemy with the primary purpose of causing delay. They were to be based mainly on road blocks, with secondary road blocks sited with a view to creating traps for enemy armoured fighting vehicles. Additional preparations were then to be made for attack and destruction of trapped vehicles. 'Defended localities' were to be prepared to cover the anti-tank obstacles and other areas through which enemy infantry might infiltrate.

The terms 'centre of resistance' and 'defended locality' were intended to be part of a hierarchy of defence features. In theory, anti-tank islands were at the top of the league table, and included the major towns with a defence garrison of about 1,000 men. Then came centres of resistance, providing defence for parts of these larger towns, the whole of smaller towns, large villages, airfields and major river crossing points. These would have a garrison of 200 or more men and could comprise two or more defended localities. The role of centres of resistance was to deny whatever they defended to the enemy, delay his advance and strike at him if he endeavoured to bypass the position. Third came defended localities which consisted of two or more mutually supporting posts each comprised of three of more fire trenches, capable of all-round defence, but under the control of one commander and within his shouting distance. The garrison was to be not less than 80 men and their role was to protect some important point. A post was to be sited to cover a defile, a road block or to protect a weapon of offence, such as a 6 pdr Hotchkiss or Blacker Bombard.

In practice, the terms were interpreted flexibly by local defence planners and the scale of the defence feature was not always the obvious criterion. Some specific areas in Worcestershire appear to have changed status between one defence plan and another! Droitwich, for example, attained the status of anti-tank island at one stage, only to be demoted to defended locality later. On a smaller scale, certain of the defence features of the Worcester anti-tank island might be described as a defended locality in one defence scheme but at another time the same feature might be described as a centre for resistance. It might also be designated as a 'vulnerable point' (see Chapter 7). Analysis of the few surviving defence plans in Worcestershire produced between 1940 and 1944 is therefore complex and to some degree confusing. The following description of the various stand-alone defence features of the county has therefore been simplified somewhat to make some sense of the changes in defence approach over this period.

In Worcestershire, during the 1940/41 period, only the three major urban areas — Worcester, Kidderminster and Redditch — were designated as anti-tank islands but, when the Brooke approach to defence began to take full effect in 1942 and the stop lines were finally abandoned, Dudley, Evesham and Malvern attained anti-tank island status, and Droitwich too for a short time. In 1942, some of the well defended river crossings were simply re-designated as centres of resistance or defended localities and more of the smaller towns and villages in Worcestershire were prepared for all-round defence and received one or other of these designations. In effect the spirit of General Ironside's combination of fixed defences to delay enemy columns, while the Field Force and other mobile troops organised themselves for counter-attack, was retained but instead of lines of resistance and some anti-tank islands or nodal points, there was a close pattern and hierarchy of stand-alone defended areas sometimes described as a 'web defence' (see Figure 3).

In Gloucestershire, Tewkesbury was an anti-tank island from 1940 onwards and its outer defences impinged on Worcestershire.

Worcester City Anti-Tank Island

A significant amount of contemporary documentary evidence survives for Worcester's defences in a collection of Home Guard files held in the archives of the Worcestershire Regiment Museum Trust. This, together with some eyewitness and photographic sources, has allowed us to build a reasonably comprehensive picture of the city's defences from 1940 onwards. Sadly, very few of these defences remain, the city having been subject to much development since the war.

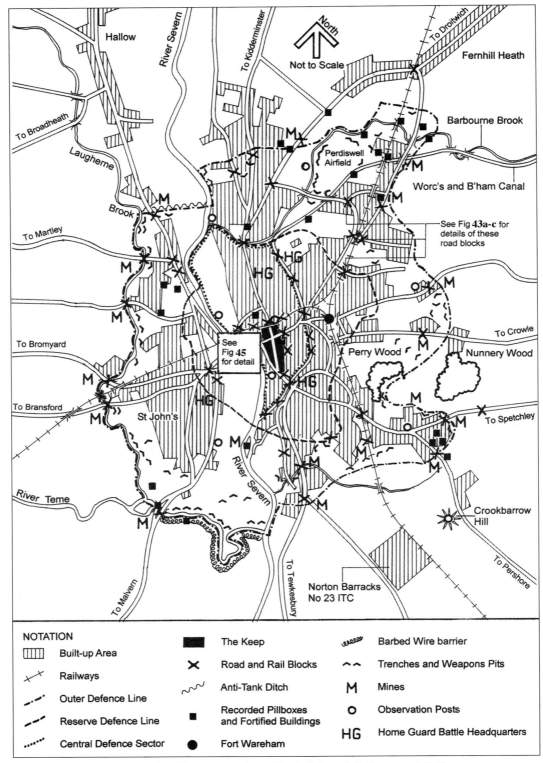

Figure 41. Worcester Anti-Tank Island defences, 1940

Figure 3 shows graphically what a key position Worcester occupies in the centre of the county; most of the county's major roads actually passed through the city during the 1940s, with a major junction at The Cross. Anyone with a memory of the city before the M5 Motorway and the construction of the more recent bypasses will recall the traffic congestion, The Cross and the approaches to the road bridge over the river being particularly notorious bottlenecks. Many of the city centre streets, including the south end of High Street, were much narrower. Some were more tortuous than they are now and closely lined with buildings, like Bird port (see Figure 45) that was to be replaced by the much wider Deansway. It was a difficult city to get through with a vehicle at the best of times, so what better place to enmesh and trap enemy armoured columns. The bridge demolition policy for Worcestershire tends to confirm the importance that defence planners attached to this idea. As noted in Chapter 2, all the bridges over the River Severn, with the exception of the road bridges at Worcester and Bewdley, were to be demolished. This suggests, although there is no written evidence for it, that enemy columns, coming from the west, were being encouraged to become entangled in the streets of the Worcester or Kidderminster anti-tank islands.

Figure 41 indicates that in 1940 Worcester was to be prepared for all-round defence based on four broadly concentric lines:

1) An Outer Defence Line
This generally followed the outer edges of the wartime built-up area with the exception of the Northwick/Claines area. The River Teme and Laugherne Brook formed the south and west defences, the former with its steep and deeply incised banks providing a significant tank barrier, while Laugherne Brook, or 'Bubble Brook', as it is known locally, was to be dammed to raise the level of water in it and improve its performance as a barrier. The means to achieve this is not described in any defence plan but it would be necessary to dam the brook at intervals, probably at each bridging point, to lift the water levels along the whole length. A purpose-built anti-tank ditch was proposed to be dug to link the Laugherne Brook to the River Severn, just north of Henwick Grange. However, there is no evidence that this was actually constructed. A barbed wire barrier is remembered as being erected along the south bank of the River Teme from the confluence with the River Severn to Powick Bridge. Elsewhere barbed wire was to be provided and anti-tank minefields laid, and all of the road and rail entry points to the city were to be blocked. The location of the majority of known pillbox sites or fortified buildings are around the city outskirts, while a pattern of trenches, machine gun posts and minefields completed the outer defences. The latter pattern can be clearly seen on Figure 41. It is interesting to note that at least some elements of this defence on the south side of the city mirror those of Charles II in 1651, prior to the Battle of Worcester.

The next chapter will deal with the defence of vulnerable points but the defences of four of these would also have contributed to the outer defence line of the city. These are the pillboxes around the former Air Ministry site at Whittington Road, now occupied by the Department of the Environment, Food and Rural Affairs and the Inland Revenue; the pillboxes around the Blackpole Royal Ordnance Factory, also known as Cadbury's factory, those of Metal Castings in the Droitwich Road and the defences around the Diglis Petrol Depot and locks. Complete pillboxes can still be found at the Whittington Road site and at Blackpole.

The Heenan and Froude company raised two platoons of Home Guards, Numbers 10 and 11, which would have had responsibility for manning Fort Wareham. Their commander, Major Richard Wareham, is seated in the centre of the second row, with his Second in Command, Captain Edmund Wedgbury DSO, MC, DCM, MM, to his left. (Courtesy of Ted McGee, who is third from the left in the front row)

As part of the outer defences, anti-tank mines were to used, but apart from a defence plan for the Diglis Locks that specifically indicates a minefield, the precise location of most of the other proposed minefields can only be guessed at. Most minefields were allotted 12 or 24 mines with only that at Nunnery Farm having a larger number, 48. Most of them were at road block locations and Figure 41 indicates the general pattern in and around the city.

2) A Reserve Defence Line

Drawn within the built-up area of the city, this line incorporated part of St John's on the west side of the river, including its main shopping area. For the main part of the city, east of the river, the line stretched as far north as Gheluvelt Park, as far south as Diglis Basins and eastwards beyond Shrub Hill Station. No details of this defence line have been found and it does not seem to follow a particularly logical route. However, it is likely that road blocks and fortified buildings on the main approaches to the city centre would have formed an important element of it. It is between the outer defence line and this reserve line that urban resistance patrols, to be considered in Chapter 12, would have operated to disrupt the attacks against the main bridgehead and city centre.

A curiously named Fort Wareham is indicated in the city defence plans for the area adjoining the former Heenan and Froude factory, at SO 857 553. This too would have contributed to the reserve defence line. No details of this so-called fort have survived and former members of the factory Home Guard there do not remember any specific or extensive defence posts at the factory. However, it is

Entry to the Fort Wareham Tank Trap! This section of Tolladine Road is in a deep brick-lined cutting with the opportunity for plunging fire and grenade attack from the high ground on either side, or the succession of railway bridges that cross it, onto any tanks that might venture in

significant that Heenan and Froude raised two platoons of Home Guard and that their commander was Major Wareham. Some of the buildings that formed the Heenan and Froude factory complex are substantial and there are signs of blocked up loopholes in one of the buildings overlooking Tolladine Road.

Another intriguing aspect of the defence of the city is a brief documentary reference to an armoured train being stored in a siding at Shrub Hill Station. This must have been a local initiative since no such train is listed in the files dealing with armoured trains at the National Archive. The layout of the railways in the city actually lend themselves well to the use of such a train in support the defence of the city against an attack from three of the main points of the compass. It would have been able to steam off through Foregate Street Station to help defend against an attack from the west, or northwards through the tunnel to help the defence in that direction and similarly to the south towards Norton Barracks. It could also have contributed to the defence of the Reserve Line, from the east, by staying in the vicinity of the Shrub Hill Station and Fort Wareham. It is therefore disappointing to find that no eyewitnesses remember the train being stored at Shrub Hill and consequently its form and armaments.

Commonly, an armoured train consisted of two armoured wagons, one at each end, two flat bed wagons adjoining them to give a clearer field of fire and observation, and the locomotive in the centre of the train, where it would have some protection from head-on fire. The high sided armoured wagons could be sandbagged on the inside, or treated like the Armadillo trucks of the RAF, to provide a small-arms proof breastwork for the garrison. Some of the armoured trains used in the coastal areas were provided with a 6 pdr Hotchkiss gun and Boys anti-tank rifles for an anti-tank role.

3) Central Defence Sector

The Central Defence Sector was a more logical defence area, where the River Severn, a more than adequate tank obstacle, formed the west boundary; the Worcester and Birmingham Canal, again an efficient tank obstacle, formed the south and east boundary, while to the north the less substantial Barbourne Brook initially formed the boundary. These three water features mirror the concept of a medieval motte and bailey castle, with a water filled moat. The addition of a keep, described later, completes the medieval simile! It is not recorded, but some means of raising the level of water in the Barbourne Brook would have been necessary to improve its efficiency as a tank obstacle.

This picture of the Worcestershire and Birmingham Canal in Lowesmoor, with the flanking walls, illustrates what a formidable barrier it would have been for tanks should the bridges have been destroyed

Later, the northern boundary of the Central Defence Sector was redrawn further south, along the line of the railway line that crosses the city centre from west to east, and is mainly on embankment or viaduct. It provides an altogether more substantial defence line than the Barbourne Brook.

As part of the defences for the original Central Defence Sector, a pillbox was remembered by the late Dick Philips as being built on the triangular traffic island at the junction of the Droitwich Road and Ombersley Road, at SO 846565. This was demolished early in the war to allow the long RAF Queen Mary trucks to negotiate the road junction. Another pillbox is remembered at the junction of Castle Street and Farrier Street, at SO 848 554, while another can be seen on contemporary defence plans and in post-war photographs, located in front of the Dents glove factory, Copenhagen Street, at SO 848548 (see also Figure 42). It is likely that many of the city centre buildings would have been fortified but, apart from a number covering the road bridge, no details of these have survived.

A 6 pdr Hotchkiss emplacement was provided near the junction of Croft Road and The Butts, at SO 844 550. From here it was intended to fire on any enemy armoured fighting vehicles attempting to cross the river from the west that sought to use either the railway or road bridge. To help aiming at and destroying any enemy vehicles on the road bridge, a steamroller was to be placed on the west side of the river, ready to push the bridge parapet into the river, a feat achieved by errant motorists several times in recent years! Two contemporary defence plans survive and indicate the Hotchkiss emplacement, one showing it on the river side of Croft Road, the other on the town side. However, the former seems the most likely, since the Riverside Hotel would otherwise obscure a significant part of the road bridge from the gunners.

All of the road and rail crossings over the water features that delineate the Central Defence Sector were to be blocked with vertical rail obstructions, supplemented with anti-tank cylinders, none more so than the road bridge over the Severn. There were two blocks on the bridge itself and others on the approaches from the west, most notably along New Road, where the avenue of lime trees were to have been sacrificed by felling them across the road to form a continuous block for the length of the road outside the County Cricket Ground. The defences around this key area of the city are looked at again later, as part of a separate defence plan for the township of St John's.

Figure 42. The location of the pillbox, Copenhagen Street

The majority of the Worcester City road blocks were of the vertical rail type with the sockets sunk into the road surface to accept the vertical rails. An amazing survival, probably from a rail block, are some lengths of rail, with angle-iron cross trees, abandoned on top of a former air-raid shelter near Shrub Hill Station, at SO 857 556. There would have been hundreds of these stored on the side of roads and the railways during the war, ready to have been lifted into the sockets. Figure 43 shows the location of known road blocks in and around the city and these mirror reasonably closely the defence lines and zones described above.

Defence schemes and accompanying notes for three of the city road blocks have survived. These are for the road blocks at the junction of Bilford Road and Astwood Road, at the junction of Blackpole Road and Brickfields Road and at Tunnel Hill. These are reproduced in Figure 43a-c and provide a good insight to the extent and layout of defences around other blocks in the city. To provide more detail for these blocks it is necessary to relate the following numbered items to the plans.

Bilford Road Block (Figure 43a)

1) Two men were to occupy this defence post with mines. This suggests that the men in this trench were to operate a mine necklace, where a number of mines would be strung together on a cord and drawn across the road at the last moment and on the approach of an armoured vehicle. A disabled enemy vehicle at this point would add to the block on Bilford Road.

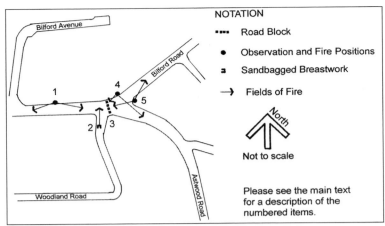

Figure 43a. The Bilford Road Block

2) Named 'The Redoubt' on the original defence plan, this sand-bagged breastwork was to have been garrisoned by a corporal and three men.

3) The barricade here is not specified, but appears to have been a line of sockets for vertical rails, and was to be manned by two men. As on road blocks elsewhere, one of the men would question any approaching motorist while the other would cover him with his rifle.

4) This was the main defence post and the trench was to be manned by the section commander and three men.

5) This trench, sited on elevated land, was to have been manned by two men.

Sergeant J.A.H. Appleton of No 3 Section, No 4 Platoon recorded the manning of this position on 4 August 1940, when he commented as follows:

> The men commenced to arrive at 8.27 pm and the parade was complete by 8.35. The men were allotted to their positions as shown on the attached diagram. [This diagram forms the basis of the layout in Figure 43a]. Some doubt existed as to which direction the barricade had to be defended. My platoon commander and myself assumed, in view of the position of the barricades at Droitwich Road, that we were to defend facing the Droitwich Road. Assuming that the enemy was attempting to enter the city coming from the Birmingham direction [presumably if Perdiswell airfield was captured or the city surrounded] and turning into Bilford Road, the position of the barricade is not a good one and the redoubt in Woodland Road is in a useless position. They are unable to concentrate fire over any radius beyond directly in front of the barricade and this is the sole extent of the vision from this point. In addition, a tank or any enemy forces could, upon coming over the canal bridge and observing the barricade, turn into Kingston Avenue and attack the men at the redoubt in Woodland Avenue from the rear.

Clearly Sergeant Appleton was not impressed with the defences here and his reference to a redoubt suggests that he was a World War I veteran who was not afraid to voice his disquiet about the quality of the defences. The tenor of this report suggests that provision of the defences here, and possibly elsewhere, was the subject of debate between those manning them and those in authority and that these discussions might lead to improvements!

Brickfields Road Block (Figure 43b)

6) This trench, or fire position as it is described on the original plan, was placed in the garden of the first house on this side of Blackpole Road and would cover any enemy approach from Thorn Avenue.

7) The window of one of the two buildings that formed part of the short-lived Astwood Halt provided an elevated fire position with 200 yards of clear observation northwards along Blackpole Road. It can be assumed that the window would have been sandbagged to provide the firing position.

8) A sandbagged firing point for an anti-tank weapon or Bren was provided on the railway embankment, covering any approach to the roadblock along Brickfields Road from the east. This position was remembered by the late Maurice Jones as being a sandbagged breast-work built into the side of the embankment.

9) The barricade here appears to have been another vertical rail obstruction, with the sockets placed diagonally from in front of the anti-tank gun position to the small shop that still exists on the south side of Brickfields Road.

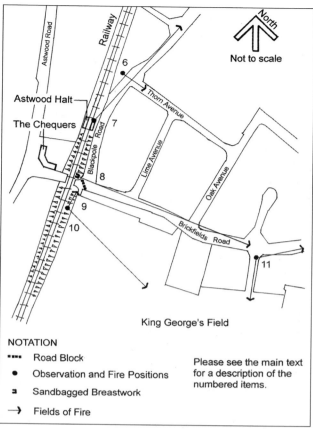

Figure 43b. The Brickfields Road Block

10) A trench in the railway embankment here provided extensive observation and field of fire over both the block and across King George's Field. The depression of this trench could still be seen in the railway embankment when the site was first recorded some years ago.

11) An observation and fire post was provided just inside the entrance road to King George's Field from Brickfields Road, near the post office, although the form is not specified. From here Brickfields Road could be observed eastwards for a distance of 150 yards.

In his notes on the undated plan of the defences here, H. Marriot, the Section Leader (part of No.5 Platoon) made the following observations:

> This post requires more advanced observers. An advanced post communication would be in a better position for contact with the Elbury Mount Post. Fire positions on each side of the railway bridge [would have] fire support from Tunnel Hill.

Section Commander Marriot also notes on his plan that the nearest telephone, water supply and lavatories were then, as now, in The Chequers pub on the corner of Astwood Road and Brickfields Road. He notes that the men from No.11 Post were to exfiltrate back to the main post via St George's Field.

Tunnel Hill Block (Figure 43c)

12) A trench on the upper part of King George's Field providing good observation and field of fire northwards over the playing fields of 500 yards.

13) A defence position at the road junction adjoining Gorse Hill School. This position on a crossroads provides observation and fields of fire along four roads but there are no details of its construction.

14) An observation post was established in the very prominent house at the top of the hill here. The house can be seen

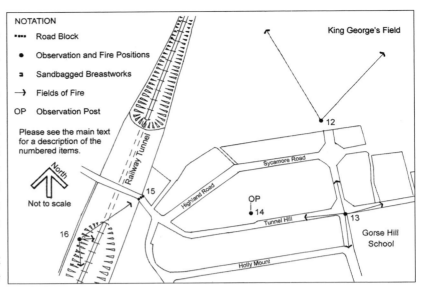

Figure 43c. The Tunnel Hill Block

from many parts of the city and so it can be assumed that the field of view is equally extensive.

15) The block is again likely to have been a vertical rail type and was located diagonally across Tunnel Hill at the east end of the bridge-like structure over the railway tunnel.

16) This fire trench was located on the embankment overlooking the tunnel entrance on the south side of the cutting. The depression of the former trench can still be seen in the land adjoining the footpath.

The plan and notes for this defence scheme also appear to have been produced by Section Commander Marriot, who notes that telephones were available at a callbox outside The Vauxhall Inn and in the Tunnel Hill off-licence, and that there was plenty of water and lavatories available for the garrison. Clearly a very practical man with an interest in the essentials!

The Keep

The keep in Worcester incorporated The Cross and what are now the main shopping streets stretching from Foregate Street Station in the north to the Lich Gate area in the south, and from Angel Place and Deansway in the west to New Street and Friar Street in the east. The railway on the east-west axis through the city is on a high embankment and, with blocks under the bridges in the Foregate, Sansome Walk and Farrier Street, and the arches blocked in the viaduct leading to the river, would have provided a formidable barrier to any enemy column moving north or south. Although no details of the defences for the keep in Worcester have survived, a combination of road blocks and fortified buildings would have made it particularly difficult for enemy armoured columns to have moved through. Tank trapping between the tall buildings and in the blocked-off narrow streets would have been a feature of the defence and a substantial delay in the movement of the armoured columns could have been achieved by a determined defence.

Observation Posts

A number of observation posts were established by the Home Guard in and around the city. The two key ones were on the cathedral tower and at Elbury Mount from where wide views of the approaches to the city could be kept under observation. The cathedral OP was also manned in 1940 by men from No.23 ITC, at Norton Barracks, and an Aldis lamp signals facility established between the cathedral tower and the keep at Norton. Both written and oral evidence from former Home Guards suggest that this key OP was also manned by men of the Home Guard from outside the central sector of the city. To protect them from the elements, the men were provided with a wooden shed, apparently erected on the roof of the tower. Use of the cathedral as an OP was a repeat of history for Charles II also utilised the cathedral tower for this purpose in 1651.

Other Home Guard observation posts were established on the tower at the waterworks in Barbourne, the tower at the sewage works in Bromwich Road, on the grandstand at Pitchcroft, on the Maypole Laundry at the top of London Road and at Perdiswell, presumably on the hall roof. All of these features of the city landscape have now gone.

Obstruction of landing grounds

In addition to the airfield at Perdiswell being temporarily obstructed with old vehicles to prevent its use by enemy aircraft, eyewitnesses tell us that Pitchcroft and Boughton Park golf course were obstructed with lengths of tram rail salvaged from the former tram depot in St John's, and the Powick Hams with wooden poles, all contributing to the city defences.

Brooke's influence on the City Defences

In the same way that the river-based stop lines were superseded in 1942 by centres of resistance and defended localities elsewhere in the county, so too were the defences of anti-tank islands evolved to change the emphasis from lines of defence to a number of area defences covering the main roads into the centre. There is good documentary evidence that there was, in any case, difficulty in fully manning the long outer lines of defence of Worcester, particularly on the west side of the city. This would have encouraged the abandonment of the earlier scheme in favour of the more concentrated form of defence illustrated in Figure 44. However, despite this change of emphasis, the pattern of road blocks on the roads into the city centre from the earlier scheme was maintained but, in addition, a series of centres of resistance were established. Some of these had been designated defended localities in earlier documents, but for the sake of simplification all have been shown as centres of resistance in Figure 44. Some of the centres of resistance were also designated as vulnerable points and so for the sake of completeness all the designated vulnerable points have been shown. They would all, in any case, have had defence garrisons and some are known to have had defence posts, including pillboxes that would have contributed to the wider defence of the city.

The keep and Fort Wareham were also retained from the earlier defence scheme but a significantly smaller central defence sector was organised with the northern boundary now drawn along the east-west railway line through the city centre. Although the viaduct from the former cattle market area westwards to the river, with its many arches, may seem to today's observer difficult to defend, it should be remembered that during the war there was a second, steeply sloping, viaduct

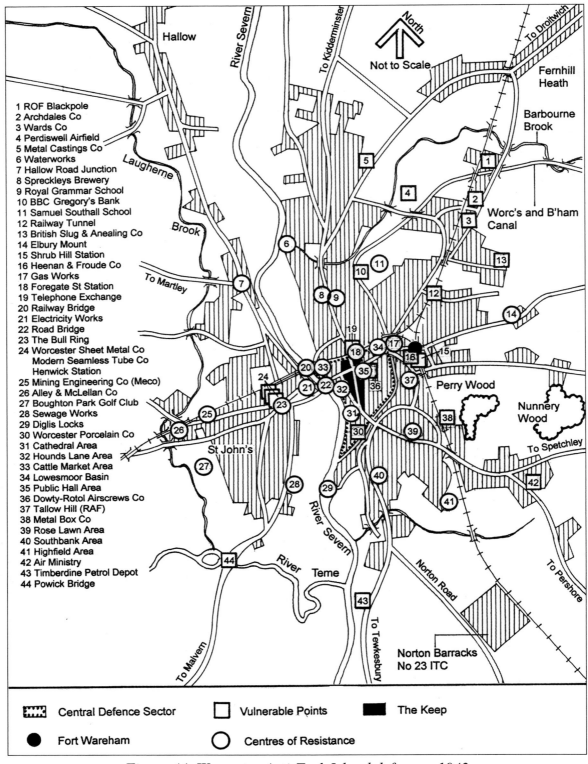

1 ROF Blackpole
2 Archdales Co
3 Wards Co
4 Perdiswell Airfield
5 Metal Castings Co
6 Waterworks
7 Hallow Road Junction
8 Spreckleys Brewery
9 Royal Grammar School
10 BBC Gregory's Bank
11 Samuel Southall School
12 Railway Tunnel
13 British Slug & Anealing Co
14 Elbury Mount
15 Shrub Hill Station
16 Heenan & Froude Co
17 Gas Works
18 Foregate St Station
19 Telephone Exchange
20 Railway Bridge
21 Electricity Works
22 Road Bridge
23 The Bull Ring
24 Worcester Sheet Metal Co
   Modern Seamless Tube Co
   Henwick Station
25 Mining Engineering Co (Meco)
26 Alley & McLellan Co
27 Boughton Park Golf Club
28 Sewage Works
29 Diglis Locks
30 Worcester Porcelain Co
31 Cathedral Area
32 Hounds Lane Area
33 Cattle Market Area
34 Lowesmoor Basin
35 Public Hall Area
36 Dowty-Rotol Airscrews Co
37 Tallow Hill (RAF)
38 Metal Box Co
39 Rose Lawn Area
40 Southbank Area
41 Highfield Area
42 Air Ministry
43 Timberdine Petrol Depot
44 Powick Bridge

Central Defence Sector
Vulnerable Points
The Keep
Fort Wareham
Centres of Resistance

Figure 44. Worcester Anti-Tank Island defences, 1942

106

carrying an additional track down from Foregate Street Station to sidings on the racecourse and along the river bank. This effectively blocked off many of the arches on the main viaduct until demolished some years ago. The road blocks on Croft Road, Infirmary Walk, Farrier Street, The Foregate, Sansome Walk, and in the vicinity of the canal would have completed the barrier.

Analysis of Figure 44 and the numbered items, indicates that while many of the defence features of the 1940 scheme, notably covering vulnerable points in the outskirts of the city, have been perpetuated, they have become a series of outlying pickets for the more concentrated defence around the city centre. In 1942 there was a series of centres of resistance around the critical city centre where the main through-roads converged and where the available defence forces could be concentrated. The distribution of anti-tank mines also changed with each river and canal bridge block now having 20 mines each and six to each of the street blocks. Although not explained in surviving documents, there is no doubt that, on the hard street surfaces, these mines would have been used in the form of necklaces, to be dragged across the street at the last moment in front of an approaching enemy tank.

Under both the 1940 defence scheme and the later scheme, the city was divided into four sectors for Home Guard manning purposes: the North Sector, that part of the city north of the east-west railway line and Newtown Road; the South Sector, the remainder of the city to the south of that railway and Newtown Road; the West Sector, which incorporated the whole of St John's, and the Central Sector, the city centre to the south of the east-west railway.

Manning the Worcester Anti-Tank Island

For most of the period 1940 to 1944, the 1st Worcestershire (Worcester) Battalion Home Guard was responsible for defending the Worcester anti-tank island. Good documentary evidence for the operational organisation and defence responsibilities of the Worcester Battalion exists for March 1942. Since such comprehensive garrisoning details have not survived for the other anti-tank islands in the county, the manpower organisation of the Worcester garrison provides at least an insight as to how the Home Guard battalions manning of the other major towns in the county may have been organised.

The Worcester Battalion was organised into the North Unit, comprising 'A' and 'B' Companies, with a battle headquarters established in the St George's Tavern, St George's Lane; South Unit, comprising 'C' and 'D' Companies, with a battle headquarters in The Angel Hotel, Sidbury; West Unit, comprising 'E' and 'F' Companies, with a battle headquarters in The Bell Inn, St John's; and the Central or Headquarters Unit, that was responsible for defence of the keep and provision of a Battalion Reserve. Their battle headquarters was to initially to be in the Royal Grammar School, in the Tything, but later it would be moved to the Southfield Street Drill Hall. Separate Railway Platoons, under the operational command of the Worcester Garrison, but part of a Railway Battalion of Home Guard based in Birmingham, were responsible for the protection of Shrub Hill, Foregate and Henwick Road stations, and defending the railway blocks on the railway bridges over the Severn, over Laughern Brook, the rail block at Highfield Cutting and the tunnel at Tunnel Hill. A Post Office Platoon, again part of a Post Office Battalion based in Birmingham, but under the operational command of the Worcester garrison, was responsible for guarding the Telephone Exchange on the corner of Pierpoint Street and The Foregate, now the

Part of the North Unit of the Worcester Garrison, No.1 (Waterworks) Platoon of the 1st Worcestershire (Worcester) Battalion Home Guard, with Platoon Commander Lieutenant Gerry Tysoe in the centre of the second row. The platoon had responsibility for the protection of the waterworks at Barbourne, as well as manning the road block on the bridge carrying the main road over Barbourne Brook. (Courtesy of the late Gerry Tysoe)

Postal Order pub. The defence of the Powick Bridge over the Teme was initially the responsibility of the 7th Worcestershire (Malvern) Battalion Home Guard, but later this was passed to the Worcester Battalion.

No.15 Platoon had, perhaps, the most onerous of the defence tasks in Worcester: defence of the road bridge over the Severn and the approaches from the west. For this the Platoon had a strength of 49 men. Their ammunition store is remembered as being in the bowling green pavilion near Cripplegate Park which was apparently stacked high with anti-tank mines. A number of detailed defence schemes have survived for defending the river bridge. These are combined to form Figure 45.

One of the few surviving Nissen huts left in the county stands behind the Leaping Salmon pub in Severn Street, Worcester, at SO 851 543. It is said to have been the headquarters of the Porcelain Works Platoon of the Home Guard, but is likely to have been erected when the Air Ministry occupied the Kings School for a short period in 1940

The defences for the bridge were extensive and would certainly have delayed any enemy column wishing to enter the city from the west, although with just 49 men No.15 Platoon would have been hard put to man all the defences adequately. However the Central Sector garrison was to provide support for the bridge defenders including manning the

Copenhagen Street pillbox, armed with a machine gun.

During the summer and winter of 1940, the 6 pdr anti-tank gun at Croft Road was manned by men of the 62nd Anti-Tank Regiment Royal Artillery, but would be handed over to the Home Guard in the spring of 1941.

The importance of St John's as a defence sector, within the overall plan for the Worcester anti-tank island was recognised by defence planners, and a separate scheme of defence of the 'township of St John's' was produced and has survived. This defence scheme is undated but appears to be from an earlier period than the Home Guard arrangements set out above. However, the scheme for St John's points out that the defence of the township was important, not only because it covered the western bridgeheads of both the railway and road crossings of the river, but that it also contained at least four substantial factories manufacturing munitions and aircraft components, the electricity power station for the city and district, and the sewage disposal works, that would need to be guarded and kept working for the general health of the city population. It will become apparent, as this account proceeds, that many of the important munitions factories of Worcestershire were within anti-tank islands and so would have benefited from the added protection that this designation afforded.

Should all of the St John's defences fail, it was recognised that the next stop would the road and rail bridges over the Severn. One of the Railway Platoons would be responsible for defending the railway bridge and a small armoured train, carrying 'at least heavy machine guns' is mentioned in the St John's defence scheme. This must be the same train mentioned earlier that was to be stored at Shrub Hill Station. Arrangements were to be made for demolition of the railway bridge in a final emergency.

The Worcester Royal Grammar School was the first battle headquarters for the Central Sector of the city, later re-designated as a centre of resistance, covering the approaches to the city centre from the north

The Bell Inn, St John's, was the Home Guard battle headquarters for the West Sector of the Worcester Anti-Tank Island

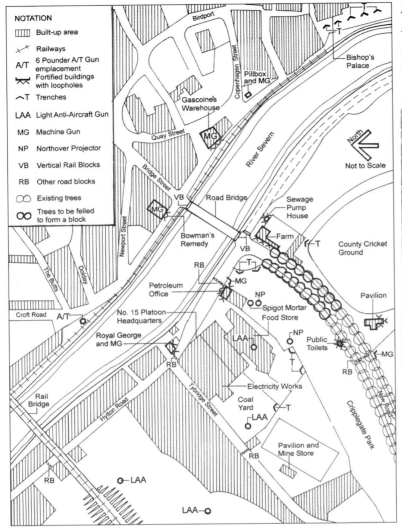

NOTATION

				Built-up area
×⌒×	Railways
A/T	6 Pounder A/T Gun emplacement
∿∿	Fortified buildings with loopholes
⌒T	Trenches
LAA	Light Anti-Aircraft Gun
MG	Machine Gun
NP	Northover Projector
VB	Vertical Rail Blocks
RB	Other road blocks
○○	Existing trees
∞	Trees to be felled to form a block

Left: Figure 45.
Plan of the defences

1944 saw the demolition of the anti-tank cubes blocking the pavement and part of the carriageway at the New Road end of Worcester Bridge. Note also the white paint applied to the edges of the cubes to help them show up in the blackout. (Courtesy of the Worcester News*)*

Left: During wartime this building was the Petroleum Office and more recently it was the Worcester City Planning Office. It was to be fortified as a defence post in the event of an invasion, with loopholes covering the adjoining road block in Hylton Road. The building was demolished recently in order to extend Cripplegate Park

The defence of Worcester Bridge and Electricity Works Vulnerable Point
(this page and opposite)

Bowmans Remedy, the warehouse to the right of the Old Rectifying House, was once fortified as part of the defence around the road bridge over the River Severn, to the right. A machine gun was located on the second floor, probably in a sandbagged emplacement in the centre door. The River Severn here displays its excellent qualities as an 'anti-tank ditch', complete with an unclimbable wall on the far bank

These 2 pounder anti-tank guns are being demonstrated by the 1st Worcestershire (Worcester) Battalion Home Guard during a 'Holiday at Home' event at the New Road Cricket Ground in 1943. (Courtesy of Mr A.E. Doughty, who can be seen with the extended arm, at the back of the nearest gun crew)

111

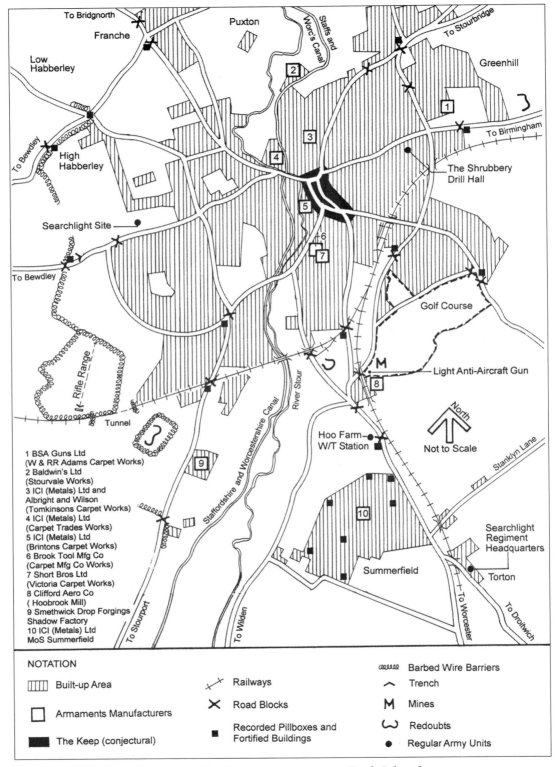

Figure 46. Kidderminster Anti-Tank Island

For the expected battle for Worcester in the 1940s, four first aid posts were to be used by the Home Guard for their casualties: Berkeley's Hospital, in the centre of the city; Christopher Whitehead School for the West Sector; Samuel Southall School for the Central and North Sectors, and Holy Trinity School for the South Sector.

Kidderminster Anti-Tank Island

Unfortunately, the amount of documentary source material for this anti-tank island is much less than for Worcester, nevertheless a combination of a single surviving defence plan for the town dated July 1940 and good eyewitness reports have given us a relatively clear picture of the proposed defences. Figure 46 summarises what is known about the town defences and indicates that the defences were not as extensive as at Worcester. Nevertheless a clear ring of outer defences in the form of pillboxes and road blocks is apparent. Other road blocks within the town suggest that an inner or reserve defence line was planned.

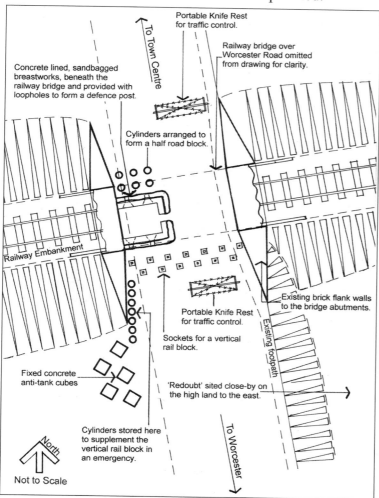

Figure 47. Road block and defence post, Worcester Road railway Bridge, Kidderminster

Of particular interest are the three strong-points occupying higher ground. The most prominent of these is to the west of the Stourport Road on the ridge at Birchen Coppice, at SO 818 744. The area was more open during the war and while post-war housing and commercial developments now surround it, the summit of the hill has been retained as open space. There is no sign of any defence-works now but from the open space it is possible to appreciate what a dominant position it would have been for covering the approaches to Kidderminster from the south.

The second strong-point was sited on the sandstone ridge to the east of and overlooking the Worcester Road, immediately to the south of the Severn Valley Railway, at SO 833 750. This has now been covered in housing so nothing remains. However, a former local resident has given us a very good description of the road block at the railway bridge here, that would have been covered by this redoubt. This reproduced in Figure 47.

The third of the strong-points was located on the low hill immediately adjoining the present built-up area of Kidderminster, on the north side of the Birmingham Road, at SO 849 774. Although this pastureland is still open, there is no sign of any earthworks.

We are told that the west side of the town had a barbed wire entanglement along the outer edge of the built-up area and it is likely that other parts of the town would have been treated similarly. Minefields would also have been planned but other than the provision of mines at Hoobrook, no details have survived. Contributing to the outer defences of the town were the pillboxes that still exist around the Summerfield establishment, as well as the barbed wire security fencing around the rifle range and Home Guard battle training area to the south-west of Sutton Park Road.

There is no indication of a keep on the defence plan for the town, yet there must have been one; all anti-tank islands had them! Bearing in mind the purpose of a keep, it is possible to speculate fairly confidently about where it was and its extent. It must have incorporated the buildings at the ends of Mill Street, Church Street and Blackwell Street, along the whole of High Street, Worcester Street, Vicar Street, Oxford Street, and the area of the junction between Green Street, Hoo Road, Bromsgrove Street and Comberton Hill in order to have defended the approaches of all the major through-roads that then converged in the centre of Kidderminster. It is also likely that the Staffordshire and Worcestershire canal and the River Stour where they pass through the town centre would have been incorporated into the defences. The location of a Home Guard wireless communications facility in the yard behind Brinton's premises and the Town Hall suggests that this was the location of the battle headquarters from where the battle for Kidderminster, and the counter-attack reserve, would have been directed.

Like urban areas elsewhere, little remains of the town defences within Kidderminster but by plotting all the recorded road blocks and surviving anti-tank cylinders around the town, an outer ring of defences beyond the built up area can also be deduced. Of these, surviving features can still be seen at the following locations:

A) anti-tank cylinders in the ditch at Stone (SO 860 735).
B) anti-tank cylinders in Trimpley Lane, Shatterford (SO 793 804).
C) cable block anchors in the road cutting at Jacobs Ladder (SO 801 783).
D) one cable block anchor in the road cutting near Shatterford (SO 799 804).

The most complete set of defence structures, including five substantial double-deck pillboxes, survive within the Summerfield establishment on the south side of the town. The defence of this vulnerable point is looked at in more detail in the following chapter, but it does raise the issue that all of the key armament factories in Kidderminster would have had their own defences and, like those in Worcester, their own Home Guard platoons or sections. These would have contributed to the overall defence of Kidderminster and so the key armaments factories are shown on Figure 46.

Responsibility for manning the majority of defences in the Kidderminster anti-tank island lay with the 6th Worcestershire (Kidderminster) Battalion Home Guard. Unfortunately, no details of the proposed disposition of their forces for the defence of the town, location of OPs or battle headquarters have been sourced so far, although a number of former Home Guards have referred

Part of A Company of the 6th Worcestershire (Kidderminster) Battalion Home Guard, photographed outside King Charles Grammar School, their company headquarters, on 3 December 1944. (Courtesy of Judith Ashcroft whose father, CQMS Lionel Howles, is standing at the right-hand end of the second row)

to reporting for duty at the golf clubhouse (SO 840 754) that suggests that it may have been a Company Headquarters. Contributing to the defence of the town would have been a number of regular troop detachments located in Kidderminster. These were to put their establishment or camp into a state of all-round defence and the following regular troops have been identified:

A) The signals staff at the military W/T station at Hoo Farm. This site was designated as a vulnerable point and so would require defending as a matter of priority anyway. It is likely that the personnel from this establishment would have manned the nearby pillbox and road blocks until their move to Park Attwood.

B) The newly formed 8th Battalion, The Essex Regiment, part of the 210th brigade of the Dorset Division were billeted at Park Attwood for a short period during 1940, before moving to Bentley Manor and The Sillins, near Redditch.

C) The succession of troops billeted at The Shrubbery Drill Hall. This former Territorial Army property was used by elements of the various Field Force divisions that were located in Worcestershire during 1940/41.

D) The searchlight crew at Summer Hill and 80th Searchlight Regiment headquarter staff at St Margaret's, Torton.

It would also true to say that the stop line defences established at Bewdley and Stourport would also have contributed to the outer defences of the Kidderminster anti-tank island and vice versa.

Redditch Anti-Tank Island

Like Worcester and Kidderminster, the defences of this anti-tank island had two principal tasks: to prevent enemy armoured columns using the main roads through the town in any attack towards Birmingham and to protect a large number of key war production factories and vulnerable points in and around the town. As elsewhere, the vulnerable points that would need protecting were the public utilities and power supplies necessary for maintaining the well-being of the town's population and for maintaining war production.

Only limited documentary sources have come to light to help establish the means to defend the town and since Redditch has been subjected to much redevelopment, new development and road building since the war under the provisions of the New Towns Act, few tangible remains can be found of its former defence works.

The layout of wartime Redditch illustrated in Figure 48 indicates that, apart from the north side of the town which had, and still has, a well defined 'urban edge', in all other directions pre-war development had spread in narrow tentacles out into the countryside, making it very difficult to establish a clear and cohesive outer defence line such as that planned for the Worcester and Kidderminster anti-tank islands. The railway penetrates almost to the centre of the town from both north and south, providing enemy armoured columns a potential route into the heart of the town without the need to use the main roads, while the pattern of woodlands, farmland and open spaces, including the town golf course, gave the opportunity for enemy infantry to infiltrate, notably from the south and west, well into the town. The golf course also provided the enemy with a potential landing ground for paratroops close to the town centre, although it was obstructed against aircraft landing with a pattern of concrete blocks. Two other large fields elsewhere were also obstructed with poles: one to the south of Salters Lane, another to the east of the BSA factory. There were probably others.

Eyewitness accounts, notably from former Home Guards, and the few scant documentary records, provide us with some locations for road blocks and weapons positions, but unless further documentary sources come to light, such as Home Guard defence schemes or instructions, the planned pattern of defence for Redditch will have to remain largely speculative. The interviews with former Home Guards also gave us some information on the disposition of their companies in and adjoining the town.

Reports of defence exercises can sometimes be revealing of methods of defence and fortunately Redditch was well served in this respect, surprisingly so in the light of wartime reporting restrictions. As an example, the *Redditch Advertiser* of 24 April 1943 describes a major military exercise involving a number of 'attacks' on towns in Worcestershire by regular troops to test the Home Guard defences. At Redditch, the attack was made from the south, the most vulnerable sector, and the most likely direction of an attack by an enemy force that had made its way inland from landings on the south coast of Britain. The newspaper records that, unsurprisingly in view of the difficulties expressed above, the outer defences were penetrated but the attack was held by the inner defences and did not reach the keep. A strong counter-attack was launched by a mobile column and at the end of the exercise the umpires expressed satisfaction, presumably with the Home Guard defence. Apparently the exercise involved the use of police radio cars and civil defence resources, but the main responsibility for defending the town lay with the 9th Worcestershire (Redditch) Battalion

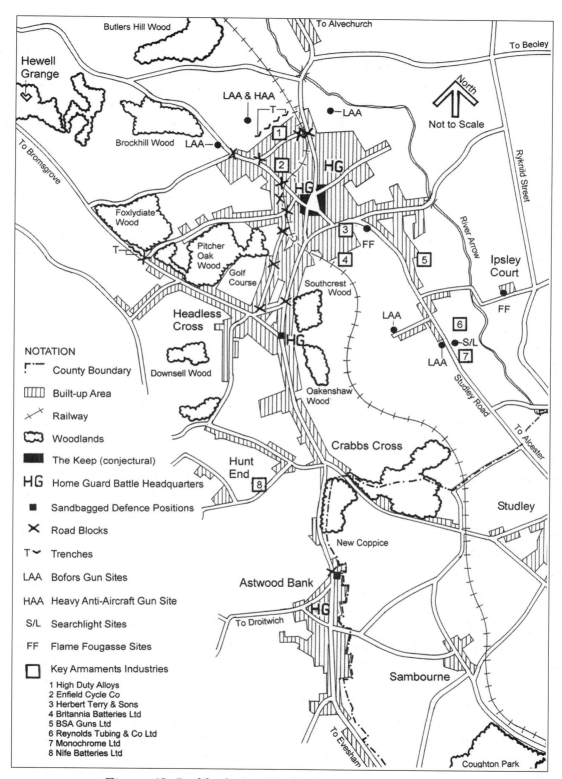

Figure 48. Redditch Anti-Tank Island, known defences

Home Guard, a defence force with a strength approaching 2,000 men. The counter-attack force is not specified but would have been either troops from Hewell Grange (SP 007 690), that was occupied throughout the war by a succession of Regular Army units, or by the 9th Battalion's own mobile column based at the Perkins Factory at Astwood Bank (SP 042 626).

Also to be gleaned from this report is the fact that in common with other anti-tank islands, there was a keep and it can be deduced, with reasonable certainty that this was located around Church Green, where the main roads through Redditch then converged. From the location of the Home Guard Zone and Battalion Headquarters in the Drill Hall, at the end of Church Road, it can be deduced that the battle for

Some of the Home Guard battalions had royal duties to perform. This is a detachment of the 9th Worcestershire (Redditch) Battalion being inspected by the Duke of Kent in February 1941. The Duke is talking to Leonard Preece, whose brother Bill can also be seen in the front rank, 6th from the right. Major Moram is the officer standing to the left of the Duke. (Courtesy of Bill Preece)

Redditch and, if necessary, the last stand in Church Green would have been directed from there. A

The former Territorial Artillery Drill Hall in Easemore Road, Redditch, was to have been the Battle Headquarters of B Company of the 9th Worcestershire (Redditch) Battalion Home Guard in the event of an enemy attack on the Redditch Anti-Tank Island

former resident of Redditch and then a boy scout, remembers that, with other scouts, he helped Colonel Scothern, the then battalion commander, to erect a wireless aerial in the trees alongside Church Green, no doubt to provide a means of communicating with the Home Guard garrisons in other sectors of the town defences and the regular troops at Hewell Grange. An observation post was provided on top of the Danilo Cinema, at SP 040 677, shared with the Observer Corps.

Nothing remains of the defences around Church Green, and no documents have surfaced to tell us about them. Even the Drill Hall has gone, although the crest of the Worcestershire

Regiment from over the main entrance has been retained and incorporated in the replacement building at SP 040 678. However, it can be confidently speculated that there would have been road blocks and covering weapons positions at the narrowest points between buildings of Prospect Hill to the north, Unicorn Hill to the west, Easemore Road and Evesham Street to the south and Alcester Road to the south-east. The other smaller side roads to Church Green would also have been blocked and the upper floors of buildings fortified to provide firing positions and bombing posts overlooking each of the road blocks. Responsibility for manning these posts and blocks would have been that of the Headquarters Company of the Home Guard and one eyewitness, Robin Moram, son of Major Moram, can recall seeing a Smith Gun stored at the Drill Hall and occasionally emplaced close-by. A counter-attack force of Home Guards would also have been held ready in this central defence zone.

The newspaper report also refers to an inner defence line and for this some evidence of defences has been recorded, including a road block on Pigeons Bridge and others at each end of Windsor Road. Further blocks were provided on Hewell Road, where it passes under the railway; on Bridge Street, where it crosses over the railway; and on Bromsgrove Road, where it too crosses over the railway. The latter is reported to have been of the vertical rail type, with permanent concrete cubes on either side of the road to narrow down the width of the carriageway, while at Pigeons Bridge the block comprised of a number of large octagonal concrete blocks stored on the side of the road, ready to roll into place. The blocks in Windsor Road are recorded as being 10 ton chain blocks.

For operational purposes, B Company of the Redditch Home Guard would have used the Drill Hall in Easemore Road at SP 045 680 in order to cover the eastern approaches to the town, and no doubt would have formed further road blocks in that vicinity. It is known that a flame fougasse was installed in the bank overlooking Holloway Lane, at SP 049 673 and it would be normal to have a road block on the town centre side of the weapon in order to bring an enemy column to a halt, before the device was fired. We have been told by a former member of their contingent that responsibility for manning and operating the defences in that vicinity was to have been that of the Terry's Factory Home Guard, while another former Home Guardsman informed us that the Britannia Batteries force were responsible for a watch being kept for any enemy approach along the

Large octagonal concrete anti-tank blocks of the type recorded at Redditch can still be found alongside the Oxford Canal at Napton on the Hill in Warwickshire (SP 457 604). This picture shows a few remaining pieces of shaped wood used to help roll the blocks into position. The round holes in the centre of each flat were to provide purchase for a steel bar used to lever the device into position

railway from the south. It is likely therefore that a rail block would have been formed where the railway went into a cutting and before entering the tunnel. Both the cutting here and on the other side of the short railway tunnel would have made very good ambush positions for Home Guards attempting to prevent enemy troops entering the town along the railway.

As for the outer defences of Redditch that were understandably penetrated by the 'enemy' during the exercise in April 1943, a miscellany of some documentary evidence and eyewitness reports provide a part of the picture. A defence scheme for the HDA Factory Home Guard describes a series of four concrete trenches spread along the northern boundary of the factory and loopholes in the wall along Windsor Road. The site also had a light anti-aircraft Lewis gun and two Vickers machine guns mounted on the factory and office roofs, the latter also providing fire cover for the road blocks in Windsor Road with one of them also covering the approaches along the railway embankment from the north. Armed police at the factory gate were also to contribute to the defence of the factory, while men of the C Company, Redditch Home Guard, were to defend a road block at the junction of Salters Lane and Brockhill Lane. A number of houses in this vicinity were to be fortified by C Company to provide firing positions overlooking this road block and the open land to the west of the HDA factory. There is also documentary evidence that a minefield was to be laid in the open land to the north-west of the factory, while the nearby Bofors light anti-aircraft gun sites would also have contributed to the defences.

To the east of the town, the River Arrow is likely to have formed a defence line with road blocks on the various crossing points. Elsewhere, due to the ill-defined urban edge of the town, the defence is likely to have been by a series of defended localities, and Home Guard informants have described a number of individual defence features that lend weight to this view, as follows:

A cache of Molotov Cocktails, stored near St Peter's Church at Ipsley (SP 065 666), together with a flame fougasse installed in the roadside in front of the church, suggest that a defended locality was to be formed around the church and court to deal with an enemy approach from the east. The church tower provided an observation post and the phone in the Rectory a means of communication with other units and the Battalion Headquarters. The BSA Factory Home Guard garrisoned this locality.

The BSA Factory Home Guard, along the Studley Road, were perhaps some of the best armed men in Redditch, provided as they were with a number of the Besa machine guns that were being manufactured on site, and with plentiful ammunition. Exercises by this factory Home Guard along the River Arrow, nearby, suggests that they would have manned part of this defence line, as well as road blocks in the vicinity of the factory.

The Reynolds Tubing Company did not itself raise a Factory Home Guard unit and a number of Home Guards from elsewhere in Redditch recall assembling there for night-time guard duty and to provide light anti-aircraft gun teams for defence of the factory. With the Home Guard from the Monochrome factory next door, the Bofors gun teams from the sites opposite the Reynolds factory, and the searchlight crew immediately to the south of the factory, a defended locality is likely to have been formed around both factory sites.

Eyewitness evidence of road blocks in the area, a sandbagged defence post on the traffic island and an observation post on the ridge overlooking the surrounding area, suggests that Headless Cross was the location of another defended locality. The road blocks here were again formed with the large octagonal concrete blocks that seem to have been a feature of Redditch defences. C Company of the Redditch Home Guard had their Headquarters in the Cooperative Hall, over the shop in the centre of the village. The Company had responsibility for defence of this vicinity as well as covering the approaches over the open fields to the west, as far north as Salters Lane. An exercise, remembered by a former member of this Company, entailed occupying positions near Foxlydiate Wood and alongside Birchfield Road, to deal with an 'attack' by Regulars, acting as the 'enemy'. This suggests that another defended locality was to be formed there, incorporating the slit trenches and explosives stores remembered by another eyewitness as being in this general area.

It is certain that the important road junctions at Crabbs Cross and Hunt End would have been blocked from all directions and a defended locality formed around the two settlements. However, no evidence for this, either documentary or from eyewitnesses, has been found and so it is not known whether C Company, from Headless Cross, or D Company, from Astwood Bank, had responsibility for the defence of these areas.

The Headquarters of D Company in the Perkins factory, at Astwood Bank, and evidence of a road block of the pivoted tree-trunk type, together with a covering weapons position on the north side of the village and another road block of unspecified type in Sambourne Lane, suggests that this village was another defended locality. It is likely that other road blocks, with weapons positions, would have been formed at all the other road entrances to the village, to complete the defences.

D Company also had a number of garrisons in the villages to the south and west of Redditch, notably at Feckenham and Inkberrow. Both of these villages had locally-constructed armoured cars to help with their defences, while Inkberrow had a key observation post on the hill near Stonepits Lane, at SP 011 570, traffic control road blocks at the north and south ends of the village, and a machine gun post on the church tower, at SP 016 573, contributing to the defence of the village. Virtually nothing is known about the fixed defences for Feckenham although the church tower was again to be used as an observation post. The Cookhill Home Guard manned a traffic control road block on The Ridgeway, while at Holberrow Green a searchlight battery detachment of regulars had a number of slit trenches nearby and a knife rest road block was observed, near Sillins.

A Company of the Redditch Home Guard, based in The Red Lion at Alvechurch, were responsible for defending this village and manning an observation post on high land at Rowney Green. Road blocks to the north and south of the Alvechurch have been recorded but there must have been other blocks on the other entrances to the village as well, along with fortified buildings within the village. A Home Guard ammunition store of the standard design once stood in the churchyard.

The common county boundary with Warwickshire follows The Ridgeway and then loops around Redditch to the east, thereby administratively separating the nearby settlements of Sambourne and Studley from the town. Nevertheless, close liaison between the 9th Worcestershire (Redditch) Battalion and the 4th Warwickshire (Stratford) Battalion Home Guard, which certainly had a garrison in Studley, and possibly in Sambourne, would have contributed to the defence of Redditch by delaying any enemy attack from those directions.

In addition to the Home Guard garrisons described above, the Regular Army had troops billeted in the area who would also have contributed to the defence of the town. Hewell Grange has already been mentioned, but Bentley Manor and Sillins, to the south-west of the town, were both occupied by regular troops during the early stages of the war, indeed until the Americans arrived to occupy these properties prior to D-Day. All three locations would have been provided with defences and would have contributed to the defence of Redditch.

Only two pillbox sites have been recorded for Redditch: one at the Brockhill Lane Bofors site and another covering the road junction outside the entrance to Hewell Grange. One eyewitness remembers others covering the open approaches to Redditch from the south and to the west of Studley Road but has no detailed recollection of where. There must have been many more around such an important anti-tank island.

A combination of known defence sites including the anti-aircraft gun sites that would also have had an anti-tank role, have been shown in Figure 48.

Evesham Anti-Tank Island

From being part of the Avon Stop Line defences, Evesham town was re-designated as an anti-tank island in 1942 when the concept of stop lines was abandoned. The loop of the River Avon around Evesham provides the town with a natural defence feature upon which to base a plan, a feature that had been exploited for military purposes at least twice before: in 1265 and again 1645, when battles had been fought here. Both times the battle was lost by the occupiers of the town so the portents were not good for the 1940s. However it was intended to try again.

Unfortunately, no official defence plans have so far been found for Evesham as an anti-tank island but as part of the commemoration of the fiftieth anniversary of the ending of World War II, Evesham Almonry Museum collected some information on the defences of the town from local people and produced their own map. The pattern of defences in Figure 49 is therefore an amalgam of that information, together with that provided by the 217th Field Park Company RE in its War Diary and used as a basis for the description of the defences along the Avon Stop Line in Chapter 4. There must have been many more defence features in and around Evesham but we shall probably not now discover these.

It is possible to predict that the keep was located around the Market Square and the junction of Bridge Street and High Street. How the Home Guard was organised to defend the town is also presently not known.

Malvern Anti-Tank Island

Malvern was also added to the list of anti-tank islands in the county in 1942 and, although, again, no overall plan of defence has been found for the town, a number of sources describe some of the defences provided in 1940. Many of those defences would have been maintained through to 1942 and beyond, although the pillboxes may have been abandoned by then. However, in 1940, the town had been turned into a veritable armed camp with troops from the 36th Infantry Brigade garrisoned here, as well as the sailors at *HMS Duke*, the Free French and the Home Guard. That concentration of troops was no accident and although no written evidence provides an answer it is reasonable to assume that this was to provide a defence force for those elements of Black Move coming to Worcestershire, and Malvern in particular, described earlier, as well as deal with any enemy attacks towards Birmingham and the Black Country from the west.

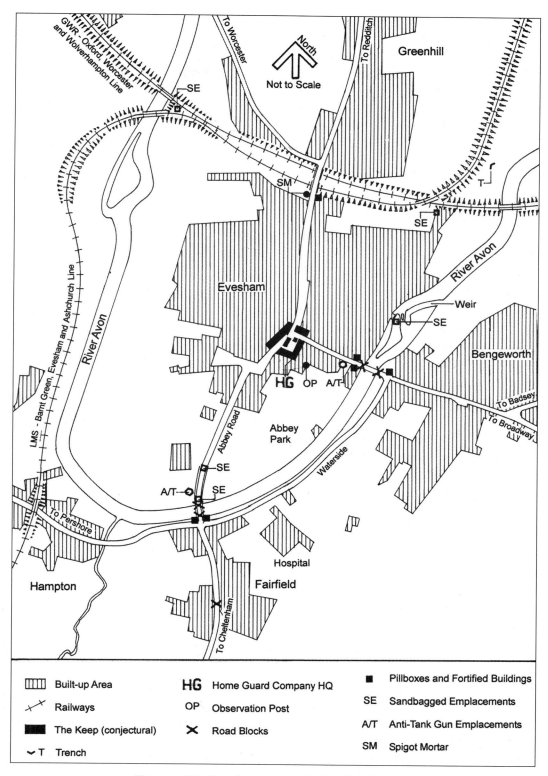

Figure 49. Evesham Anti-Tank Island, 1942

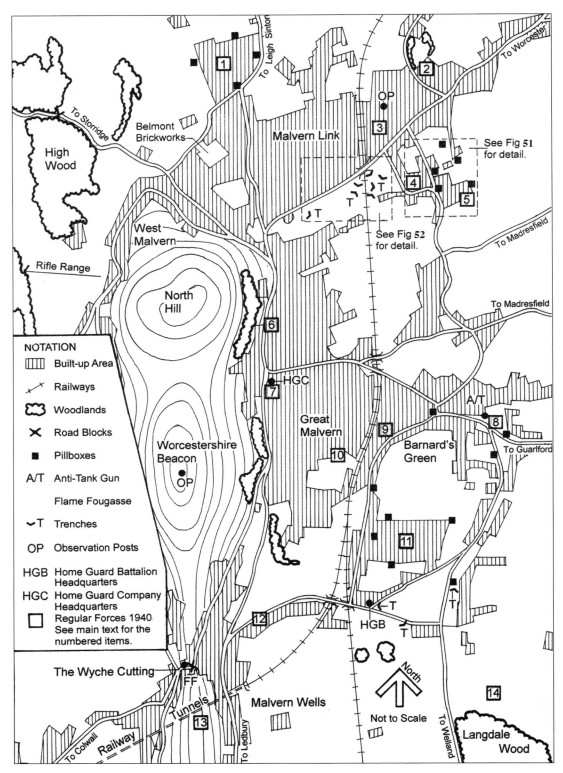

The map legend reads:

NOTATION

|||| Built-up Area

Railways

Woodlands

X Road Blocks

■ Pillboxes

A/T Anti-Tank Gun

Flame Fougasse

~T Trenches

OP Observation Posts

HGB Home Guard Battalion Headquarters

HGC Home Guard Company Headquarters

□ Regular Forces 1940 See main text for the numbered items.

Figure 50. Malvern Anti-Tank Island

124

Rather like Redditch, with its tentacles of development reaching out into the countryside, the extended and scattered form of Malvern, stretching north to south along the hills with large areas of open space and common land interspersed with the built-up area, must have provided the garrison with a difficult defence task. However, the Malvern Hills themselves do help in the defence by providing an impassable barrier for armoured columns approaching from the west and would have allowed the defenders to focus their attention on the main pass over them into the town at the Wyche Cutting, where a road block and flame fougasse were provided. Only one other road block (anti-tank cylinders) on the Storridge Road, where it crosses the Whippets Brook, has been recorded yet there must have been many other road blocks, including at the pass near the British Camp, and at each of the road bridges over the railway that is largely in a cutting where it passes through the town. A concentration of trenches recorded around the bridge over the railway at Malvern Link Station would tend to confirm this likelihood. Other blocks would have been provided at the entrance to the built-up area from each direction into Malvern, together with attendant defence positions.

One of the features of anti-tank islands elsewhere is a keep around the junction of major roads. However the form of Malvern suggests that there may have been several keeps. The areas around the small shopping centres at Malvern Link and Barnards Green, as well as the major junction at Belle View in Great Malvern are likely candidates but there could well have been others. There are several vulnerable points in the town, including most notably the Admiralty munitions store in one of the two tunnels through the hills and although no defences have been recorded for the Malvern end of the tunnels, there are a number at the Colwall end with both anti-tank pimples and anti-tank walls surviving. Yet there must have been defences provided for the defence garrison on the Malvern side of the hills. Pillboxes were provided around a number of key sites and the location of those that are known about are shown on Figure 50. These were identified from eyewitness evidence and air photographs but there were probably many more of these too. Certainly there would have been many more trench systems than those recorded and shown on Figure 50.

Two observation posts for the Home Guard have been recorded: one on the Worcestershire Beacon and a second on the church tower in Church Road, Malvern Link. There must have been others in a town with so many opportunities for observation from elevated positions.

All static regular forces were expected to provide defences around their billets or camps and while there is good documentary evidence for the location of troops accommodated in Malvern, there is little evidence of the defences that they would have provided around their billets and camps, other than a map produced by a key witness to the Malvern of 1940. Ken Davies, son of the local Air Raid Warden in Pickersleigh Road, recorded not only every item of use for civil defence purposes within his father's area of responsibility, but also every military defence too. Although only for one fairly limited area of Malvern Link, it does include two of the military camps and so Ken's map provides a wonderful impression of how many defences there must have been elsewhere in Malvern, particularly around the other army camps and billets. It is therefore appropriate to highlight the locations of other regular forces in the town from 1940 onwards and these are shown on Figure 50. The numbers on Figure 50 relate to the following paragraphs which provide a guide to the distribution of troops in 1940, and consequently a location for many of the defences of the town, if not the detail:

1) Pale Manor (SO 772 482), built for occupation by the Home Office, the site was provided with at least four pillboxes for defence. It was to become Alma Barracks and occupied by Numbers 167 and 168 Officer Cadet Training Units in 1941, then No.5 RAF Signals School until May 1942, when it was occupied by Air Defence Research and Development Establishment, with its own platoon of Home Guard responsible for defence of the site. Post-war, the site was combined with the former *HMS Duke* for use by the Radar Research Establishment and known locally as North Site. More recently the site was again used by the army and is now due to be redeveloped for mainly housing purposes.

2) Camp C, Lower Howsell (SO 787 482). This site is now occupied by the Regency Road residential estate but during the war contained Nissen huts used to accommodate elements of the 36th Infantry Brigade. Later, the 70th Battalion, the Royal Warwickshire Regiment would occupy the camp and finally the Americans of the 12th Medical Hospital Centre. In 1940 the camp would have had its own defences although no details have survived.

3) Cromwell Road Drill Hall (SO 783 477). Built before World War 1 for the Malvern detachment of the 8th Territorial Battalion, The Worcestershire Regiment, the drill hall was occupied by elements of the 36th Infantry Brigade in 1940, later the 70th Warwicks and finally the Americans of the 12th MHC. The site was redeveloped for housing in recent years.

4) Camp A, Pickersleigh Road (SO 787 473). Built for elements of the 36th Brigade, the site was heavily defended (see Figure 51). Later the 70th Warwicks occupied the site and finally the Americans of the 12th MHC. The site was redeveloped for local authority houses in the post-war years

5) Camp B, Pickersleigh Road (SO 788 472). Again built for elements of the 36th Brigade, it too was heavily defended. Afterwards the 70th Warwicks and finally the Americans would occupy the site. This site was redeveloped for housing post-war.

6) Oriel Villa, Worcester Road (SO 776 464). Occupied by the HQ staff of the 7th Battalion, Royal West Kents in 1940, later occupants not known. The property still exists.

7) The Abbey Hotel (SO 775 458). Occupied by the original signals station

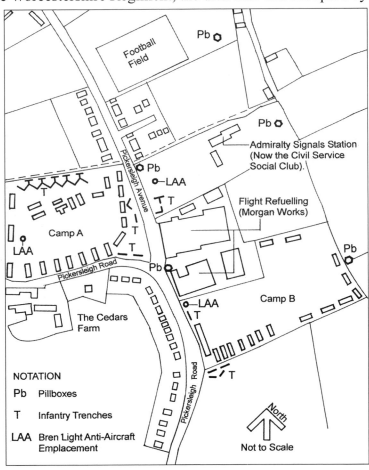

Figure 51. Defences around the Pickersleigh Road and Pickersleigh Avenue Junction, Malvern Link

for the Admiralty, it was later the HQ of the Belgian Army in Britain and then of RAF Malvern. The property remains in use as an hotel.

8) Crown Lea (SO 792 456). This large house has now gone and has been replaced by modern apartment blocks. However, in 1940 it was occupied by the HQ staff of the 36th Brigade. Besides the known pillboxes and anti-tank gun emplacement in the vicinity, there must also have been defence positions within the immediate vicinity of the house. The house was later occupied by Belgian forces and then civilian staff of TRE.

9) Clarence Road Drill Hall (SO 783 454). Built before World War 1 to accommodate the Territorial gunners of Malvern Battery of the 67th Field Regiment Royal Artillery, it was occupied by elements of the 36th Brigade in 1940. The later occupants are not known until the Americans arrived and occupied it in 1944. The site was redeveloped for housing recently.

10) No.5 House, Malvern College (SO 780 453). Occupied from 1940 to 1942 by the Free French OCTU, it would then be occupied by TRE along with the remainder of the College build-

Belle Vue, Great Malvern, May 1943. Men of the 7th Worcestershire (Malvern) Battalion Home Guard parading for their '3rd Birthday' celebration. The salute is being taken by Captain Spencer-Cooper RN, of HMS Duke, outside the entrance to the Post Office. Major Kendall, M Company Commander, can be recognised from his left-handed salute. A severe wound to his right arm sustained during World War I prevented him from saluting with his 'correct' right hand. Note also the large 'V for Victory' banner and the sailors from HMS Duke in the foreground. (Courtesy of Sheila Edmunds)

Members of M Company (Malvern) Home Guard at some of their battle stations at a public demonstration on Malvern Link Common in May 1943. Apparent are the Northover Projector and crew in the foreground and the spigot mortar and crew in the middle ground, to the left. The photograph illustrates the trench system shown adjoining the spigot mortar position on Figure 52. The trenches are not as precisely constructed or maintained as the Royal Engineers designs in Chapter 8 might suggest. (Courtesy of Sheila Edmunds)

ings until 1946. The site must have had defences but no details have been found, although the civilian staff of TRE formed a substantial element of the Malvern Company Home Guard. No 5 House returned to dormitory use for Malvern College and still exists, adjoining Woodshears Road.

11) *HMS Duke* (SO 785 447). The site is now occupied by QinetiQ and has changed significantly since 1940 when it was built to accommodate the Admiralty. It was heavily defended in 1940 with at least five pillboxes and several trench systems and the naval staff provided a number of mobile columns for counter-attack purposes.

12) Hatherley, Peachfield Road (SO 775 441). Latterly the Youth Hostel for Malvern, but in 1940 this large house and a number of Nissen huts alongside Peachfield Road were occupied by the HQ staff of the 6th Battalion, Royal West Kents. Later the 70th Warwicks and finally the RAF would occupy the site. No details of the defences are known.

13) The older railway tunnel, Malvern Wells. Utilised as an Admiralty munitions store, a guard for this vulnerable point was provided by numerous units, including *HMS Duke*, and the Home Guard, who would occupy huts in the station yard of the former Wells Station. Two of the three huts provided for the guard survive to this day and are now used for commercial purposes (SO 778 441). Two further huts remain at the rear of Colwall Station and have been converted to residential use (SO 757 424).

14) Blackmore Park (SO 798 437). Originally a tented camp to accommodate elements of the 36th Brigade, a hutted camp would later be built here to be occupied by an American hospital. Like all Regular Army camps, in 1940 the site would have had defences although no details have survived.

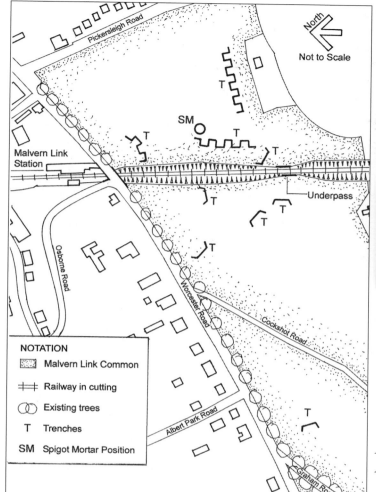

Above: Home Guards digging trenches on Poolbrook Common, adjoining Peachfield Road, Malvern. Lance Corporal Reg Moss looks on while 'Pop' Davis does the digging. (Courtesy of Dennis Burrows, former Home Guard)

Left: Figure 52.
Infantry trenches, Malvern Link

By 1942, much of the Regular Army had left Malvern and two key scientific research establishments had arrived. The prime responsibility for defence now fell upon 'M' Company of the 7th Worcestershire (Malvern) Battalion Home Guard, with their headquarters in Lyttelton House (SO 775 458), near the Post Office. The RAF presence in support of Telecommunications Research Establishment (TRE), the naval forces at *HMS Duke* and much later, the Americans of the 12th Medical Hospital Centre based in the town would also contribute. Unfortunately, nothing survives of M Company plans for the disposition of the forces for the defence of the town, other than a map of trenches around the railway cutting across Malvern Link Common and covering the nearby roads. The form of some of these trenches to the east of the railway reflect the experience of the World War I veterans in the Home Guard with their zig-zag complex of traverses, while those to the west of the railway are much simpler and are probably of later vintage. The spigot mortar position would have been added in 1941. These are all shown in Figure 52 which, in addition to the details recorded by Ken Davies, provide evidence of just how well defended this area, and possibly other parts, of the town was to be.

Centres of Resistance and Defended Localities

This loop-holed wall, at SO 948 750, is one of two in the centre of Fairfield village, to the north of Bromsgrove, and is indicative of the web of defences created throughout rural Worcestershire in 1940/41

Figure 3 shows where the key centres of resistance and defended localities, outside those incorporated in the anti-tank islands, were in Worcestershire by 1942, but this is not the whole defence story for the county by any means. Every village would have had its defence plan, worked out by the local Home Guard commander, but few documents survive to tell us what they were. However, the scatter of individual defence sites so far recorded throughout the county provide confirmation that a complete web of defence had been planned and constructed. Two surviving loopholed walls and a cable block anchor at Fairfield, north of Bromsgrove, at SO 948 750 and a loopholed building at Hanley Swan, at SO 812 437, are good surviving examples.

Two rural defence plans for the Home Guard have been found, one for the defended locality at Beckford, between Tewkesbury and Evesham. This was produced by Lieutenant H.W. Denbeigh of Sedgeberrow, Commander of No.20 Platoon, of the 4th Worcestershire (Evesham) Battalion Home Guard. This is reproduced in Figure 53 and illustrates how a key road junction on the route from Cheltenham to Evesham was to be defended. The spigot mortar pedestal behind the Beckford Hotel, at SO 981 354, is all that remains of the defences.

The other defence plan is for the small village of Wickhamford, between Evesham and Broadway and is reproduced in Figure 54 The author of this plan for No.6 Platoon of C Company is not known but may be the Platoon Commander, Lieutenant H.T. Horsfield AFC, of Knowle Hill, Evesham. The defence centred on the Sandys Arms, at SP 067 414, that is still in existence, as are the houses close-by that were to be fortified, but all else has gone and a great deal of imagination is needed to visualise wartime Wickhamford, or indeed Beckford. The numbered items on the Wickhamford defence plan were described as follows:

1) Two men were to man what is described as 'the barricade' at Three Ways Orchard. No details of the form of barricade are available but the original illustration implies a barbed wire barrier, possibly along the lines of the Wallace Bagnet described in Chapter 8 and possibly supplemented by anti-tank cylinders that were widely used for road blocking elsewhere in Worcestershire. The siting of this road block suggests that an enemy attack from the south, via Willersley, was expected. To protect the riflemen manning this post when under attack, a wall was constructed across the wide grass verge on the south-west corner of the junction. Again no details are available but a sandbagged breastwork with loopholes and capable of being used in either direction seems likely from the indicated fields of fire on the original plan.

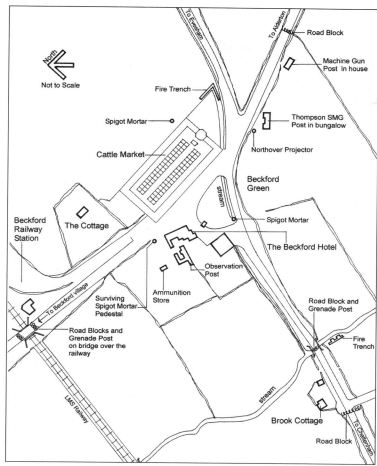

Figure 53. Beckford defended locality, 1942

2) A reserve of four riflemen for the Three Ways Post were to be stationed in front of the house adjoining the road junction and it is likely that a fire trench would have been provided for their protection.

3) Described as a traffic control point on the original plan, this probably involved the use of a knife rest (see Chapter 8) to draw traffic to a halt and was to be manned by two riflemen. Typically, one of the men would question anyone approaching the barrier and check their identity documents while his colleague would cover the people being questioned with his rifle, from the roadside. This control point would also act as an outer piquet for the village, able to warn the men manning the main defence posts at the Sandys Arms of any enemy reconnaissance vehicles approaching from the Broadway direction.

4) Two additional riflemen were to be stationed on the village side of this traffic control point with a field of fire over the adjoining countryside to the west in order to deal with any enemy troops attempting to bypass the block.

5) Two riflemen were to occupy the semi-detached houses at this location to provide observation and fields of fire over the countryside to the front and rear. No doubt upstairs windows would have been used for the purpose.

6) The same arrangements were to be made for this house nearer the Sandys Arms.

7) A reserve of seven riflemen were to be stationed in the car park at the rear of the Sandys Arms in readiness to make their way to defence posts at the rear of the house at No 6 on the defence map. This arrangement implies that an attack from the Broadway direction was expected and that enemy troops would attempt to bypass the blocks on the main road.

8) The garrison commander intended to station himself at the front of the Sandys Arms in order to direct the defence of the two main roadblocks here. A one-man trench in the grass verge in front of the pub would seem to be the likely provision for this exposed position or perhaps he would have conducted the battle from one of the pub windows, suitably sandbagged.

9) A defence post was located on the opposite side of the road to the pub and was to be manned by two riflemen and two 'bombers'. Bomber was a World War I term for grenade thrower and

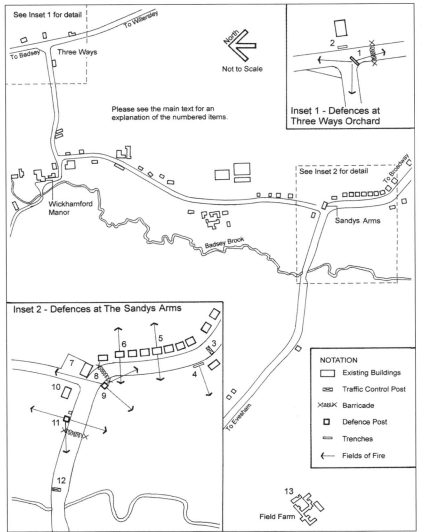

their use here would imply that the defence post was an open-topped structure, probably a sand-bagged square breastwork to provide all-round protection for the occupants against small-arms fire. The fields of fire indicate that the men here had responsibility for covering the barricade as well as the approaches from Broadway, from the village centre or across the field from the west.

10) One rifleman and one bomber were to be stationed in the house that still exists, close to the road junction. A telephone earmarked for Home Guard use was available and would have been used to alert the Evesham anti-tank island garrison of any enemy approach.

11) A second defence post occupied by two riflemen and two bombers was located close to the telephone call box, to cover the barricade and provide fire over the surrounding fields and towards the traffic control point on the Evesham side of the village.

Figure 54. The Sandys Arms and Three Ways Orchard defence posts, Wickhamford

12) A traffic control point was established on the village side of the Badsey Brook bridge, to be manned by two riflemen.

13) One rifleman was to be stationed at Field Farm and, although no indication is given on the original defence plan of his role, it is likely that he would have been an observer/sniper able to report by telephone to his Company and Battalion commanders progress on the battle of Wickhamford and pick off any small parties of enemy troops infiltrating through the surrounding fields, towards the village.

The Wickhamford defence plan is the only one of its type to be found so far for a small village in Worcestershire but it does illustrate the methods and extent of defences that must have been a feature of the web defence pattern in villages throughout the remainder of the county.

CHAPTER 7

The Defence of Vulnerable Points and War Production

The second of General Ironside's objectives, in his strategy of June 1940, after the prevention or limitation of any enemy landing and then dealing swiftly with scattered enemy forces, was to prevent the enemy from interrupting or destroying the vital resources of the country. Only very general references could be made to the protection of the so-called vulnerable points in his broad defence plan; nevertheless, sites were identified and lists of them supplied by the Area Commands. The Central Midland Area Defence Scheme consequently listed the key vulnerable points in Worcestershire for protection.

A priority system was established for these sites that was to determine the level of defence provided. Priority 1 sites were to have protection from units of the Regular Army, while Priority 2 could be either the Army or the LDV/Home Guard, with Priority 3 by the LDV/Home Guard. However, in the same way that other aspects of defence policy were never as black and white as planned, Home Guards did provide the guard for some of the Priority 1 sites.

The 11th Battalion of the Royal Warwickshire Regiment were moved to Hewell Grange (SP 003 690) during the summer of 1940 to provide a defence force for many of the key vulnerable points (VPs) in Worcestershire. Later a contingent of Military Police was trained at Norton Barracks for this purpose. Sam Beard, who was the depot runner at the time, remembers these so-called Vulnerable Points Police with their blue police flat caps and khaki uniforms, and that they were generally older men with lower than normal medical grades.

The vulnerable points listed for Worcestershire in the Central Midland Area defence Scheme, and in order of priority are as follows:

Priority 1
RAF Hartlebury, No 25 Maintenance Unit
Constructed in 1938 and occupying seven widely dispersed sites in the countryside to the east of Hartlebury village, this former storage facility is still largely intact, although it has long since been relinquished by the RAF. The seven sites can be found at SO 854 700, SO 863 700, SO 857 725,

SO 867 720, SO 863 710, SO 874 708 and SO 878 700. 25 MU originally stored everything the RAF might need, except apparently bombs and bullets. The site is interesting from an architectural viewpoint because it came at the end of the so-called RAF expansion period when, encouraged by the Royal Fine Arts Commission, some well constructed and attractive buildings, of mock-Georgian appearance, were built in order to limit the visual impact of their airfields and

This former guard house of 25 MU Hartlebury reflects the quality of architecture of the RAF expansion period

barracks on the countryside. Although perhaps little could be done to make the vast storage buildings of 25 MU attractive, the quality construction of the expansion period are in marked contrast to the strictly utilitarian buildings put up on RAF establishments after the war started. Strangely, no military defence structures have survived at 25 MU, although it did have its own Home Guard platoon recruited from the civilian staff and must have had defence positions. The wide dispersal of the seven sites are an obvious attempt to limit the effects of an air attack but some other passive defence features also remain, including a gas decontamination building, an air raid siren, as well as the remains of a bombing decoy site located at Hampton Lovett, at SO 892 665, to lure the Luftwaffe away from the Hartlebury complex. There is also photographic evidence of blast walls having been provided around some of the buildings.

The Hartlebury 25 MU Home Guard Platoon marches past the Air Officer Commanding. Note the earth blast protection wall for the building on the right and the external window shutters, which appear to have been camouflaged. (Courtesy of Bewdley Museum)

RAF Aviation Fuel Reserve Depot, Upton upon Severn

This is the Ripple Depot and it is still largely intact at SO 866 389, although it appears to be unused now. Some of the underground storage tanks are apparent from ground level, with their turf covering to camouflage them from the air. Air raid shelters and one pillbox remain. The railway that once served the depot, and distributed the fuel to RAF stations, has now gone, as has the jetty on the adjoining river bank where the petrol tankers from Avonmouth off-loaded their

The former aviation fuel depot at Saxons Lode, near Ripple, can still be seen from the ground and in air photographs. The railway and sidings that served the site have gone from this 1960s photograph, but their location is clear. (Courtesy of WHEAS)

aviation fuel. The construction of the oil pipeline through the county during the war, as part of the Pluto scheme, eventually brought to an end the tanker traffic on the River Severn.

RAF Aviation Fuel Reserve Depot, Stourport
Nothing is presently known about this site.

RAF Cased Fuel Depot, Hinton on the Green
Set in the countryside to the south of Evesham, at SP 020 405, only a former security gate adjoining the site betrays its former military use. It is now a trading estate and the railway that once served it has long-since gone as a result of the Beeching cuts. Apart from a small camp for the staff, the site was largely open with the fuel apparently stored in containers on large hardstandings. An official, and now very rare, defence scheme for this vulnerable point survives and is reproduced in Figure 55. It illustrates just how extensive the defences for the other key VPs in Worcestershire must have been.

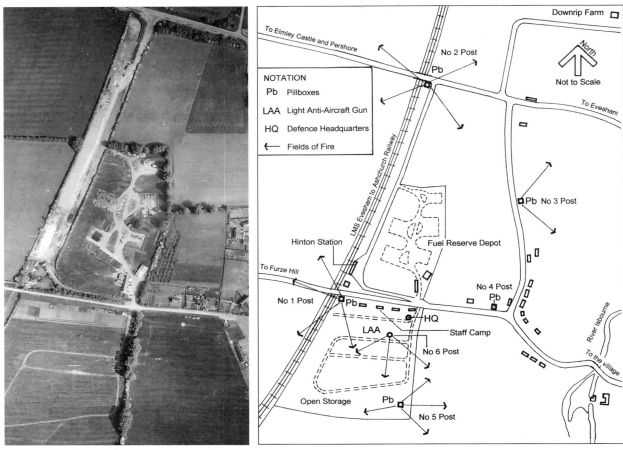

Figure 55 (right) is a plan of the RAF Cased Fuel Depot defences at Hinton the Green, whilst the late 1960s air photograph shows the layout of the hardstandings for the 'cased' aviation fuel, and the later extension into the field to the south. The location of the railway and sidings that served the site can be seen on the left of the photograph, whilst the edge of the village can just be seen on the right. (Courtesy of WHEAS)

BBC Station, Wood Norton Hall

As part of the scheme to evacuate government departments to Worcestershire, the BBC established a broadcasting and radio monitoring (Y Service) facility in September 1939 to the west of Evesham, at SP 017 472. The BBC still occupy the site that now also includes a Cold War period, nuclear bomb-proof, underground broadcasting studio. Many of the wartime huts remain on the site, as does the infamous 'Mrs Smiths House' used by the monitoring service. Gilbert Harding, of Twenty Questions fame, was one of the staff listening-in to foreign services here in order to glean intelligence. The information collected would be sent to Whitehall in a daily digest. Apparently the accents of some of the other foreign language monitoring staff caused concern about Fifth Column activity in the Evesham area! The staff were then largely billeted out in the surrounding area and people asking for directions to the BBC in a foreign accent must have appeared to be very suspicious to the locals. An emergency broadcasting studio was located at Abbey Manor House (SP 033

457) and took the form of an innocuous air raid shelter. This building was demolished some years ago but it is said that Alvar Liddell, one of the BBC's wartime news readers, used the facility during the war. The BBC raised its own Home Guard for defence of the site and an Auxiliary patrol, but only a crumbling explosives store has so far been recorded, on the wooded hillside behind Wood Norton Hall, at SP 020 475.

BBC Station, Droitwich

This is the BBC Wychbold transmitter station at SO 929 666. Established between the wars, the facility was designed to relay broadcasts to the rest of the world. The broadcasts would come into the Wychbold station from the BBC's studios elsewhere via normal telephone lines. A secondary function of the powerful transmitter was to provide a homing beacon for British bombers returning from raids on Germany and the device was switched on at appropriate times, even when not broadcasting, to fulfil this function. A by-product of this was that the Luftwaffe also used it as a navigational aid and this is often given as a reason for the site *not* being bombed during the war. The 11th Battalion, The Royal Warwickshire Regiment, provided a guard for the site initially, in the summer of 1940, but the mainly

Wood Norton Hall, the former house of the Duc d'Orleans, was occupied by the BBC in 1939 in order to provide alternative broadcasting facilities should London have become untenable through bombing or invasion

This emergency broadcasting studio at Abbey Manor, near Evesham, had the appearance of an air raid shelter, and was used temporarily by the BBC's wartime newsreader Alvar Lidell. It has now been demolished. (Courtesy of Malcolm Atkin)

male staff of the establishment also formed a Home Guard platoon for defence of the site. In fact every man was expected to join the Home Guard, unless he had a very good reason for not doing so! The BBC Home Guard would patrol the inside of the perimeter fence, while the Stoke Works Home Guard Platoon would patrol the surrounding roads. A number of air raid shelters still exist on the site but no military defences have so far been identified.

The BBC Transmitting Station at Wychbold

Admiralty Tunnel Magazine, Colwall

The original railway tunnel through the Malvern Hills that runs alongside the present tunnel, was abandoned in the 1920s as a result of a rock fall. This abandoned tunnel was offered by GWR to the Admiralty in 1939 and it was to become a major store for bombs, shells and mines. A narrow gauge railway was provided to move the munitions from the store to the mainline sidings. A permanent guard was provided and their living huts still survive, two at each end of the tunnel. There is evidence of road blocking materials above the tunnel entrance in Colwall, with both anti-tank pimples and small anti-tank walls visible in Broadwood Drive.

Petroleum Board Reserve Storage Depot, Worcester

This was the Diglis Depot (SO 848 534) and adjoins the locks on the River Severn, to the south of the city. A defence plan for this locality has survived (see Figure 28), the defences contributing both to the Severn Stop Line and the outer defences of the Worcester anti-tank island.

Petroleum Board Reserve Storage Depot, Stourport

This site adjoined the former power station described below but little is known about it or its defences. However, pipelines from the depot to the former Leapgate railway siding have been exposed by soil erosion on Hartlebury Common at SO 825 706.

The Electricity Power Station, Stourport

This generating station, at SO 814 707, was demolished some years ago and the site redeveloped for housing. It is remembered as being painted green and brown during the war with a mock house painted on the top as part of the camouflage. Defence against air attack was extensive with 20 Lewis guns and one 40 mm Bofors gun, manned by 187 Troop of the 70th LAA Battery Royal Artillery. These weapons were installed on 24 August 1939, eleven days before war with Germany was declared by Neville Chamberlain! One of the Lewis gun positions still survives as an earth-works on Hartlebury Common, at SO 824 707. Eyewitness accounts tell of three other LAA sites: one on Stagborough Hill, at SO 788 722, another in the Stourport Memorial Park, at SO 805 718 and a third to the north of the former church, at SO 718 816. No doubt other positions would have been established on and around the power station itself, although they have yet to be identified. The station would have been an essential source of power for maintaining war production in the Stourport/Kidderminster area. By February 1941 two mobile Bofors guns were added to the defences and by March 1942, two Troops of the 79th LAA Regiment. Despite the improving war position, a surprise air attack was obviously still considered to be a possibility.

Priority 2 Vulnerable Points
There were apparently no Priority 2 Vulnerable Points designated in Worcestershire in 1940.

Priority 3 Vulnerable Points
Military Wireless Transmitting Station at 'Hoobrook Farm'
This is actually Hoo Farm which occupied the high land south of Hoobrook and has now been redeveloped for industrial uses. The farm used to stand a little to the north of where the present estate entrance is now, at SO 837 744. A pillbox standing on the roadside nearby, and primarily part of the Kidderminster anti-tank island, two road blocks, and probably a flame fougasse in the nearby road-cutting were provided for defence of the area. The Army Signals staff at the W/T Station would have provided their own defence garrison. This W/T Station was later moved to Park Attwood, north of Kidderminster, at SO 797 797.

Military Wireless Transmitting Station at Wribbenhall
Bewdley Historical Research Group have identified the site of the aerials for this facility as being on Maypole Piece, an area of high land at SO 794 754, with the Army Signals staff accommodated in nearby Storrage House, on the south side of the main road to Kidderminster. These wireless facilities apparently provided overseas communications and were later moved to Park Attwood. A sand-bagged defence post was provided at the Catchems End road junction and may have been part of the defences for the transmitting station.

Admiralty Wireless Transmitting Station and buildings, Malvern
Originally established in the Abbey Hotel, Malvern, the wireless station was moved to a purpose-built facility off Pickersleigh Avenue, Malvern Link. The building still exists at SO 788 474 and

Located just off Pickersleigh Avenue, the present Civil Service Club was once an Admiralty signals station. Should 'Black Move' have taken place, and the Admiralty have moved to Malvern, this is from where contact with the fleet would have been made

is now the Civil Service Social Club. The number of defence positions here and at their site off St Andrew's Road, occupied by *HMS Duke*, suggests that the Admiralty were going to defend their interests here to the last man.

Parkfield House (Home Office), Malvern

Nothing is known about the proposed defences for this location.

The foregoing list of vulnerable points is not the full story by any means; the LDV/Home Guard listed others of local importance for protection, such as public utilities, railway infrastructure and communications facilities and there appears to have been an amazingly inconsistent approach to both listing such facilities in Worcestershire as VPs and the level of defence provided for them.

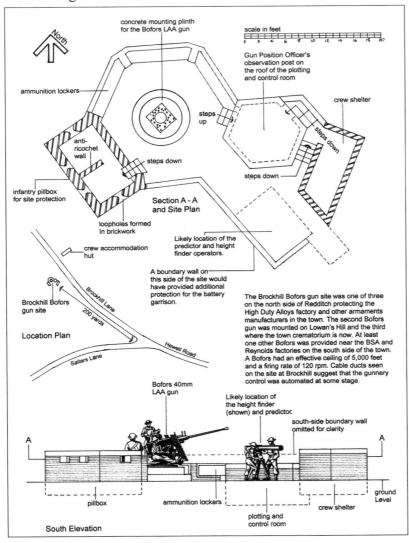

It has been noted that Lord Beaverbrook was as anxious as anyone to see that his Ministry of Aircraft Production (MAP) factories and storage facilities were well protected, and to this end a number of the Worcestershire factories were provided with additional light anti-aircraft protection with weapons issued from Air Ministry stores. Evidence collected so far suggests that many MAP factories had at least one roof mounted Lewis gun to be operated by the factory Home Guard or paid guards. However some of the air defences were more substantial: the Ackles and Pollocks Tube Works in Oldbury had five light anti-aircraft guns, while High Duty Alloys in Redditch had three 40mm Bofors guns protecting the factory. An almost complete fixed emplacement for one of these survived until recently alongside Brockhill Lane, at SP 029 685. It was demolished to make way for new housing but the recorded details of the gun site are illustrated in Figure 56.

Figure 56. The Bofors light ant-aircraft gun site at Brockhill Lane, Redditch

140

A general view of the excavated Brockhill Lane Bofors site with the Bofors gun mount in the foreground, together with signs of ready ammunition shelving etched into the concrete around it. The pillbox would have contributed to the outer defences of the Redditch Anti-Tank Island

The wide dispersal of some companies engaged in munitions work into Worcestershire was clearly a passive form of defence and one of the more impressive dispersals by MAP was the enormous underground factory at Drakelow, north of Kidderminster. Surprisingly, the facility does not appear on any lists of key vulnerable points and little evidence of defences that might have been expected has come to light. Designated Rover Factory N1D — the 'D' for dispersal — it was constructed under Blakeshall Common at SO 824 814, together with a workers' hostel in Sladd Lane, at SO 819 814. The decision to construct this underground factory came as a result of bombing raids on the existing Rover shadow factories at Acocks Green and Solihull in the winter of 1940-41, where the company were producing Bristol aircraft

One of the tunnel entrances to the former underground factory at Drakelow, north of Kidderminster. Photographed during a visit to the tunnels by Subterranea Britannica some years ago

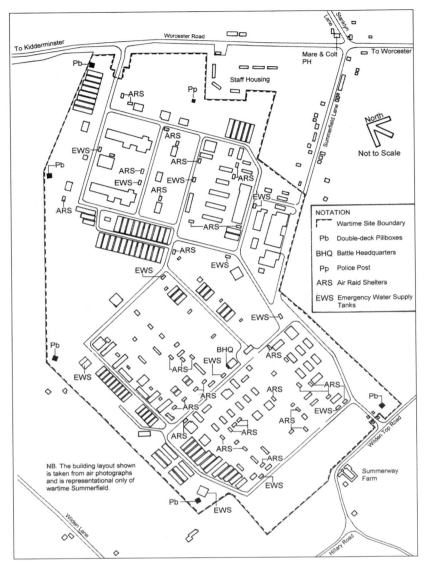

This unusual defence post is sited near the centre of the former Summerfield ROF. Its elevated position suggests that it had a function as a battle headquarters

Figure 57. Plan of the site and defences

Defence of the ICI (Metals) Ltd site at Summerfield, Kidderminster
(this page and opposite)

Right: Not strictly a pillbox, this small structure is described as a 'police post' and would have provided protection for the security staff during an air raid. It is sited behind the MOT Testing Establishment on the main Kidderminster-Worcester road

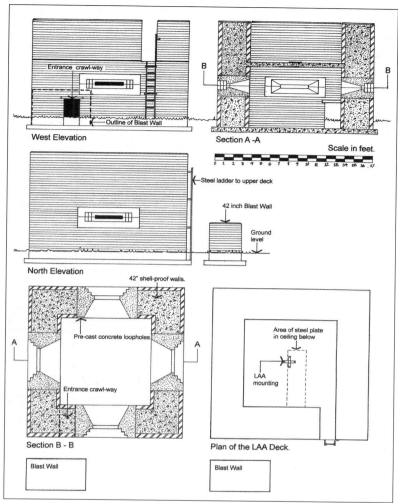

West Elevation

Entrance crawl-way

Outline of Blast Wall

Section A -A

B

B

Scale in feet.

0 1 2 3 4 5 6 7 8 9 10 11 12 13 14 15 16 17

North Elevation

Steel ladder to upper deck

42 inch Blast Wall

Ground level

42" shell-proof walls.

Section B - B

Pre-cast concrete loopholes

Entrance crawl-way

A

A

Plan of the LAA Deck.

Area of steel plate in ceiling below

LAA mounting

Blast Wall

Blast Wall

Figure 58. Type FW3/26 double-deck, shell proof variant pillbox at Summerfield (SO 839 739) with, below, another of the five surviving such pillboxes at the site

engines. Construction of the new factory began in 1941 by creating a series of inter-connected tunnels, giving almost 300,000 square feet of production, stores and office space. When completed, the Drakelow factory produced mainly spares for Bristol engines during World War II. After a brief period producing tank engines following the war, the complex of tunnels was taken over by the Ministry of Supply as a storage facility. By the 1960s, its value as a nuclear-proof Regional Seat of Government was recognised and something less than half the tunnels were converted for this purpose. Even the BBC was provided with a broadcasting studio, the aerial for which can still be seen on the hill above. The site was sold off in the early 1990s.

The Ministry of Supply (MOS) provided both air and ground defences, often of considerable extent, for some of their factories in the county. The MOS were responsible for construction of the extensive Summerfield establishment to the south of Kidderminster, at SO 835 735, in order to produce small arms ammunition and, again, it is surprising that this establishment does not appear on the priority lists for protection. The workforce were largely directed to Kidderminster from elsewhere in Britain, many coming from South Wales, and so a workers' hostel, on two sites, was also constructed to the south of Stone at SO 855 740. In addition, a number of carpet factories

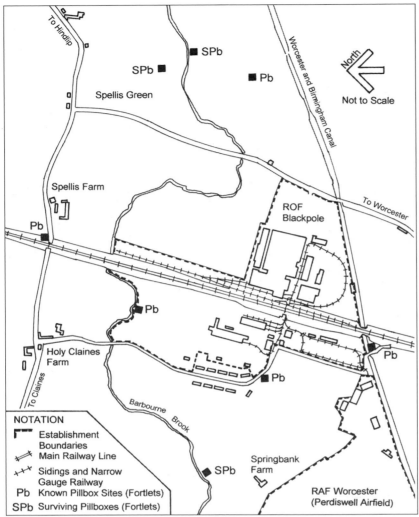

Figure 59. Blackpole Royal Ordnance Factory, Worcester

This is one of three open-topped pillboxes that survive of the Blackpole ROF defences. The design appears to be unique to Worcester and has been dubbed the 'Worcester Fortlet'

in Kidderminster were requisitioned to disperse production and make use of the now largely redundant carpet workforce. Although the manufacture of the components, including the cartridges and projectiles (bullets), was dispersed in this way, the filling with cordite and final assembly of the ammunition was carried out at Summerfield. Yet despite not appearing on the official lists of vulnerable points, survival of many of the defence structures at Summerfield illustrates just how extensive the defences of this key munitions establishment was (see Figure 57).

ROF Blackpole, initially known as Cartridge Factory No.3, was constructed during World War I for the manufacture of small arms ammunition by the Kings Norton Metal Co Ltd. The site was then bought by Cadbury's in 1921, only to be requisitioned again in 1940, becoming The Royal Ordnance Factory, Blackpole. Fortunately the dies for producing .303 cartridges had been kept in store and so manufacture could quickly re-start. The factory was returned to the Cadbury Company in 1946. The complex is sited at SO 866 578, where the main buildings still exist and are still in use for commercial purposes, although no longer occupied by Cadbury's. The survival of three pillboxes,

Once one of the well-defended and key Vulnerable Points of Worcester, the main building of the Royal Ordnance Factory still exists as part of the Blackpole Industrial Estate

together with evidence from air photographs and a number of eyewitness accounts of other pill-boxes that have now gone, provide some indication of how well this Royal Ordnance Factory was to be protected (see Figure 59), yet the site appears only on a local Home Guard list.

The three surviving pillboxes at Blackpole are unusual in that they do not have the normal protective concrete roof. This suggests that the greatest threat was thought to have been an airborne attack and that there was a need for the defenders to be able to fire into the air. Another possibility is that the builders were trying to economise on the use of concrete!

On a more modest scale, and appearing on a Home Guard list for protection, the Meco Company were provided with a Browning machine gun by the army, *after* the air raid on the factory on 3 October 1940, when a number of staff and nearby residents had been killed and injured. Geoff Devereux, who was part of the works' aircraft spotting team, was made responsible for operating the Browning which sat within a sandbagged emplacement on the roof of the main office building that still remains at SO 833 544. Geoff recalls that the workforce were usually fairly slow in making their way to the shelters after the air raid warning was sounded, until on one occasion he fired a volley in the direction of a German Dornier aircraft making its way up the Severn valley. Although the aircraft was not apparently harmed, the effect on the staff was quite dramatic, as they dashed for the shelters. The Managing Director was so impressed that he made his way up on to the roof and suggested to Geoff that: 'in future, loose off a few rounds when a raid is imminent to get the staff into the shelters!'

By 1942 the possibility of a German invasion of Britain had considerably reduced. Nevertheless there was still concern about the protection of key facilities and Home Guard instructions explained that, during normal states of readiness, the risks to which vulnerable points were liable to attack could be defined as a 'destructive raid' by enemy troops landed by sea (near coasts) or air; a 'smash and grab' raid carried out with the object of, for example, capturing a piece of secret apparatus and taking it back to the continent; or armed sabotage carried out by a small organised party of determined men, who might either be already in the country or else have landed by sea or dropped by parachute several days beforehand. Such a party might be prepared to use whatever force might be necessary to achieve their object of causing major damage to the installation or establishment. The target might be anywhere in the UK. Petty sabotage carried out by one or two individual agents relying on stealth or cunning rather than force and taking the form of stealing documents or otherwise obtaining secret information, the disruption of machinery by covert means, arson, etc might also occur.

The inclusion of the 'smash and grab' raid as a threat is significant, and no doubt was a realisation that the Germans could copy the successful operation carried out by British paratroops to capture parts of a German radar station at Bruneval, on the French Coast. This possibility, and the fact that there was a concentration of German parachutists in France, had led Professor R.V. Jones to point out to the government that the Telecommunications Research Establishment, then located on the Dorset coast, at Worth Maltravers, was vulnerable to just such a retaliatory attack. With this in mind, both TRE and ADRDE from Christchurch were moved to Malvern in May 1942, but clearly the government thought any of the key vulnerable points could be the subject of such an attack.

In light of the possibility of parachute troop sabotage attacks from 1942, a comprehensive scheme for Home Guard defence of key factories was arranged and coded 'Vitguard'. Each Home Guard battalion would contribute a number of armed men to the scheme and a 24 hour guard would be mounted. The duty proved to be too demanding and placed a terrific strain on the men involved, resulting in a reduced work output.

In early 1944, with the allied preparations for the invasion of Europe progressing under 'Operation Bolero', it was considered necessary to prevent enemy troops or agents from interfering with communications, petrol supplies and airfields and further lists of VPs were drawn up for protection by the Home Guard in Worcestershire.

The Appendix on page 225 lists the known MAP and MOS factories in Worcestershire, together with local vulnerable points designated by the Home Guard for defence. Many of these have yet to be investigated and their activities and/or defences established, but it will be clear just how widely munitions manufacturing was dispersed into the county — the BSA Company being a good example — and how many of the small motor repair garages became involved. It is accepted that this is not a comprehensive list for Worcestershire.

CHAPTER 8

Pillboxes, Emplacements and Field Works

A number of references to 'pillboxes' appear in the preceding chapters and it is thought that the shape of the round cardboard Victorian pillboxes led to the British Army using the term to describe small round concrete fortifications of World War I. Another term, in widespread use then and again during World War II, since many Home Guards had fought in the Great War, was 'blockhouse'.

Faced with the possibility of a German invasion of Britain, the War Office Directorate of Fortifications and Works established a branch called Fortifications and Works No.3 (FW3) in May 1940. It quickly produced drawings for a number of pillbox designs for the various forms of weaponry then available for the defence of beaches, stop lines, nodal points and vulnerable points, including airfields.

Pillboxes could be constructed with two thicknesses of wall: a small-arms bullet-proof or a shell-proof 42 inches. The latter was considered to be adequate protection against the then relatively small calibre tank shells, but would not have been adequate against the German 88 mm Flak guns that had been very effectively used to demolish some of the fortifications along the River Meuse in France. Calculations by FW3 suggested that a massive six feet wall thickness would have been necessary to provide protection from that particular weapon! A saving grace in any German invasion of Britain would have been the fact that these guns were heavy and required a powerful vehicle to move them. Neither would have been easy to transport across the English Channel in barges and the capture of a deepwater port would have been necessary before these weapons could make an appearance on the home battlefield.

Nearly 100 pillboxes have so far been recorded in Worcestershire, of which only 16 remain. However, some of the common types designed by FW3 are represented together with an interesting variety of local designs, although the small overall numbers surviving mean that some designs are now down to just one example in the county.

The hexagonal Type FW3/22, with equal length sides, was used to protect the Admiralty establishments at Malvern and Pershore airfield, but now just one remains at Tilesford (SO 963 501). The hexagonal Type FW3/24, with irregular length sides, was used extensively to protect the government evacuation sites, but of these just two remain, with their loopholes bricked-up, at

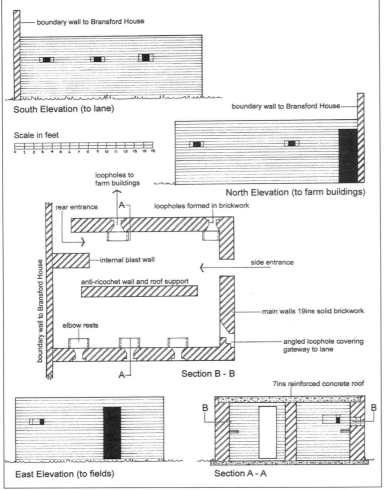

South Elevation (to lane)

boundary wall to Bransford House

boundary wall to Bransford House

North Elevation (to farm buildings)

Scale in feet

0 1 2 3 4 5 6 7 8 9 10 11 12 13 14 15

loopholes to farm buildings

rear entrance

loopholes formed in brickwork

A

internal blast wall

side entrance

boundary wall to Bransford House

anti-ricochet wall and roof support

main walls 19ins solid brickwork

elbow rests

angled loophole covering gateway to lane

A

Section B - B

7ins reinforced concrete roof

East Elevation (to fields)

Section A - A

Figure 60. Type FW3/26 variant pillbox formerly adjoining Bransford House at SO 806 531

Whittington Road, Worcester. Called the 'LDV' pillbox by the 217th Field Company RE, the FW3/24 was also used along the Avon Stop Line. Just one of these survives in fine condition at the Fish and Anchor Ford (SP 065 472). The single octagonal defence post at Summerfield, Kidderminster, thought to be a battle headquarters, appears to be unique.

Given the designation, FW3/26, there are a number of variations on the square pillbox in the county. Two of the prefabricated version of the FW3/26 manufactured by the Stent Company, survive: one at Droitwich railway station (SO 895 636), the other at Eckington Bridge (SO 922 424) although this one is crumbling fast. The five shell-proof, double-decked pillboxes at Summerfield are a variation on the FW3/26 and appear to be unique to Worcestershire, as are the open topped, fort-like structures around Blackpole ROF. Two examples of the small square police posts survive, with their distinctive narrow observation slits: a standard example at Summerfield, and a larger version at Witton, Droitwich. The smallest square defence post of them all can be seen on the canal bridge at Perdiswell.

Left: This Norcon pillbox can still be seen overlooking Bridge Sollers, from the north side of the River Wye. Its small size is apparent and its origin as a sewer pipe, with loopholes, is recognisable. There are none left in Worcestershire now

148

The Royal Engineers of III Corps and 293rd Field Park Company, who were responsible for the Severn and Teme Stop Lines, were apparently unconstrained by FW3 designs and constructed some unique rectangular structures that in some cases clearly demonstrated the tactical needs of particular locations; none more so than the pillbox recently demolished at Bransford, where two loopholes faced the inside of farm buildings and one was angled to cover a farm gate (see Figure 60). The Stanford Bridge pillbox is a good surviving example of their individuality of design.

No round pillboxes, designated FW3/25, remain in Worcestershire, although the base of one can still be found at SO 852 577, on the Droitwich Road, Worcester. Eyewitness accounts refer to Norcon structures in the Bromsgrove area but although none of these appear to have survived in the county, one exists near Bridge Sollers, in Herefordshire, at SO 413 426. It is also necessary to travel to Warwickshire to see any of the Oakington variety of round pillbox that were once numerous on some of the airfields of Worcestershire.

At least seven of the brick and concrete emplacements for the 6 pdr Hotchkiss anti-tank gun were built in Worcestershire, and the design seems to be unique to the county. Only the emplacement at Holt Bridge remains in unaltered condition, although the original structure of an emplacement can be seen inside the pumping station at Pershore Bridges.

Issued to the Home Guard from 1941, the Blacker Bombard, or Spigot Mortar, was to be used primarily as an anti-tank weapon from an ambush location. While a portable mounting for the weapon was available, a fixed pedestal was preferred and metal reinforcement spiders were provided for use in their construction. Figure 61 is based on a drawing by FW3 and illustrates the form of the emplacement and pedestal. No complete emplace-

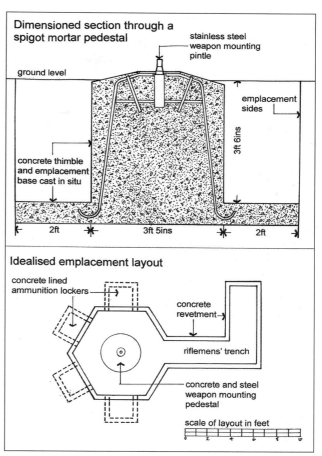

Figure 61. Recommended form of a fixed spigot mortar emplacement

One of the most accessible spigot mortar pedestals that survive in Worcestershire can be seen at the entrance to the picnic place adjoining Eckington Bridge at SO 922 422

Pollarded willows have provided overhead camouflage for the Stent pillbox at Eckington Bridge since 1940, but the photograph graphically illustrates the need for a screen over the loophole if a rifleman using it is not to present a clear target

ment remains in the county but a number of the concrete pedestals survive along the Avon Stop Line, the most accessible being at Eckington Bridge Picnic Place (SO 923 422).

The experiences of the BEF in France had demonstrated how efficient German battlefield low-level air reconnaissance was. Anything or anyone spotted could expect a Stuka attack or heavy artillery bombardment within half an hour. Camouflage of defence positions in Britain was therefore given high priority to frustrate pre-invasion photo-reconnaissance by the Germans and post-invasion battlefield-reconnaissance. The end-of-war discovery of caches of Luftwaffe air photographs of British defences suggests that the concealment was not always successful! Concealment of defence works from ground observation was also considered to be most important if the attacking troops were to be taken by surprise by the likely to be out-gunned and out-ranged defence force. The Home Guard were therefore coached in the art of concealment both from the air and the ground and a number of official instruction books on the subject were available to help them.

Pillbox building came to an end in 1941 when doubts were expressed about their value and instructions were issued for their replacement with well-sited, well-concealed and well-constructed earthworks. Military instruction books tell us that such fieldworks took several forms: from the simple pit for a single rifleman, to fire trenches that could be many yards long, and of zig-zag plan form to reduce the effects of enfilade fire. A number of trenches could be linked to form a defended locality. A limited number of fieldworks have been recorded

Henschel He 126 aircraft were extensively used by the Luftwaffe for battlefield reconnaissance, flying as low as 50 feet to spot enemy defence positions and troop concentrations. Camouflage would therefore be a key factor in constructing and locating defence works.
(Courtesy of the late Howard Inight)

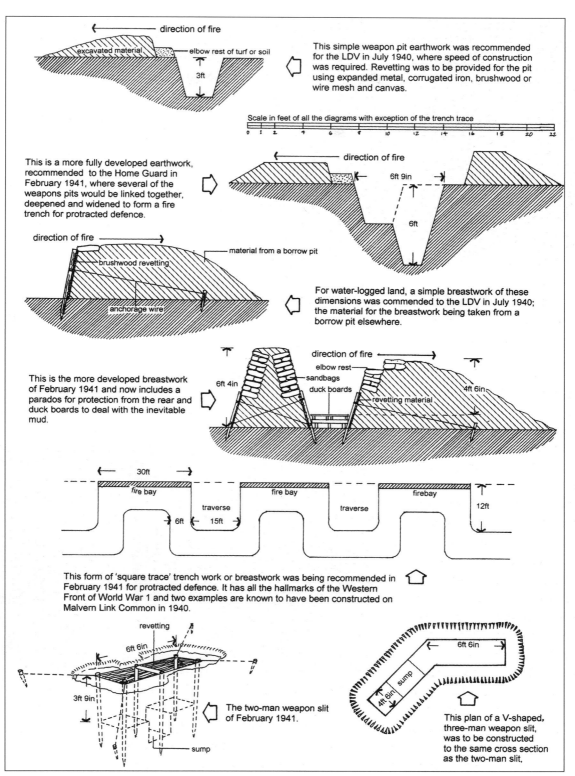

Figure 62. Some of the recommended fieldwork defences for the LDV/Home Guard

in the county, although the majority were filled in at the end of the war and only slight hollows and ridges can now be seen. Figure 62 illustrates the main types of field work recommended to the LDV/Home Guard, examples of which once existed in the county.

CHAPTER 9

Road and Railway Blocks

Western Command summarised and clarified the principles of road and rail blocks in an Instruction issued on 3 September 1940. The object of the blocks was twofold and they were to be categorised as:

1) Those to stop enemy vehicles of all types up to and including medium tanks from penetrating stop lines, entering large towns or nodal points or obtaining access to aerodromes or other vulnerable points.

2) Those to stop enemy motorcyclists as well as enemy personnel in captured vehicles dashing about the country, and to enable civil traffic to be controlled and searched when this might be necessary. Such blocks were also considered to be of value to Home Guards in the local defence of the smaller towns and villages. These blocks could be of a considerably lighter type until labour, material and money was available to strengthen them up to a scale that would stop light tanks.

It was considered essential that roads should not be prematurely blocked, while in the case of Red and Blue Roads, and certain uncoloured roads (not specified) that were important traffic routes, it was essential that two-way traffic should be possible until the last possible moment. In consequence a block on a Red or Blue Road and the 'certain uncoloured roads' had to leave a gap of at least 20 feet wide, while those on other roads had to leave a gap at least 13½ feet wide. Figure 63 indicates the known Red and Blue Roads designated in Worcestershire and these have been related to the location of mobile counter-attack columns of the Regular forces and the later Home Guard mobile columns. The Red Routes are primarily the trunk roads through the county from the south and south-west, while the Blue Routes are those for east-west movement. Related to the bridge demolition strategy referred to earlier, the importance of not demolishing the road bridges at Bewdley and Worcester becomes clearer. The mobile columns at Bewdley and Worcester would be considerably hampered if the bridges were to be destroyed.

The gaps in road blocks along the Red and Blue Routes had to be capable of being rapidly closed if the approach of the enemy was anticipated and of rapidly being re-opened if it was then found that the road was required for use by our own troops. To achieve this, it was suggested that suitable blocks in Category 1 above could be rails in slots (sockets), filled trucks on rails, or cylinders rolled into position, together with wire, while suitable blocks in Category 2 could be created with filled carts, old cars, or even coils of barbed wire.

In the case of blocks in Category 1, it was considered to be essential that enemy tanks should not be able to circumvent them, and that they had to form part of continuous anti-tank obstacles, incorporating natural obstacles, ditches, concrete blocks or mines. The blocking of railway lines was to be carried out by Railway Companies. It was an advantage if blocks could be sited so that they would come as a surprise to the enemy.

In all cases, the blocks were to be covered by fire positions sited so as not to be obvious to the enemy and offering good protection for those manning them. It was considered to be essential that enemy infantry should be prevented from capturing the block by working round

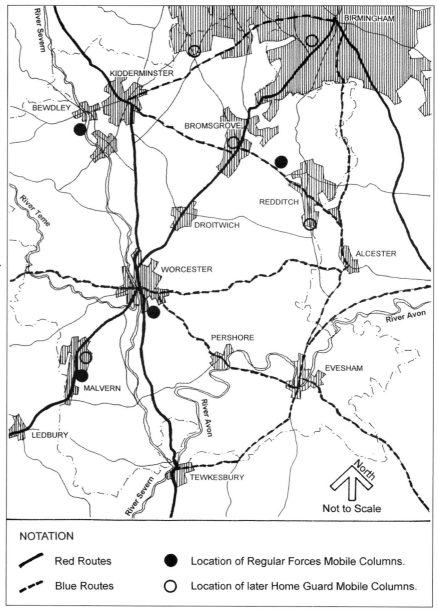

Figure 63. Designated Red and Blue Routes in Worcestershire

a flank. Full use was to be made of houses, walls, etc and where loopholes could not be made immediately, preparations were to be made for them to be made at short notice.

Area Commanders were to control the erection and alteration of road blocks and arrange that night lights be placed at all blocks that encroached on the carriageway.

Rehearsals by those responsible for closing and defending the blocks, usually the Home Guard, were ordered. The rapid closing of gaps, and the re-opening of them, to allow mobile columns through was recognised as requiring practise and, in some cases, the provision of 'special

154

appliances'. These were usually toggle ropes and steel bars, used to haul and lever the elements of the block into position.

In the event of an enemy landing, from the sea or air, Area Commands were to be the authorities for ordering the closing of gaps in the blocks. Once gaps had been closed personnel from those provided for defending the block were to be stationed at, or very close, to the block in order to re-open it to allow mobile columns, and other essential traffic, to pass through. It was expected that some enemy troops would be dressed in British uniforms and be in the possession of satisfactory passes. It was considered that a few words of conversation would suffice to ascertain whether the troops really belonged to the British Army! A reply to a question that would result in utilising words beginning with 'w' and 'v' was thought likely to catch out the unwary German masquerading as a British soldier or civilian, though it may have made life difficult for some of our allies from the Dutch, Belgian, Polish and Czech armies, that were helping with our defence.

A third type of road block not covered by this instruction was the 'sham block' where, by means of screening or the laying of mine-like items across a road, an armoured column could be brought to a halt while the obstruction was investigated and cleared. These techniques had been successfully used by the International Brigade during the Spanish Civil War, where blankets were sometimes hung across a road to obscure what might be beyond them or soup plates used to represent anti-tank mines. This would encourage them to waste ammunition firing into the sham block without really knowing what was behind the screen, or try to circumvent the sham block and blunder into a minefield. Hessian was issued to Home Guard units to be used for screening purposes and an issue of 450 yards of this material per battalion was indented for in the Worcestershire Sub Area in July 1941. Pioneer officers were invited to indent for more if required.

Surprise was to be a key element of road blocking. By locating the block around a corner, or over the brow of a hill, it was hoped that the German column would blunder into the block before making any attempt to go round it or destroy it by tank fire. While hessian could also be used to disguise or hide elements of a road block from the ground, to hide it from the prying eyes of Luftwaffe reconnaissance aircraft, was more difficult. The block would disrupt the normally smooth surface and regular width of a road and so virtually all that could be done was to tone down the tops of white concrete blocks with paint.

Locating a road block in a defile, such as a road cutting, would create a tank trap so that when the enemy column had drawn to a halt there was no opportunity to go round the block and time would be needed to reverse out of the trap, causing maximum delay to the enemy. One of the best examples of a tank trap in Worcestershire was on the south side of Holt Fleet Bridge, at SO 824 632, and referred to in Chapter 5. Another is located in the rock cutting on the Dunley to Heightington road. The War Office, through their instructions to the LDV issued in 1940, were determined to dispel the myth of Panzer invincibility as were as people like Tom Winteringham and Hugh Slater who had had experience of the early German tanks in the Spanish Civil War. They were writing articles for popular magazines and publishing books to help overcome any fear people then had for German armoured columns, and explain the techniques for trapping and attacking that could be used against them. In his book, *The Peoples' War*, Tom Winteringham had the following to say about tanks:

Towns and villages, and main cross-roads, can be held for hours and Blitzkrieg loses its pace and effectiveness. During fighting in built-up areas the two principal weapons of Blitzkrieg are at a disadvantage. Tanks cannot carry enough ammunition to flatten more than a few houses. As soon as they attempt to break into a built up-area, tanks are in immediate danger from attack at close quarters from buildings on each side of the street. Each street is a defile which can be blocked by a tank or a lorry turned over; and although tanks can butt their way through flimsy buildings, they cannot do so without risk to their tracks and armament. Tanks trying to make their way through or over shattered buildings or improvised road blocks must necessarily slow down so that they are good targets for hand grenades and Molotov Cocktails. Even if tanks succeed in mastering the streets of a city, they cannot dig the defenders out of the broken buildings on each side of the streets.

The official view, set out in LDV instructions, was that campaigns in Spain and Finland had indeed shown that tanks could be destroyed by men of resource, bravery and determination and that a tank, for all its hard skin, mobility and armaments, had serious weaknesses, including:

1) Blindness. At least 90% of the surrounding area was invisible to a tank closed down and none whatever within a radius of 15 feet from the tank.

2) Guns. The guns of tanks were incapable of firing at anything within ten feet of the vehicle or above 25 degrees. The tank could not, for example, engage targets in its immediate vicinity that were on the tops of banks or in first-floor windows. Gun turrets revolved slowly and a simultaneous attack from several directions would find serious gaps in its defence. It was incapable of firing into deep slit trenches except in enfilade.

3) Tracks. The tank was mobile only while the tracks held out. These could be broken with an anti-tank rifle or removed by crowbars or wooden spars rammed in between the driving sprocket and track while the vehicle was moving at a slow pace. The British anti-tank mine would completely remove a track from any tank.

4) Crew Exhaustion. Crews would become exhausted over long distances or several hours in closed down tanks and required frequent rests for sleep and food.

5) Fuel. The tank was dependant on a fuel supply which may be by local resources or petrol lorries, both unarmoured and easily set on fire.

One of Worcestershire's Home Guard tank traps? Two cable anchor eyes can be seen, one above the other, in the rock face on the left of this picture, set in concrete, while the hollow near the hanging ivy is almost certainly the housing for a flame fougasse. These features are located in the rock cutting on the Dunley to Heightington Road, at SO 785 695

6) Night. This was the biggest ally of the tank hunter and provided opportunities for stalking, sniping and attacking with grenades and incendiary bombs.

What Tom Winteringham and the LDV Instructions did not say, but this was pointed out to me by a former Auxiliary, is that tank engines relied on a basic, and vulnerable, ignition system with a distributor and HT leads to plugs, just like any other petrol driven vehicle and that fans were necessary to draw cooling air through louvres to a radiator. A phosphorous grenade bursting on the louvres on the top of the engine compartment would result in the burning phosphorous and benzine being drawn into the engine compartment by the cooling fan. This would destroy the ignition system and then start a petrol fire fed by the tank's own fuel pipes. The tank would then stall and could be subjected to more grenades or petrol bombs until it was destroyed. Flames and toxic phosphorus smoke would also be drawn into the crew compartment making the tank untenable. Any crew attempting to escape would be easy prey to Home Guard marksmen.

Besides formal War Office organised tests of the various forms of road block, the Home Guard and locally based Regular troops would, as advised in the instructions from their Area Commander, practise the act of blocking a road and attacking the road block to test both it and the defenders' efficiency. Two accounts of such exercises in Worcestershire have survived which provide both local interest and an indication of the efficiency, or otherwise, of the techniques being used.

The first is by C.H. Digby-Seymour, the then Town Clerk for Worcester City, in a letter dated 22 July 1940, to Colonel Cotton at the Silver Street Home Guard HQ. He records his impressions of an exercise involving the Bromyard Road Bridge over Laughern Brook, on the south-west side of St John's. The presence of a loud speaker van suggests that this was a demonstration for the benefit of the local Home Guards or perhaps even the public. Colonel Melville Lee is identified as the organiser of the exercise. He was at the time the Commanding Officer of No.23 Infantry Training Centre, at Norton Barracks. Digby-Seymour's letter includes the following:

1) The fire posts were insufficiently manned for the concentration of rapid fire to be effective in repelling an attempt to break through the Laughern Bridge; more men would be required, I think to man the posts in actual operations and a further trench might well be sited on the Railway Line, just above the position where the Loud Speaker Van stood.

2) The attack by a light tank and two motorcyclists might be misleading to the many LDVs who were present. It is probable that if an attack were made at this point the enemy units would be much more substantial; there would be more tanks and, what should not be lost sight of, rapid moving armoured motor cars and mechanical troop carriers. The latter filter more rapidly through opposition and their crews are capable of extensive deployment and after leaving their vehicles, of enfilading the defence posts, their object being to menace and take possession of the Factory temporarily as a strong point and to cover their further attacking troops.

3) We saw yesterday the tank crew leaving their vehicle in operation against concrete pillars. I was always under the impression that the Tank's crew stayed put as it were and left this sort of thing to sidecar carried troops and units conveyed in armoured motor cars. I think if

an attack were to be put into operation in this Sector it would be preceded by Motor Cyclists and Armoured Cars and not by Tanks and this apparently seems to be the German practice. In any event, in view of the position of the barriers on the City side of the Bridge, I take it that the Bridge would have been demolished and any Tanks approaching, even though perhaps the Bridge were in situ, blocked, they would not hesitate in crossing the Brook on either side. Except for its weight and unwieldiness an 8' section of railway line might be considered more effective for smashing the track of a tank than the scaffold pole which was utilised. A section of railway line could always lie at the road strong points but it would have to be operated by two men. Wood would be crunched and splintered by the tremendous power of a heavy tank.

The pillars of slabs of concrete are the wrong shape, a chain or wire hawser put round them from a tank or mechanised unit put into reverse gear in an attempt to pull them away would not really break in actual practice and indeed if it were utilised on loose slabs of concrete it would slip the blocks off from one another. The blocks themselves should be solid and larger and heavier at their base; they should be placed on wheels and rolled into position when required and on a definite attack the wheels could be broken off. The operation of putting the barricade in situ took about twelve minutes and it would take considerably less time if they were move-able and only a few moments longer if the wheels had to broken.

It occurred to me that a sawn-off 12 bore shotgun is a much handier weapon than the one the sentries carried when investigating vehicles. The cartridge should contain very heavy shot and be almost cut through with a knife round above the brass. The effect is terrific, the wad and contents being discharged almost as one solid projectile. In my view it is the most deadly of all manual weapons, save perhaps a Bomb, up to an effective range of 10 yards.

This letter suggests that the local government officers of the City were very much involved with the defence of their area and that this Town Clerk in particular had had at least some military training in the past. Colonel Cotton's reply noted:

1) I have already noted this point. My difficulty of course is an acute shortage of men who are available for duties such as these. You will realise that 80% of the men are working 12 hours a day and are engaged upon munitions and other essential services. We are, of course, forbidden to take such men from their factories.

2) It has already been explained to my men that an attack would be much greater and heavier than the one demonstrated on Sunday. Here again, we suffer from a lack of numbers, but for an emergency such as this, I retain an expert mobile unit at Headquarters for reinforcement.

With regard to your suggestion that a sectional railway line could be used for smashing a tank, I rather wonder what the Tank Personnel would be doing while two LDVs were strug-gling with such a heavy object.

With regard to the question of concrete slabs, I agree with you that pillars are better if they were solid and better still if they were shaped like pyramids. They are of course intended only for the basis of the barricade as any vehicles, tree trunks, etc ... would be piled up round the barricades and the whole entangled in barbed wire. This would prevent the tank crew from attempting to pull the blocks away. Here again, I wonder what our personnel would be doing when they got out of the tank to carry this manoeuvre out.

Your suggestion with regard to sawn off shotguns is noted, but arrangements somewhat on the lines of your suggestion have already been made.

I thank you for the interest shown by you in this matter, and I shall make use of a number of your suggestions.

A postscript was added: 'I regret the speed of movement in making these Barricades is somewhat slow.'

Clearly, at this early stage in the war more refinements and practise were needed in blocking roads, defending the barricades and dealing with tracked vehicles.

The second account is a report, by an unknown hand (but thought to be Major Kendall), of an incident involving No.10 Platoon of the 7th Worcestershire (Malvern) Battalion Home Guard and local Free French forces, and is entitled: 'A Road Block Proves Itself'.

> During an exercise with Mobile Free French Forces, the Road Block at Leigh Sinton was partly erected with strong words and sweat by members of the platoon.
>
> After viewing the work with some satisfaction, the men of the platoon whose pigeon it was, retired to their respective positions of defence to await the battle.
>
> Some short time elapsed, when armoured forces were reported approaching the village from the direction of Hereford. Not a man could be seen except the local policeman outside his house. On came the vehicles towards the RB. The leading AFV (an armoured car) treating the obstacle with contempt continued on its way at a fair speed to brush the block aside. The innocent looking 40 gallon drums, being full of concrete, withstood the assault with such good effect that the AFV ricocheted off a drum, crashed into a brick wall, completely demolishing it. The effect of this contemptuous action against the platoon RB brought many faces with broad grins appearing from the most unexpected places.
>
> Instead of a volley of murderous fire being directed onto the unfortunate vehicle, the crew were subjected to curses, ribald jests and riotous laughter from the HG supported by the local PC.
>
> On further examination, it was found the front axle, gearbox, etc ... had been completely smashed.
>
> Two officers following closely in a car made a quick appreciation, (too quick) for when turning their car to make a quick getaway, crashed themselves into a telegraph pole, thus completely blocking the road and holding up some 20 lorries and other transport for close on 30 minutes.
>
> Overcoming their momentary surprise, it was felt that this was time for action and the platoon quickly brought their weapons, imaginary and otherwise to bear with great effect (according to the umpires). But like in all exercises, men prefer not to die, and one Home Guard was to be seen appearing with great care from behind a brick wall, clout a Frenchman on the head with a clod of earth with the words: 'Now will you die you b . . . . . . !'
>
> Incidentally, the wrecked armoured car was not removed for two nights and a day. It is thought that the crew at least learned a lesson and the platoon claimed another victory to its list.

It is not known where this road block had been sited in Leigh Sinton but a location near the road junction between the main road through the village and the B4503 to Malvern would seem likely. This road junction was covered by a concrete pillbox.

A number of Category 1 blocks have already been referred to in earlier chapters, but the most common of those recorded are the anti-tank cylinders. Manufactured largely by the County Surveyor, concrete cylinders were stored on roadsides throughout the war, waiting for the signal to the Home Guard to roll them out into the road and upending them to create an efficient anti-tank block. Most have now disappeared in the post-war clearance of defence material and it is thought that they were dumped into landfill waste sites, a process that continues today, with the remaining cylinders gradually disappearing from the county's roadsides.

The more portable and more commonplace small concrete cylinders weighed, typically, 10 to 12 cwt each and were provided in collections of 20 or more. Each cylinder would require four men to roll it into position. It was found that the 27 cylinders required to block a 30 feet wide gap could be placed in position in 20 minutes by a team of eight men.

Test results on concrete cylinders as an anti-tank block varied, but the official view was that they were an efficient barrier capable of bringing 25 ton tanks to a halt, exposing their vulnerable undersides or even breaking a track. The cylinders were, however, recognised as being vulnerable to gunfire by tank main armament and could be smashed. This was in fact also an advantage since a tank carried a limited number of shells for its main gun, and any ammunition used up in smashing a road block would then not be available for attacking other targets.

Concrete cylinders were best used in combination with 'vertical rail' or 'hairpin' blocks, where the cylinders were placed in front of the steel elements of the block and used to absorb the initial shock of a charging tank.

The evidence collected so far suggests that, after cylinders, vertical rail blocks were the most numerous anti-tank block in the county, being used for most of the main blocks in and around the Worcester anti-tank island and along the Severn and Teme Stop Lines. This type was used for both roads and railways, it being recognised that German armoured columns were just as likely to use a rail track bed to reach their objective, as a road.

When not in use for their intended purpose, the sockets for the vertical rail blocks were covered with a metal or concrete plate so that the road or railway could be used by

Some of the sockets for the hairpin block can still be seen at the ford near the Fish and Anchor pub, Offenham. Two of the sockets can be discerned in the centre of the photograph; others will be buried beneath the turf to the right

normal traffic, and each socket was kept free of debris. The socket caps could sometimes come loose and cause problems to traffic using the roads, notably damaging tyres. When a vertical rail block was erected, it was found that each rail required two men to lift it into position and that a six man team could erect 38 rails in 35 minutes. To prevent enemy troops from lifting out the rails, pea gravel was provided for the defenders to tamp down around the socketed rails to jam them into position.

In testing, it was found that a medium tank charging a vertical rail block at 25 mph could bend the rails and so it was recommended that this type of block should be supplemented with concrete cylinders placed on the enemy side of the block to slow down the tank. Concrete cylinders within the area occupied by the vertical rails were also found to be effective in raising the tank in such a way that it could be spiked by the rails through the thin under-plates and trapped.

A more robust anti-tank block than the vertical rail type was the hairpin or bent rail variety. Documentary sources record that this type of block was used to obstruct crossings over the Avon Stop Line, although the only evidence remaining of these blocks are the sockets in the ramp down to the Fish and Anchor Ford (SP 065 471), near Offenham. However, sockets were exposed some years ago when the road surface on Abbey Bridge, Evesham, was renewed, but an eyewitness thinks these were removed at the time. It seems likely that this type of block was also used on at least some of the Severn Stop Line bridges, for photographs clearly show hairpins stored near the bridge at Bewdley (see Figure 34). These appear to be of the welded variety, rather than bent, resulting in a sharper angle at the apex more likely to spike the belly of a tank. Each rail was a four-man load but it was possible to erect 30 rails in 45 minutes with an eight man team. This type of block was capable of stopping a 25 ton tank and imposing a greater delay on heavier tanks than vertical rails. Evidence collected so far suggests that in Worcestershire the recommended design was not followed and that the layout for the formation of the rails was divided so that two rows only were located at each end of a bridge.

Most of the steel provided for vertical rail and hairpin blocks was salvaged in 1944 when the danger of invasion was over, in order to make up for the losses of steel in Europe after D-Day, and so surviving examples of this element of the blocks are rare. However, a few rails, with angle iron cross-trees have been recorded near Shrub Hill Station, stacked on top of an air raid shelter and were no doubt a relic of a block near the station.

Several examples of the cable block have been recorded in the county but it is thought that they were probably quite numerous, being simple to construct and quick to erect. A 1 inch diameter steel cable, properly anchored, was capable of stopping a 25 ton tank but could be severed by gunfire or pulled away by the successive charging of a tank. Cables were anchored to suitable trees, RSJs set into the bank on either side of a road, or into steel eyes set in concrete. The latter type of fixing was used in the road cuttings through rock to the north of Kidderminster: at Jacob's Ladder, SO 802 782; another just south of Shatterford, at SO 799 804; and in the rock cutting to the west of Dunley. RSJs were used as anchoring points at Fairfield, north of Bromsgrove, at SO 947 754, and at Titton, near the petrol depot, at SO 827 697. A variation of the cable block was the chain block and two of these are recorded as being used at each end of Windsor Road, Redditch. These apparently utilised '10 ton chains', although no further details are available.

Only one instance of the felled tree block has been recorded in Worcestershire and this was planned for the avenue of lime trees in New Road, Worcester, at SO 845 546, but it is likely that many other roadside trees in urban areas would have been similarly used to hinder enemy columns. Trees would have been felled so that their trunks remained attached to their stumps and the crossed trunks would have been firmly fixed to one another with spikes, cables and chains. The saw cut

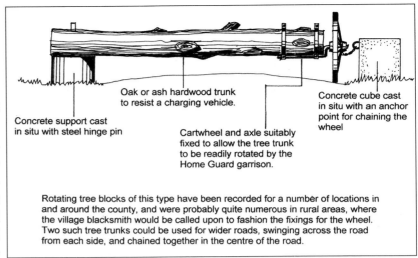

Concrete support cast in situ with steel hinge pin

Oak or ash hardwood trunk to resist a charging vehicle.

Cartwheel and axle suitably fixed to allow the tree trunk to be readily rotated by the Home Guard garrison.

Concrete cube cast in situ with an anchor point for chaining the wheel

Rotating tree blocks of this type have been recorded for a number of locations in and around the county, and were probably quite numerous in rural areas, where the village blacksmith would be called upon to fashion the fixings for the wheel. Two such tree trunks could be used for wider roads, swinging across the road from each side, and chained together in the centre of the road.

Figure 64. Use of trees for road blocking

for felling the trees was to have been two feet above the ground to give height to the block. The block would have been further strengthened with booby traps, anti-tank and anti-personnel mines, together with barbed wire.

Another use of trees for road blocking involved a single large trunk being rotated across the road and chained to a suitable concrete anchorage point to create a block capable of bringing all but the heaviest tanks to a halt as illustrated in Figure 64. Examples of this type of block have been recorded at the Hundred House, Great Witley (SO 752 662); Mythe Bridge, Tewkesbury (SO 887 337); Finger Post, Rock (SO 736 739), and at Astwood Bank, south of Redditch (SP 044 630), although many more of these simple blocks are likely to have been used in the county.

Concertina wire laid out as in Figure 65 was capable of stopping wheeled vehicles but if a series of these blocks were laid in succession, then it was possible to bring a tank to a halt. The concertina block laid lengthways along the road would snarl the tank driving wheels and idlers and bring it to a halt. In one demonstration, it took 24 men two hours to clear the sprockets of a tank after it had attempted to get through such a barrier. However, to achieve this, the ends of adjacent coils needed to be wired together and the obstacle anchored to the side of the road. Eyewitnesses can remember coils of barbed wire being stored on roadsides in a number of locations in the county and these were almost certainly held ready to create such a block.

An intriguing form of barbed wire block, for which local documentary evidence has been found, but so far no drawing, was the 'Wallace Bagnet'. Since Captain Wallace was the Chief Engineer attached to the Central Midlands Area Headquarters at Droitwich, it seems likely that he was the architect of this particular type of block, which appears to be unique to Worcestershire. Introduced in 1941, a demonstration version of the Wallace Bagnet was erected at Powick Bridge, at SO 836 525, and described in contemporary papers as 6 feet 6 inches in height and constructed with triple Dannert wire. (Triple Dannert is essentially three coils of barbed wire linked together to form a high and wide barrier and is illustrated in Figure 65.) The barrier is said to have been capable of being stretched across a road in a very few minutes and that the triple Dannert formed an efficient and rapidly erected obstacle. Jack Hawks remembers coiled barbed wire fixed on a wooden frame at the south end of Pershore Bridge and also at Eckington Bridge. There is also documentary evidence that confirms the provision of Wallace Bagnets at Pershore Bridge, as well as others being provided at some of the blocks around Worcester City Anti-Tank Island.

The most rudimentary type of Category 2 Block was described by former Cookhill Home Guard, Egbert Ganderton as being no more than poles placed on top of oil drums and erected across The Ridgeway, in Cookhill, at SP 057 584. On the north side of Redditch, a more substantial traffic control block was constructed just outside the Police Station in Alvechurch, at SP 027 728. This consisted of a concrete block wall, built half-way across the road from the east side so that only one vehicle from either direction could pass at one time. The means of blocking the remainder of the carriageway is not recorded but it is likely to have been the ubiquitous and portable 'knife rest'. Figure 65 illustrates the form of a knife rest (or rack) that was essentially a light frame of angle iron, forest poles or squared timber, lashed together and braced with plain wire to form a support for a 'cats cradle' of barbed wire. Handles were provided at each end of the main horizontal support pole to enable the structure to be quickly placed into position or removed to allow traffic to pass. The knife rest was a relic of the Western Front in the Great War, where such structures would be carried out from the trenches at night for a quick repair to damaged barbed wire.

It was the traffic control road block sited on the approach roads to even the smallest of villages and the towns in the county, manned by over zealous Home Guards, that were to gain a reputation for delay and nuisance for the law-abiding citizen. It is therefore interesting to note some of the comments made about such road blocks to the County Council and reported in the press in June 1940.

Alderman Palfrey complained that road barriers were causing great loss of time, especially to those travelling by bus. In some cases, he said, this meant missing trams in Birmingham. Alderman Palfrey asked if it was possible for the Chief Constable to issue chits to members of the County Council to support their identity. He reported that a member of the Stockbridge Water Board was taken away by a man with a bayonet

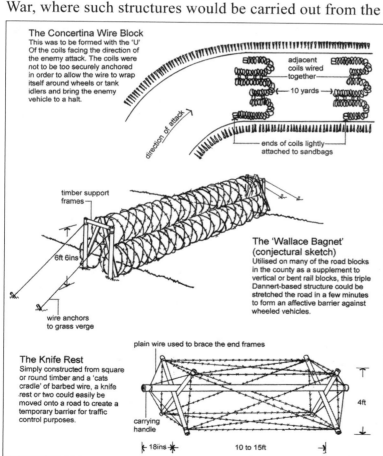

The Concertina Wire Block
This was to be formed with the 'U' Of the coils facing the direction of the enemy attack. The coils were not to be too securely anchored in order to allow the wire to wrap itself around wheels or tank idlers and bring the enemy vehicle to a halt.

adjacent coils wired together

10 yards

direction of attack

ends of coils lightly attached to sandbags

timber support frames

6ft 6ins

wire anchors to grass verge

The 'Wallace Bagnet' (conjectural sketch)
Utilised on many of the road blocks in the county as a supplement to vertical or bent rail blocks, this triple Dannert-based structure could be stretched the road in a few minutes to form an affective barrier against wheeled vehicles.

The Knife Rest
Simply constructed from square or round timber and a 'cats cradle' of barbed wire, a knife rest or two could easily be moved onto a road to create a temporary barrier for traffic control purposes.

plain wire used to brace the end frames

carrying handle

4ft

18ins

10 to 15ft

Figure 65. Use of barbed wire for road blocking

and was detained until he could establish his identity. In response, the Chief Constable, Captain J.E. Lloyd-Williams, said that barriers had been erected on the orders of the military authorities and that he had yet to learn that membership of the County Council was necessarily a sign that a man was not subversive. He pointed out that some persons 'put temporarily away [presumably for not being able to prove their identity] were members and officials of various councils'.

In almost complete contrast, Alderman Terry said that he had been stopped twice that day. He had apparently not got his identity card but explained that his name was Terry of Redditch. The person who stopped him had said that he had played golf at his place and allowed him to proceed.

One incident involving Home Guards manning a check point at Holt Heath ended in tragedy. A 20-year-old Fleet Air Arm gunner, Norman Searle, who was home on leave, failed to respond to a challenge at Holt Fleet Bridge, and in the subsequent altercation, received a bayonet wound to the abdomen and died before reaching hospital. In reaching a verdict of accidental death, the jury at the inquest asked the Coroner to recommend to the Home Guard authorities that 'greater care should be given as to the proper use of the bayonet.' This appears to have been the only incidence of a fatality at a road block in Worcestershire.

CHAPTER 10

Air Defences in Worcestershire

We have already seen that light anti-aircraft guns were used to protect individual vulnerable points (VPs) or groups of such sites against air attack, but the range of other air defences in the county was extensive and included heavy anti-aircraft gun sites, searchlight sites, balloon barrage sites, radio counter-measures sites, operational as well as experimental radar sites and that more basic means of spotting for enemy aircraft provided by the Observer Corps. In addition, the construction programme for air raid shelters to protect the workforce, schoolchildren and the 'man in the street' was extensive and varied in form.

Some of the air defences were to have a dual role, and in the event of an invasion were to be turned into defended localities and expected to take on invading troops in their vicinity. The primary role of ADGB (Air Defence Great Britain) troops was to engage and defeat the enemy in the air, until enemy ground troops had almost reached their position. As, in those circumstances, it was unlikely that equipment could be evacuated, the personnel were expected to stand and 'fight to the last man and last round'.

In the same way that the ground defences in Worcestershire, dealt with earlier in this account, provided defences for Birmingham and the Black Country as well as the county itself, so too did the majority of air defences.

The Observer Corps

One of the earliest elements of the air defence system to be established in Britain, the Observer Corps (Royal Observer Corps from April 1941) pre-dated radar as a means of spotting, tracking and reporting the progress of aircraft over the country. The Observer Corps had its origins in a rudimentary spotting system during World War I watching for and reporting the presence of enemy Zeppelin airships and later bomber aircraft around London. The service was reactivated in the south-east of the country in the late 1920s and expanded throughout Britain during the 1930s in the light of the growth of German air power.

The Observer Corps relied on enthusiastic volunteer spotters to identify the type, number, height and direction of both hostile and friendly aircraft over-flying their area (20-mile radius from their post), utilising rudimentary visual aids, including binoculars to spot the aircraft, a Heath

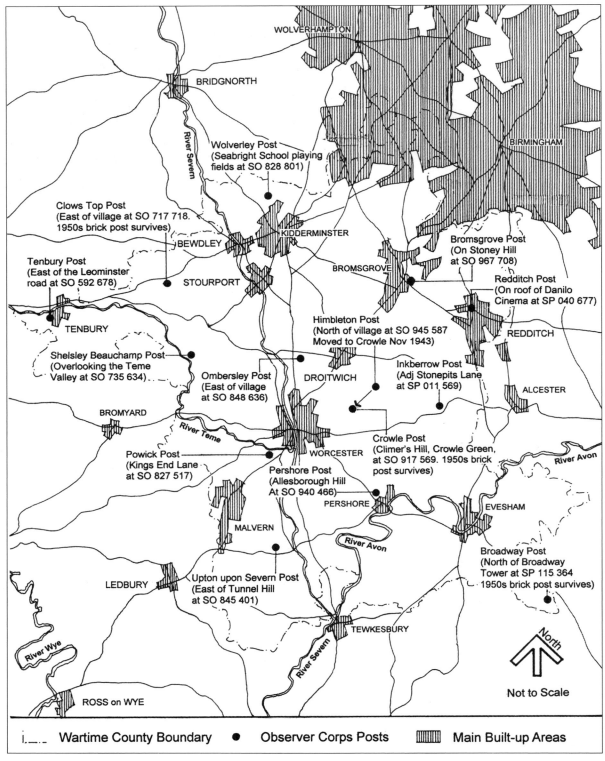

Figure 66. Wartime Observer Corps posts in Worcestershire

Robinson-like device incorporating a Micklethwaite Height Correction Attachment to determine the direction and height of the aircraft, and a telephone line to report what had been seen to an Observer Corps Operations Room at a Group Centre. From here the information would be passed on to RAF Fighter Command where, together with information from Chain Home radar stations on the coasts, it would be used to judge the appropriate response. The Observer Corps was always a volunteer organisation but administered by RAF Fighter Command.

This simulation of a wartime Observer Corps Post can be seen at IWM Duxford. It illustrates well the rudimentary nature of a typical post, with little protection from either the weather or the enemy, but the Micklethwaite Height Correction Attachment on its table and tripod, and operated by a 'volunteer observer', is clear for all to see

The wartime Observer Corps posts were little more than a protective sandbagged surround for normally two or three observers and their plotting table, located on high ground at intervals throughout both town and country, so that all sections of the visible airspace over Britain was under their gaze. After the first winter of the war, a wooden hut resembling a garden shed was provided at the posts for shelter, cooking, resting and the essential Elsan. In Worcestershire, Observer Corps posts were established during November and December 1937 at the locations shown in Figure 66.

The Broadway, Frankley, Inkberrow and Redditch posts reported to the No.5 Group Observer Corps Centre at Coventry, while the remainder reported to the No.24 Group Centre at Gloucester.

As early as November 1939, the possibility of Observer Corps Centres reporting the presence of invasion troops or parachutists in their vicinity was discussed between the then Commander in Chief Home Forces, General Sir Walter Kirke, and Air Chief Marshall Sir Hugh Dowding, Air Officer Commanding, Fighter Command. The latter took the view that the prime function of the Observer Corps was to be the RAF's overland air intelligence network for reporting aircraft and that any other function would be secondary. By 22 May 1940, with the evacuation of the BEF from Dunkirk looming and an invasion of Britain becoming a possibility, at least some Observer Corps posts were issued with rifles, bayonets and ammunition, with revolvers for officers, so that they could defend themselves. The Observer Corps were, apart from the Police, the only civilian organisation to be officially armed. At this stage the Corps had no uniform and it was expected that their wearing of a brassard and a badge would be sufficient to protect observers under the Geneva Convention. Rather like the LDV, it is likely that if observers were captured, the Germans would have considered them to be 'franc tireurs' and shot them anyway.

On 11 June 1940, Fighter Command issued the instruction that, in the event of an invasion by sea or parachute, observers were to remain at their posts for as long as possible, giving information on enemy movements. When they were no longer able to remain at their posts due to the approach of the enemy, they were to evacuate them, after cutting the telephone line, taking their Micklethwaite with them. If circumstances did not allow this, they were to smash their instruments!

By August that year, the Observer Corps was included in the wireless telegraphy scheme, codenamed 'Beetle', for the transmission of information on enemy air or sea landings in Britain to the Army Area Commands. For onward transmission of information received from their posts and groups, long-wave radios were installed in Area Headquarters.

In May 1941, instructions from the RAF to the Royal Observer Corps for reporting enemy forces clarified their role further. Observers were to report the landing of troop carriers, gliders or six or more parachutists. It was considered that six or less were likely to be a friendly air crew escaping from a crippled aircraft. In the event of a hostile attack, the ROC controller was to report this to the ROC Liaison Officer at the associated RAF Group or Sector, the Chief Constable of the district concerned and the local Army Command Headquarters. By this stage ROC posts were also equipped with pyrotechnic signals: a red flare emitting red stars to signify that enemy forces had been sighted on land, and a green flare to signify enemy forces had been sighted on the sea. These instructions remained in force until December 1944.

Some ROC posts were given a third task to perform. This was to monitor visibility and use red flares to warn low-flying friendly aircraft if there was any danger of them flying into high land. Code-named 'Granite', this function was performed by the following posts in Worcestershire: Broadway, Clows Top, Inkberrow, Pershore, Tenbury and Upton upon Severn.

The ROC was stood down in May 1945 but was reactivated again on 1 January 1947, to then serve through the Cold War period.

The Balloon Barrage

Designed to be flown to a maximum height of 5,000 feet, barrage balloons were intended to force enemy bombers to fly at higher levels and so reduce their accuracy in bombing the intended target. Any aircraft flying at a lower level ran the risk of striking the balloon cable and crashing. Eyewitnesses tell of a complete barrage of balloons around the Austin Aero Factory at Longbridge, while a defence plan for part of the Birmingham fringe indicates others in the Moundsley/Highters Heath/Haslucks Green area. It is likely, therefore, that a complete barrier of balloons surrounded Birmingham and would have impinged on Worcestershire.

Although the number of balloons flown in anger in Worcestershire may have been limited largely to the northern fringe of the county, the Royal Air Force did establish No.6 Barrage Balloon Centre, occupied by Numbers 914, 915, 916 and 917 Squadrons, near Wythal (SP 073 753), in 1939. This Balloon Centre was responsible for organising and maintaining the balloon barrage defending the southern part of the Black Country, Birmingham and Coventry.

Searchlight Sites

Before World War II, searchlights were operated by Territorial Battalions of Royal Engineers that would train in liaison with the Royal Artillery units responsible for operating anti-aircraft guns. There were no fixed positions for the searchlights in those days, their role being to illuminate the night sky near the guns. Early in the war, responsibility for operating searchlights was transferred to the Royal Artillery under the control of Anti-Aircraft Command so that an Anti-Aircraft Division or Brigade would be responsible for both guns and lights. A Searchlight Regiment would comprise nominally of four Batteries.

Several changes in the policy relating to the location of searchlights occurred during World War II with firstly, lights concentrated *in* the gun defended areas (GDA). This had the effect of highlighting the target areas for the Luftwaffe and so the lights were drawn together into clusters of up to half-a-dozen, on the approaches to the potential target areas. Finally, from 1941, the lights were dispersed singly through the countryside on the approaches to target cities. An 'indicator belt', with the lights at about 10,000 yard spacing was to provide an early warning of the approach of enemy aircraft; followed by a 'killer belt' with the lights at 6,000 yard spacing. These would use sound locators or later radar controlled lights, code-named ELSIE, to locate approaching enemy aircraft. Similar spacing was used for an area 12,000 yards beyond the GDA to illuminate the targets for the heavy anti-aircraft guns and using the strong glare to reduce the enemy bomb aimers ability to drop their bombs accurately.

While at least some of the lights in the county would have had a role in the defence of vulnerable points in Worcestershire, the whole layout is

This wartime searchlight comes complete with its miniature tracked and steerable chassis, which would have been used to manoeuvre the 'projector' into its prepared emplacement. The long control arm and wheel for rotating and elevating the projector are missing from this example, which can be seen at IWM Duxford

very much part of the outer defences of the Birmingham and Coventry GDA, the county being under the flight path of Luftwaffe aircraft, based in France, making their way to and from this target area. Many eyewitnesses have referred to hearing and seeing German aircraft following the Severn Valley before making a right turn at the Stourport Power Station to go on to Birmingham or the Black Country. At night the River Severn probably did show up as a strip of light in the darkened landscape and so would have made an ideal navigational aid for Luftwaffe aircrews. If the Stourport Power Station was such an obvious navigational aid, the camouflage paint scheme that is remembered being applied to this massive brick-built structure was ineffective. Perhaps its survival, unscathed by any air attack, is owed to this supposed usefulness to the Luftwaffe?

The reference to a 'killer belt' relates to the activities of RAF night fighters that would orbit this area, waiting for enemy aircraft to be illuminated by the searchlights, before making their kill.

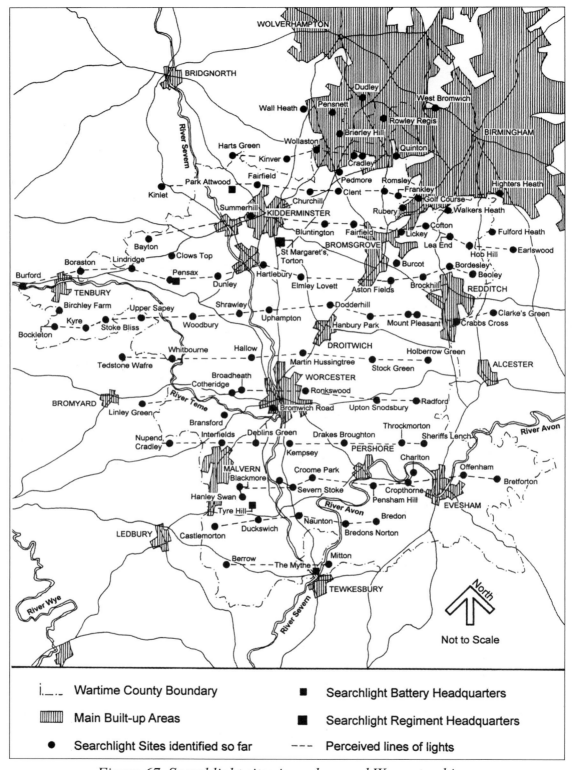

Figure 67. Searchlight sites in and around Worcestershire

Most of Worcestershire was covered by the killer belt for Birmingham, the Black Country and Coventry.

It is this final layout of lights that the majority of eyewitness reports and documentary sources relate to in Worcestershire. Figure 67 indicates the sites that have been recorded in the county and they do appear to broadly accord with the last policy with clear lines of lights although some are obviously missing and have yet to be recorded. The lights linked together are where lights have been moved to adjust the layout, and the jumble of lights nearest Birmingham probably reflects the locations of lights of the earlier GDA based layout. There was probably also difficulty in siting lights to a pre-set pattern due to the topography of the area.

A typical searchlight site would have a cluster of sandbagged emplacements, a large circular one for the light, a second circular one for a sound detector and a third for the generator. In addition a small emplacement, usually circular in shape or of a spiral form, would be provided for a light anti-aircraft Lewis gun. The German bomber aircrew often fired down the beam in an attempt to put out the light; the Lewis gun crew were to fire back up the beam to dissuade them! In addition to the operational equipment, each site would have two or more Nissen huts or sectional wooden huts to accommodate the crew. Few of the former searchlight sites in Worcestershire display any tangible remains now. However, one Nissen hut can be seen on the site to the south of Offenham, at SP 058 452, while a sectional wooden hut that was removed from Hanbury Park now stands at SO 959 642.

Not Bronze Age ring barrows! This post-war air photograph of the searchlight site at Nupend, near Cradley in Herefordshire, illustrates the degree of earthwork protection provided. The circular form of the main projector position can be seen on the right, with an emplacement for the diesel generator in the centre. Two ground defence trenches adjoin the generator emplacement. The three smaller circular emplacements are relics of the earlier cluster system, where three projectors were gathered together and then the layout abandoned as the projectors were redistributed in accordance with the final scheme (see Figure 67.) Two of the earlier sites were retained, probably to accommodate a sound locator and a light anti-aircraft gun. All of these emplacements have now been ploughed out, but the circular shadows of former searchlight emplacements do occasionally show as crop marks and are easily mistaken for earlier archaeology. (Courtesy of WHEAS)

The most substantial searchlight earthworks recorded so far lie in the edge of the woodland at Lickey Hills Country Park, north of Twatling Road, Barnt Green, and can be seen at SO 996 745. In addition to the somewhat eroded searchlight or projector emplacement, there is a well preserved, spiral form, light anti-aircraft emplacement and the associated concrete height-finder plinth. A less pronounced projector earthwork can also be seen on Castlemorton Common, at SO 779 388. This has in the past been mistaken for a Bronze Age ring ditch.

To complete the picture of searchlight sites recorded in Worcestershire, associated Battery Headquarters have been identified at Park Attwood, north of Kidderminster, at SO 797 797; Pensax Court, to the north-west of Abberley, at SO725 691; The Grange, Halesowen at SO 970 828; and Tyre Hill, near Hanley Swan, at SO 810 418. The Battery at Park Attwood moved to The Woodlands, Trimpley, at SO 803 781, later in the war. The 80th Searchlight Regiment RA established their headquarters in the former girls school of St Margaret's, Torton, at SO 844 731.

Erected originally as an accommodation hut for troops manning the nearby searchlight, this 16 ft Nissen, one of very few left in the county, survives to the south of Offenham, at SP 058 453. It is on private land but can be seen from the B4510

Like the ROC posts above, searchlight sites and battery headquarters also had a secondary defence role to play in the event of an invasion. Each was to be considered as a defence island, where possible linking up with local town or village schemes. The importance of linking with the Home Guard was emphasised in instructions issued to Anti-Aircraft Command troops, in view of the excellent system of communications existing on all AA sites, including a wireless set. In isolated locations, the plan was to deny the enemy the use of roads through or near each site. All were therefore considered to be adaptable to a platoon defence organisation, with section posts arranged for all-round defence and within voice control distance of one another. Evidence of defence posts in the form of earthworks can still be seen in Hanbury Park in the vicinity of the former searchlight site there, at SO 945 638, and in Lickey Country Park, while others are remembered by Mike Johnson, near the Holberrow Green searchlight at SP 027 595.

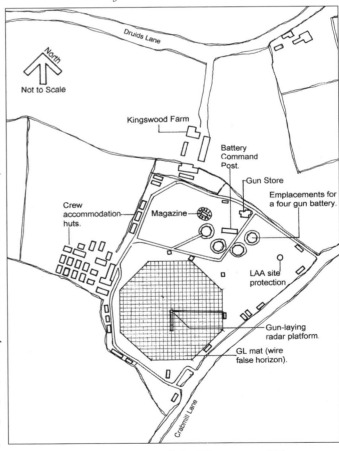

Figure 68. Layout of the Kingswood Farm, Hollywood, HAA battery (SP 072 781)

Anti-Aircraft Gun Sites

As mentioned earlier, protection of individual sites in Worcestershire from air attack relied primarily on light anti-aircraft guns, the most numerous being roof-mounted Lewis guns. These would have been effective against low-level dive bombing attacks only. The heaviest concentration of weapons deployed in Worcestershire for vulnerable points were the 40 mm Bofors gun sites located around Redditch. However, there were a few sites within or close to the northern edge of the county with heavy anti-aircraft guns (HAA) that were part of the Birmingham Gun Defended Area. At the height of the night Blitz, the Birmingham GDA had a hundred HAA guns, including 4.5 inch calibre, 3.7 inch and 3.0 inch. The latter were ex-World War I guns brought out of store to boost the numbers of weapons available and some of these, on mobile mountings, were seen temporarily sited in Worcestershire, usually near some of the searchlight sites.

Records of HAA gun sites in or near wartime Worcestershire have been found for Derby Hill, just to the west of Oldbury, at SO 970 891; Mons Hill, Dudley, at SO 934 926; Harts Green, in the Woodgate Valley, at SP 017 842; Longbridge at SP 000 777; Frankley at SO 987 787, and at Kingswood Farm, to the north-west of Wythall, at SP 072 782. The location of these indicates a clear line of defence for Birmingham and the Black Country from an attack from the south and south-west.

Mk II GL Receiver
Mk II GL Transmitter
GL Mat
The general arrangement of the components of Mk II GL Radar.
The Mk II GL Radar system was introduced in 1941 and resulted in improved accuracy from heavy anti-aircraft guns. The GL Receiver stood on a concrete plinth in the centre of, and above, a wire GL Mat that created consistent ground returns and more accurate readings from the Receiver. The GL Transmitter stood to one side of the GL Mat and would transmit signals which, reflecting off the approaching aircraft, would provide data on height, distance and direction at the Receiver. This allowed more accurate gunnery and fuse setting on the shells.
aerial support structure and stays
elevation aerials
aerial support structure
bearing aerial
bearing aerial
entry doors to operators cabin
range aerial
hand rail
concrete block ramp construction
adjustable feet
brick and concrete plinth
The plinth with Mk II GL Receiver emplaced.
Figure 69. The gun laying radar plinth, Kingswood Farm

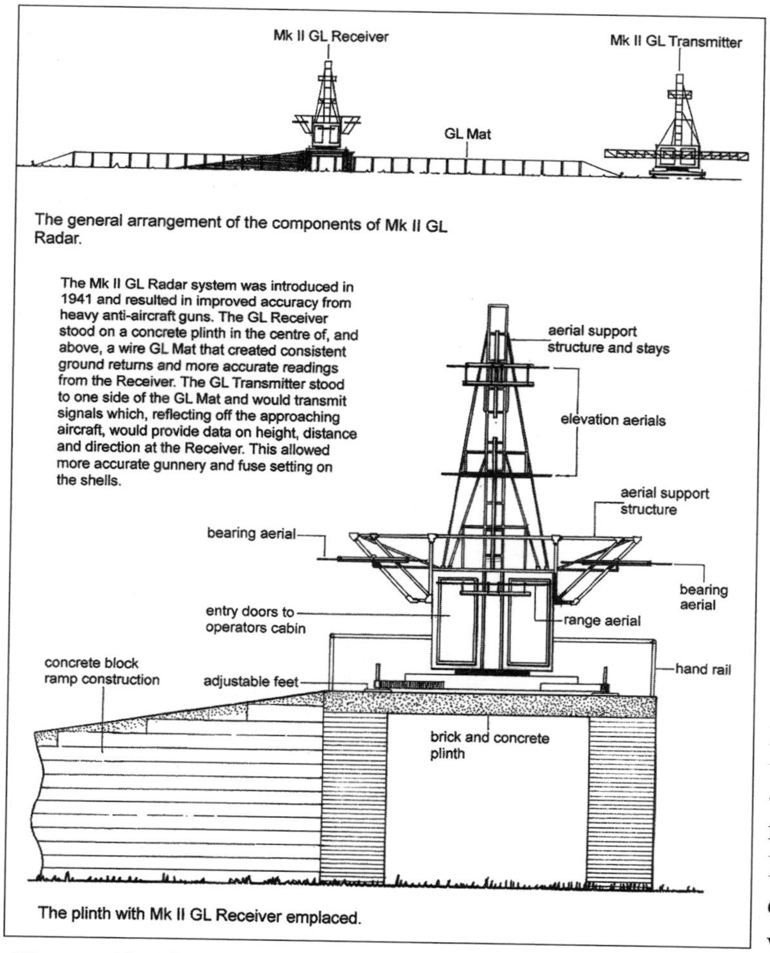

Only the Frankley and Kingswood Farm gun sites are within the current county boundary. The layout for the Kingswood farm gun site, including the GL Mat and its ancillary buildings is shown in Figure 68. This layout has been established from post-war air photos and a site inspection. The four guns on the site were 3.7 inch controlled by the GL radar equipment. Records show that this site was taken over by the 20th Anti-Aircraft Regiment of the Warwickshire (Birmingham) Home Guard in the latter part of the war.

Little now remains of the site at Kingswood Farm, just a few concrete hut bases, some of the site roads and a concrete and brick plinth for the GL radar receiver set, at SP 071 780. The latter structure incorporates a long double ramp, up which the radar set would have been dragged to its plinth (see Figure 69). The GL Mat was a

Left and above: The crumbling ramps and plinth for a GL MII gun-laying radar set can still be seen at Kingswood Farm, near Wythall, at SP 072 782

large area of chicken wire supported on wooden posts around the radar set to provide a consistent, but false, horizon.

Figure 70. Layout of the Frankley HAA battery (SO 987 788)

Figure 70 shows the Frankley HAA site layout. As at Kingswood, most of the structures have been cleared away, except for a partially demolished command post that can still be seen at SO 988 789.

A temporary HAA gun site was briefly sited to the north of Redditch, where some local residents recall that the noise created was tremendous. However, these mobile guns were quickly moved away but the earth emplacements show on early post-war air photographs as being close to Lowan's Hill Farm, at SP 033 687.

The HAA and LAA sites, like other elements of the air defences, were to have a secondary role in the event of an invasion. Although the anti-aircraft gunnery was to be their primary task, where enemy armoured vehicles approached them, they were to take on an anti-tank role. The 3.7 inch HAA gun had shown in France that it was just as effective as the German 88 mm Flak gun in destroying enemy tanks and was expected to take on that role as part of home defence. The Bofors crews elsewhere were also issued with anti-tank ammunition.

Another form of anti-aircraft weapon introduced as an alternative to, and to make up for the shortage of HAA guns, were multiple rocket batteries. These were coded 'Z' Batteries and the rockets were sometimes referred to in official records as unrotating projectiles and the launchers or projectors as UP Batteries. Several rocket batteries were sited around the Austin Aero Factory at Longbridge, one being located in the fields to the south of the factory, in Worcestershire, at SP 015 766. The Z Batteries in this area were operated initially by the 10th AA Z Regiment, that had its headquarters at 'Winsford', Twatling Road, Barnt Green (SO 994 746). This house has now gone and the site redeveloped with a small housing estate. The Longbridge Z batteries were later manned by the 108th Warwickshire Home Guard Rocket Battery. A small two-rocket projector is illustrated in Figure 71, although projectors accommodating up to 20 rockets were also produced.

The Z Battery in this illustration could simultaneously launch two anti-aircraft rockets, but launchers capable of accommodating up to 20 rockets were developed. It is not known what number and size of projectors were installed at Cofton Common, to protect Longbridge, so the illustration can only be considered to be representative. The rockets, or unrotated projectiles (UP), were 6 feet 4 inches long and carried a 22 pound warhead up to a maximum of 19,000 feet altitude. The rockets would be adjusted explode at a preset time.

Figure 71. The Z battery anti-aircraft rocket projector

Radio Counter-Measures

During 1940, Professor R.V. Jones, who was attached to Air Ministry Intelligence, became aware that the Germans were using radio beams to direct their bombers to targets in Britain. This early scheme was code-named 'Knickebein' by the Germans, who were using two beams: one to act as a director beam along which the aircraft flew; the second, a cross beam, to indicate the target area. The radio transmitters were initially located in Germany and then later, in France. It is interesting to note that one of the German stations was located at Kleve, the German city now twinned with Worcester!

Once the method of working had been deduced by Professor Jones, a means by which to jam the signals was developed by the Telecommunications Research Establishment (TRE), and No.80 (Signals) Wing of the RAF was formed to operate the equipment. This work had strong support from Winston Churchill. The first task of 80 Wing was to jam the radio beams so that enemy aircraft could not use them. The codename for this initial jamming process was 'Asprin', so named, apparently, because the beams were causing something of a headache! Later, a method of masking the German signals by picking them up and redirecting them so as to confuse the enemy pilots was developed. This process was known as 'Meaconing', a corruption of 'Masking Beacon' and involved making certain that the German pilots could not recognise the redirected beams as false. There is an oft-quoted case of a Luftwaffe pilot being completely bamboozled by meaconing, eventually running out of fuel, crash landing at Lydd and providing scientists with the latest German homing equipment.

To protect Birmingham and other targets in the West Midlands, 80 Wing outstations were established at Hagley, with the jamming equipment sited on Clent Hill, next to the Four Stones, at SO 932 803, and at Cookhill, on the Ridgeway, south of Redditch at SP 053 592. The latter is confusingly referred to in official documents as being at Alcester, the postal address of the area. The Cookhill outstation is known to have been operating by June 1940 and the Hagley site by August of that year. To help cover the West Midlands target area another outstation was established on the hill at Birdlip, in Gloucestershire. The Knickebein system was replaced by the Germans with two further systems: X-Gerät and Y-Gerät that provided greater accuracy and allowed the Luftwaffe to bomb individual targets, rather than areas. A subsequent bomb plot of a raid on Birmingham, in October 1940, when related to the known radio beams transmitted for that raid, indicated that a high degree of accuracy was being achieved. The counter-measures systems for these more accurate beams were code-named 'Benjamin' and 'Bromide' and both systems were installed at Hagley and Cookhill.

By April 1941, the Hagley Outstation had been expanded to become the administrative centre for a number of 80 Wing outstations in the West Midlands and a signals establishment sited at Furlongs Farm, Hagley, at SO 917 809.

The two 80 Wing sites in the county were operated in the strictest secrecy and even now are known simply as radar sites by locals. The key installation was a wooden hut of approximately 25 feet by 12 feet, surrounded by a blast wall of sandbags up to eaves height. Inside would be the operations room with transmitters and receivers, while on the ridge of the roof were several circular direction finding aerials. Outside the hut would be a mobile generator and various other aerial arrays. The operating crew were billeted out in nearby properties and a close guard kept on the sites to deter prying locals. At Cookhill, this task was shared between RAF Police and the local Home Guard. Nothing now remains of either of the counter-measures sites in Worcestershire, although the concrete pads for the hut supports were visible until recently to the west side of the Four Stones on Clent Hill. These disappeared under topsoil spread on the area to prevent further erosion at the top of the hill.

Bombing Decoy Sites

Decoy sites were a passive means of protecting individual vulnerable points, airfields and towns or cities containing armaments industries, by replicating a feature or an area under night attack. Decoy fires or lights were sited in open countryside to encourage the Luftwaffe to waste their bombs there. A significant number of decoy sites were established in the Worcestershire countryside, the first appearing about two weeks after the heavy bombing raid on Coventry on 14 November 1940. The first decoy sites constructed were very rudimentary fire systems comprising of little more

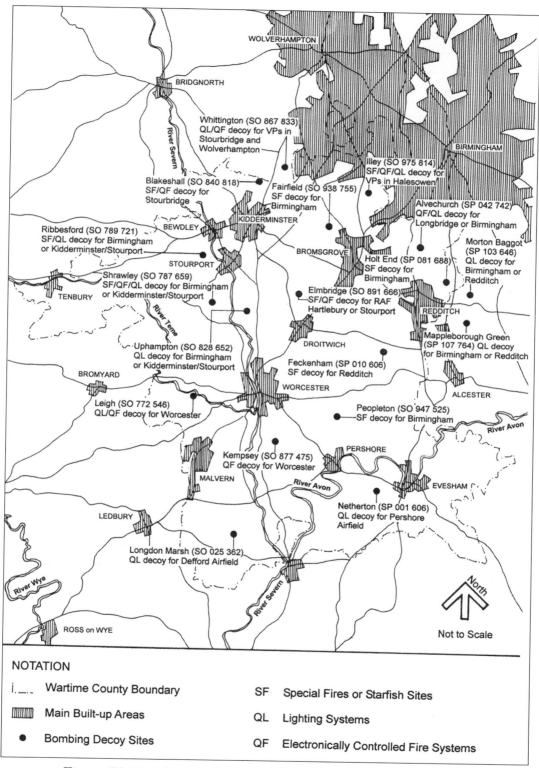

Figure 72. Bombing decoy sites in and around Worcestershire

This brick and concrete shelter for the RAF crew at Netherton (SO 999 429) is a standard QL decoy site control bunker. To the left can be seen the blast wall protecting the entrance. The nearest section of the building housed the generators for powering the dummy airfield lighting systems set out over the fields to the south, while the section to the left of the entrance was the crew room and housed the switching gear for the lighting system

than hastily dug trenches or pits filled with inflammable materials, fired by hand. These were known as SF Decoys, denoting Special Fires. These would later to be called Starfish decoy sites.

From the initial batch of Starfish sites, the number and range of sites in Worcestershire was expanded during 1940 and 1941 to include more sophisticated means of replicating an incendiary attack, triggered electronically by remote control and designated QF sites. Other decoys were constructed to replicate airfield lighting, railway sidings or industrial units, and were known as QL sites.

The timing of the activation of decoy sites was found to be critical: too soon and the Luftwaffe pathfinders would recognise the sites for what they were and be able to warn the main force; too late and the raid would be over. The ideal timing was immediately after the target marking aircraft had passed over and before the main bomber force arrived expecting to find the initial incendiary fires started by the pathfinders.

All the decoy sites were operated by the RAF and the crew would be either billeted in nearby properties or transported in daily from a nearby RAF establishment.

Decoys in Worcestershire were provided for the main industrial areas of Birmingham and the Black Country, Worcester, Kidderminster/Stourport and Redditch and for the RAF establishments at Hartlebury, Defford and Pershore. The locations of decoys in and around the county, their type and function are shown in Figure 72.

On the majority of the decoy sites in the county, only the access road survives and is easily recognised by the particular limestone course aggregate used in its construction. Used now as farm accommodation roads, they have lasted particularly well. Another good survival is of the strongly built crew shelter and generator room, found on QL sites. These were of a standard design, rather like a communal brick and concrete surface air raid shelter, with the addition of an earth surround. One of the best preserved examples in the county is at Netherton (SO 999 429). Where a decoy site was sited close to a village, air raid shelters were provided for the villagers. In Worcestershire, only Kempsey and Severn Stoke seem to have benefited from the policy and a number of small, above-ground brick and concrete shelters can still be found in both villages.

Ground Controlled Interceptor Radar

From the autumn of 1940, the night fighter activity of the RAF relied largely on the eyesight of pilots, helped by searchlights, to intercept intruders and make an attack. Using essentially day fighter aircraft, only the very best of pilots were successful in this type of operation. The development of Centimetric Airborne Interceptor (AI) radar that could be mounted in aircraft, initially the Bristol Blenheim, but later the Bristol Beaufighter and De Havilland Mosquito, improved the RAF night fighting performance, but the introduction of Ground Controlled Interceptor (GCI) radar brought more significant success. With this equipment the radar operators could guide a nightfighter to the vicinity of an intruder, where the navigator using the on-board AI set would obtain a signal, enabling him to guide the pilot to the enemy aircraft and make an attack.

Inland GCI radar sites were established during 1941 to obtain complete radar coverage of Britain, one of these sets being sited to the north of the village of Wick, near Pershore, at SO 966 462, and operated under the name of RAF Comberton. Initially a temporary, transportable set was provided, with the RAF and WAAF crew operating from a wooden hut. When off-duty, the crew were billeted in a number of the large houses in the village, including Vandyke Court and Wick Manor. An RAF Maycrete hut can still be seen in the back garden of Vandyke Court at SO 960 453.

Nothing now remains of this early, temporary, GCI radar site but the facility was replaced and considerably upgraded in 1943, with the installation of a Type 7 Radar system, capable of controlling a number of night fighters to a greater range and height. A new brick-built, much larger operations room and ancillary buildings were built on an adjoining site. Most of the ancillary buildings have now gone, some only recently, but the operations room, known as the 'Happidrome', and a generator building can still be seen and form part of Glenmore Farm. These are now probably the most substantial remains of the wartime air defences in Worcestershire and the Happidrome still contains the original operations board, with the last orders chalked on!

RAF Comberton continued to serve as a radar site well into the Cold War period and was again to be upgraded with a further and larger prefabricated operations room and multiple radar aerial arrays to form part of the ROTOR system of early warning. The later operations room has gone, although the concrete base remains, and the radar aerial plinths of this later system can still be seen in the surrounding fields.

As the radar station at Wick grew the need for more crew accommodation led to the construction of a separate camp at Pinvin. Of this camp, only the Braithewaite water tank on its steel lattice tower can be seen at the entrance to what is now the Pershore Trading Estate, at SO 952 479.

Now incorporated into the Glenmore Farm complex at Wick, near Pershore, the former wartime 'Happidrome' or operations room of the RAF Comberton GCI Radar facility survives

Why should the radar facility at Wick be called RAF Comberton when the Combertons are some miles away? This apparently stems from the fact that there was an RAF station in the far north of Scotland called Wick and it was to there that the first radar equipment, intended for the Pershore site, was initially delivered!

A second GCI radar site was established at Sledge Green, immediately to the east of Berrow Airfield, at SO 807 338. This was an experimental facility used by Telecommunications Research Establishment (TRE), and was built after the move to Malvern in May 1942. The facility was used to develop GCI radar for operational use elsewhere, including RAF Comberton. Most of the buildings built for TRE have now gone from Sledge Green, but the building that contained the former Operations Room still exists.

Air Raid Shelters and Blast Walls

Air raid shelters were a passive form of air defence, designed to protect the population from the effects of bomb blast and flying debris. They were built mainly in the urban areas by local authorities throughout the county in anticipation of the Luftwaffe destroying each town ahead of an invading ground force. The shelters took various forms, some more efficient and user-friendly than others. The numbers involved are probably uncountable now but they were considerable.

The first phase of shelter provision involved digging trenches in public parks and open spaces in towns and the strengthening of basements under easily accessible buildings. It is not believed that any of the trench shelters remain in the county, although many are remembered by eyewitnesses being dug and then filling with water after the first rainstorm. Some of the trench shelters were later covered over with timber and corrugated iron, with the excavated soil being spread over the top to provide overhead protection. They continued to fill with water, however, and were almost useless.

Basement shelters came next, and were normally adaptations of existing cellars beneath public buildings. These required the ground floor shoring up with either heavy timber or, in the more sophisticated versions concrete, to prevent the occupants being crushed if the building above collapsed as a result of the bombing. One of the most prominent buildings to be converted was the Refectory, overlooking College Green, behind Worcester Cathedral. This is located at SO 850 545. Another was under the former St Nicholas' Church in The Foregate, Worcester, at SO 850 550, where the concrete strengthening over the entrance to the shelter can still be seen at pavement level from St Nicholas' Street. The cellars of some private houses were also converted in this way as shelter for the use of the occupants, and usually referred to as a domestic shelter.

Perhaps the air raid shelter most synonymous with the Blitz was the surface communal version, of brick construction, with a flat concrete roof. These were built in various sizes to accommodate 25, 50 or 100 persons. Most were built in the streets of towns or on open spaces and were quickly demolished at the end of the war to clear the roads of obstruction, improve the appearance of open spaces, and provide a ready supply of hard-core for the post-war reconstruction of damaged towns and cities. Few survive now in Worcestershire, but perhaps the best preserved example can be seen at Elm Place, Cookley. Located at SO 845 799, it still has its 'Shelter S here' sign showing, albeit very faded. Other, smaller versions of the surface shelter still exist to the rear of Claines Village Hall at SO 846 578. Similar shelters were built at schools throughout the county,

There were once hundreds of communal surface air raid shelters in the streets and open spaces of Worcestershire, but there are only a few left now. This double-length shelter is one of the best examples left and can be found at SO 845 799, Elm Place, Cookley. The larger of the two signs on the end wall is very faded, but 'Shelter S Here' can just be discerned from close-to

and a good example of a school shelter can still be observed in front of Wribbenhall Middle School, at SO 794 751, although tree foliage is now obscuring it somewhat.

Another shelter synonymous with the Blitz was the Anderson Shelter and although the corrugated steel sections can still occasionally be seen, re-erected as a garden shed or chicken shed, or used in the construction of Home Guard ammunition stores, none have so far been found in the county in their original semi-sunken form with the excavated earth spread over the top for added protection. The Anderson Shelter was supplied to householders, on request and in kit form, by local councils. They were free to those where the household income was less than £250 per annum and supplied at a cost of £8 to those earning more.

Many householders chose to have the small brick and concrete type of domestic shelter that can still be seen in town gardens, where their robust construction has survived well and they form very satisfactory potting sheds. Some have had windows inserted to improve their utility.

Not normally found in rural areas, a surprisingly large number of these small shelters survive in the villages of Kempsey and Severn Stoke.

As an alternative to having air raid shelters, some houses were provided with blast walls. These were commonly built of concrete blocks, high enough to absorb the blast and protect ground-floor windows. Eyewitnesses can remember these being provided at the backs of houses along the Birmingham Road, Redditch, at SP 040 687. It is likely that these were built due to the proximity of the HDA Factory, a designated vulner-

This small domestic brick and concrete air raid shelter can still be seen in Backfields Lane, Upton upon Severn, at SO 851 403, and is the last survivor of several provided for the residents of the properties fronting Old Street

So far no Anderson air raid shelter has been found in the county and recorded in its original wartime semi-sunken and earth-covered state, although a number can be seen that were excavated post-war and re-erected as garden sheds or farm shelters like this one at Birtsmorton, at SO 801 358

Charles Purcell of the Bewdley Historical Research Group and Bewdley Museum staff show us the pre-fabricated air raid shelter in the grounds of the museum. This once provided shelter for workers at the nearby Brass Foundry. For many years thought to be an Anderson Shelter, this example displays a markedly different cross-section to the normal Anderson, but shares its semi-sunken and earth covering characteristics

able point, and likely to be attacked from the air. Similar blast walls were provided behind the houses on Pickersleigh Road, Malvern, at SO 787472.

All the factories involved in war work and other vulnerable points were provided with either surface or semi-sunken shelters to provide protection for their workforce during air raids. Both types still exist in the county but they are disappearing rapidly as the older factory sites are redeveloped. Many of the factory shelters were of the same brick and concrete form as the public shelters but others utilised a preformed concrete arch shaped form, produced by the Stanton Company. Some of these still exist near Shrub Hill Station but are inaccessible to the public, while earth covered shelters survive, out-of-sight, at the Steel Stamping Works, Cookley.

In the early stages of the war so much production time was being lost during air raids as the workforce trooped out to their shelters, usually sited some way from the factory, and then waited there until the all-clear was sounded, that a different approach was introduced. Shelters were built within the factories and the workforce would stay at their workbench or production line until the last possible moment before going to their shelters. To make this late reaction feasible, volunteer roof spotters were used to look for the attacking aircraft and then signal when an attack was imminent.

CHAPTER 11

The Local Defence Volunteers and the Home Guard

The threat of an attack by enemy parachutists on Britain that had been brought into sharp focus following the attacks on Norway in April and then the Low Countries, resulted in a call for volunteers to form a home defence force. The action that set in motion the establishment of this force was a radio broadcast appeal by Anthony Eden, the newly appointed Secretary of State for War, in the evening of 14 May 1940, just after the nine o'clock news.

He explained that the function of enemy parachutists was to seize important points, such as aerodromes, power stations, villages, railway junctions and telephone exchanges, either for the purpose of destroying them at once, or holding them until the arrival of reinforcements. The success of their attack depended on speed and consequently the measures to defeat such an attack must be prompt and rapid. Since the war began, the government had received countless enquiries from men of all ages who wished to do something for the defence of the country. Now the government wanted large numbers of such men who were British subjects and between the ages of 17 and 65, to come forward and offer their services. He said that the name of the force, Local Defence Volunteers described their duties and he emphasised that it was a spare-time job; there would be no need for any volunteer to abandon their present occupation. The period of service was to be for the duration of the war and although the volunteers would not be paid, they would receive a uniform and be armed. Reasonable fitness and knowledge of firearms were necessary, but the duties would not require them to live away from their homes. In order to volunteer, the men were asked to give their name to their local police station. They would be informed when they were required.

The British government moved quickly to legalise the formation of the new defence force by passing, on 17 May, 'The Defence (Local Defence Volunteers) Regulations, 1940' under the provisions of the Emergency Powers (Defence) Act of 1939. The regulations made it clear that the Local Defence Volunteers were members of the armed forces of the Crown and subject to military law as soldiers. How much this legal status would have influenced any invading Germans, when faced by men dressed in civilian clothing with only an arm band declaring that they were the LDV, is debatable.

In Worcestershire, as elsewhere, the reaction to Anthony Eden's call was immediate and reports in local newspapers indicated the high level of response, the *Worcester Evening News and Times* being typical in their reaction by describing the scenes in the city. A number of volunteers had turned up at the City Police Station shortly after the broadcast, the first to enrol being the Town Clerk, Mr Digby Seymour, just beating Colonel F.M. Buck, the former Commanding Officer of the 8th Battalion of the Worcestershire Regiment. By noon the next day, 50 men had registered, including one who had been in the Cambridge University Rifles in 1899, claiming he was still fit aged 64½, and 'could not stand being out of things at such times as these'. Another one-legged veteran of the Great War was heard to say, as he signed on, that 'he had a good packet at them last time and I'm ready for another'. The newspaper also reported that the Worcester Royal Grammar School had requested 20 forms for boys over the age of 17 who, because of their OTC training should make valuable members of the new force. Many of the city factories had also made requests for forms.

Not everyone called in person and it was reported by the Press that the city's Chief Constable, Mr E.W. Tinkler, whilst declaring his admiration for their patriotism, was concerned that people were making heavy demands on the telephone system for particulars. He explained that the role of the police was that of registration and not administration and was at pains to say that it did not follow that all who registered would be called upon. This latter point is significant because a recent study of LDV/Home Guard enrolment forms indicates that it was about a month after registration that men were formally enrolled in the force, giving time for the police to investigate each man's background and so avoid the enrolment of Fifth Columnists or enemy agents. It was also noted from this study that some men were discharged from the force as being 'unsuitable', whatever that might have meant!

Over at Malvern, a steady stream of volunteers was reported to have been registered by Police Sergeant Mound and Police War Reservist Pollard, including one youth of 17. As at Worcester, by noon the next day 50 had been enrolled, a considerable number of whom claimed to have had experience of fire-arms and were former members of OTCs, or had served in the last war. At Evesham, the story was much the same, with two clergymen from country parishes outside the town being amongst the first

One of the early volunteers for the LDV/Home Guard was Earl Beauchamp of Madresfield Court, who served as the local Platoon Commander until leaving to join the Regular forces. He is seated in the centre of the front row in this picture taken at the Court. The wearing of armbands indicate that this picture was taken in 1940. (Courtesy of Mrs Smith)

to arrive, while at Kidderminster the first man had registered almost before Anthony Eden had finished his broadcast and the police there were inundated by several hundreds volunteering — and so, apparently, it went on throughout the county.

It is interesting to consider just how many of these volunteers had had previous military experience. Analysis of LDV/Home Guard enrolment forms, held by the Army Medal Office when it was at Droitwich, indicates that in Worcestershire approaching 20% of the volunteers had been members of the armed forces during or before the Great War, the Bromsgrove area showing a higher figure of 28%. One man was noted as having served in the Sudan, like Corporal Jones of *Dad's Army*. Many had served in South Africa during the Boer War, but a higher proportion in the Great War and had already been 'shot over' as one retired officer put it! Add in an average of 10% having served between the wars, before being released from service, together with about 5% of former cadets, and it can be seen that a large proportion of the new force had already had some military experience. Official estimates for the country as a whole put this figure at 40% of the LDV/Home Guards.

A significant number of the volunteers had been officers in the British Army and were now stalwarts of the local Territorial Association. It was to them that the Lord Lieutenant of Worcestershire turned to organise the new force at a meeting called at the County Police Headquarters, at Castle Street in Worcester, on the evening of 18 May. Colonel W.H. 'Bill' Wiggin, then of St Cloud, Callow End, and the then Chairman of the TA Association, had already been appointed as the County LDV Organiser, with Colonel Mallett as his assistant and Major H. Heath as Acting Adjutant. In turn Divisional Commanders were appointed for each area of the county based upon the then Police Divisions. These commanders, initially referred to by their former Regular Army ranks organised meetings and appointed local organisers, so creating a hierarchy of experienced officers to lead and administer the LDV. At this stage the county LDV were organised on the basis of companies, one for each Police Division, and platoons or squads for the Police Districts and Stations.

Members of the Malvern Company Home Guard indicate a certain pride in their Observation Post on the side of Worcestershire Beacon. The location of this post can still be recognised on the path up from the Wyche Cutting. (Courtesy of Sheila Edmunds)

One function of the Police was to investigate the background of each LDV, and later Home Guard volunteer, to ensure that Fifth Columnists and enemy agents were not enrolled. A number of the Worcestershire candidates had distinctly Germanic names; two in the Stourport area even declaring themselves to be former members of the Austro-Hungarian Royal Family, which must have caused a bit of head scratching at the local Police Station, but nevertheless they were enrolled. Each enrolment form was endorsed and signed by a local police officer that the man was 'Approved by the Police' and returned to the appropriate LDV or Home Guard commander.

In the early weeks and months of the existence of the new force, the older experienced men were able to instruct the younger volunteers in the skills of soldiering and discipline, while former officers instilled a sense of pride and purpose in the force. The seriousness with which these officers and experienced men treated their duties, and their standard of soldiering, is at odds with the impression given by the *Dad's Army* series, a programme which still rankles with many former Home Guards. The main duties of the force was to keep watch and ward; to give police information of any attempt at parachute landing; to interrupt any such landing by armed force to the utmost of their ability, pending the arrival of a properly organised military force; and to act as guides to elements of the Field Force operating in their area, using their intimate knowledge of the locality.

In pursuit of their duty to observe and report any suspicious activity, observation posts (OPs) were established and perhaps the most effective was that in the Abberley Clock Tower. From the tower it was possible to observe parts of six counties. Others with extensive views across Worcestershire were those on Bredon Hill, the Worcestershire Beacon and on the reservoir at the top of Ankerdine Hill, from any of which almost the whole of the county could be observed on a moonlit night. In the flatter and lower parts of the county, the local church tower would often provide a suitable OP, good examples being the cathedral in Worcester, or the church in Powick, overlooking the lower Teme valley. Where a suitable high point was not available, LDVs would patrol in pairs along the roads and lanes in their area of responsibility.

A number of vicars had joined the LDV in Worcestershire, one in the Evesham unit becoming a platoon commander a factor that, perhaps, had an invasion actually occurred, may have compromised their Christian beliefs! However not all men of the cloth were so militaristic and at least one vicar would not allow rifles in his church in Malvern Link, the men having to haul their weapons, by rope, up the outside of the church tower to their OP!

Shortage of suitable armaments for the LDV to carry out any offensive action against parachutists was immediately apparent and patrols were armed with a miscellany of weapons with which to meet the enemy. At a meeting of LDV leaders on 5 June General Ironside, who was painfully aware of the shortage of weapons, amongst other things extolled the virtue of the Molotov Cocktail; a bottle filled with resin, petrol and tar that, if thrown on top of a tank would ignite, 'and if you throw half a dozen more on it you have them cooked. It is quite an effective thing'. Regarding other arms, he thought that about 80,000 rifles had been issued with more coming and he did not want his audience to misjudge the shotgun:

> I have now coming out over a million rounds of solid ammunition, which is something that will kill a leopard at 200 yards. It makes a decent bullet and you will have large numbers of them, though perhaps only three or four in men's pockets to start with ... In a city, I do not want a high velocity rifle being let off; that is not the place for it. In dusk, in the evening, and in the woods a shotgun is about as useful a weapon as you can possibly want.

To increase the weaponry available to the LDV, Sir Edward Grigg, Under Secretary of State for War in 1940, made a national appeal on radio, while Colonel Wiggin made a similar appeal for Worcestershire through the local newspapers, for more shotguns to be handed into the police. To encourage some of the more reluctant owners it was reported that the King had already handed over his shotguns for use by the LDV. It was claimed that the new ball cartridge would not damage a sound shotgun! Apparently this was not the case and the choke of a typical sporting shotgun would cause the barrel to be stretched if ball cartridge was fired.

In August, the Evesham LDV began to receive a trickle of weapons including SMLE (Short Magazine Lee Enfield) and Ross rifles but the shortage of ammunition continued. This was remedied by local villagers, who, having had numbers of troops billeted on them after the Dunkirk evacuation, would charge five rounds of ammunition for a hot bath. Over at Upton, the late Home Guardsman, John Leighton, remembered the guard on the road bridge over the river being supplied with an elephant gun from the armoury at Croome Court, together with three rounds of ammunition. They felt that they should at least have a test firing of this fearsome weapon but the first round was a dud. However, the kick from firing the second was so terrific that the grip on the gun was almost lost with the weapon at risk of dropping into the river. Despite much fumbling, it was safely held, but the guard was now down to one round of indeterminate quality with which to face the invaders!

A month after the establishment of the LDV, the Army Council issued an instruction to the effect that the county Territorial Army Associations should take over the administration of the new force and the retired General, Sir George Weir of Kings End Lane, Powick, was asked to take on the role of Worcester Zone Commander, while Colonel Wiggin continued with the administrative duties. At the same time the previously desig-

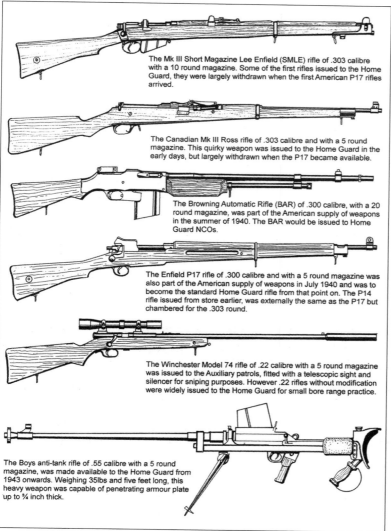

The Mk III Short Magazine Lee Enfield (SMLE) rifle of .303 calibre with a 10 round magazine. Some of the first rifles issued to the Home Guard, they were largely withdrawn when the first American P17 rifles arrived.

The Canadian Mk III Ross rifle of .303 calibre and with a 5 round magazine. This quirky weapon was issued to the Home Guard in the early days, but largely withdrawn when the P17 became available.

The Browning Automatic Rifle (BAR) of .300 calibre, with a 20 round magazine, was part of the American supply of weapons in the summer of 1940. The BAR would be issued to Home Guard NCOs.

The Enfield P17 rifle of .300 calibre and with a 5 round magazine was also part of the American supply of weapons in July 1940 and was to become the standard Home Guard rifle from that point on. The P14 rifle issued from store earlier, was externally the same as the P17 but chambered for the .303 round.

The Winchester Model 74 rifle of .22 calibre with a 5 round magazine was issued to the Auxiliary patrols, fitted with a telescopic sight and silencer for sniping purposes. However .22 rifles without modification were widely issued to the Home Guard for small bore range practice.

The Boys anti-tank rifle of .55 calibre with a 5 round magazine, was made available to the Home Guard from 1943 onwards. Weighing 35lbs and five feet long, this heavy weapon was capable of penetrating armour plate up to ¾ inch thick.

Figure 73. Rifles issued to the Home Guard in Worcestershire

nated LDV 'companies' became battalions, platoons became companies and so on, creating an organisation and command hierarchy more akin to the Regular Army.

In these early days in the LDV, men would do two or possibly three nights duty each week, in addition to evening and Sunday morning training, and a number of former LDVs have told me that they experienced a constant feeling of tiredness during those days. Since the men of the LDV were in reserved occupations, many on war production if they were in the towns or working long hours on the land if they were countrymen, the result was that often they would come off a stint of LDV night patrolling, go home and have breakfast, change their clothes and go straight off to work. It was therefore not unusual for them to be nodding off while at work which was potentially very dangerous if they were tending machinery. LDV night duty involved patrolling or OP observing, or guarding vulnerable points, for two hours on watch and then four hours off while other members of the watch carried on with the active duties, from dusk to dawn. In theory the men off watch should have been sleeping but in practise many found this to be impossible and whiled away their time playing cards.

Instigated by Winston Churchill, and set out in an instruction issued on 31 July 1940, the name of the new force was changed to Home Guard. No doubt the derogatory comments by the comedian Tommy Trinder that the initials LDV actually meant 'Look, Duck and Vanish' had something to do with the need for a change in the name.

Most of the units in Worcestershire were described as General Service Battalions and would be tasked with manning the OPs, road blocks and static weapons positions, and provide a guard for the vulnerable points within their respective areas of responsibility. Factory units were formed in most of the towns in the county and their role initially was to protect their own factory from attack or sabotage and not take a part in the more general defences. The size of factory unit inevitably varied according to the size of the factory workforce: some would be no more than a section, others, such as Heenan and Froude, in Worcester, would raise two platoons, while some, such as the HDA and BSA works at Redditch, would be large enough to raise a company. As a variation on factory guards, pit guards were formed by the coal miners, not only in the Black Country, but also at Mamble, to the north-east of Tenbury.

One of many 'Factory' Home Guard units raised in Worcestershire, this is the Enfield of Redditch Company, led on this route march by the Managing Director and Company Commander, Major Frank W. Smith. Note the air force wings and medal ribbons on his battledress blouse. (Courtesy of Barry Smith via Mike Johnson)

The complication does not end there: the General Post Office raised sections and platoons from their staff to protect post offices and telephone exchanges throughout the county, the control of them being conducted from a headquarters in Birmingham although the units would liaise and train with their local Home Guard General Service battalion. Similarly, the Midland Red Bus Company raised sections and platoons in the main towns of the county, as did the Staffordshire, Worcestershire and Shropshire Electric Company that ran the larger power stations.

The railway companies, LMS and GWR, also raised separate detachments in Worcestershire and were again controlled from their regional headquarters, in Birmingham. It was considered that railwaymen were the best people to protect railway installations since they knew the detail of what they were guarding: the bridges, the signal boxes, tunnels, etc and would relieve the regular forces of the task. These men would also know how to immobilise the railways in the event of an invasion and be better placed to recognise bogus orders and misinformation given by enemy agents, as had happened during the attacks on France and the Low Countries. Instructions received by telephone would, for example, be treated with suspicion.

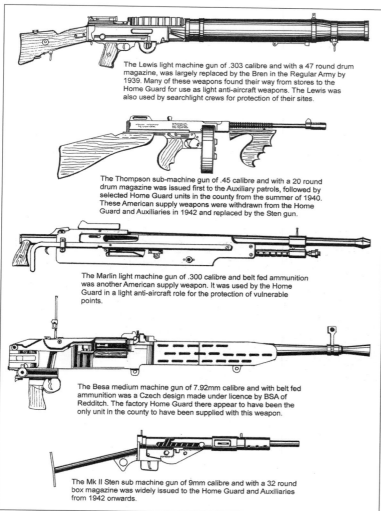

The Lewis light machine gun of .303 calibre and with a 47 round drum magazine, was largely replaced by the Bren in the Regular Army by 1939. Many of these weapons found their way from stores to the Home Guard for use as light anti-aircraft weapons. The Lewis was also used by searchlight crews for protection of their sites.

The Thompson sub-machine gun of .45 calibre and with a 20 round drum magazine was issued first to the Auxiliary patrols, followed by selected Home Guard units in the county from the summer of 1940. These American supply weapons were withdrawn from the Home Guard and Auxiliaries in 1942 and replaced by the Sten gun.

The Marlin light machine gun of .300 calibre and belt fed ammunition was another American supply weapon. It was used by the Home Guard in a light anti-aircraft role for the protection of vulnerable points.

The Besa medium machine gun of 7.92mm calibre and with belt fed ammunition was a Czech design made under licence by BSA of Redditch. The factory Home Guard there appear to have been the only unit in the county to have been supplied with this weapon.

The Mk II Sten sub machine gun of 9mm calibre and with a 32 round box magazine was widely issued to the Home Guard and Auxiliaries from 1942 onwards.

Figure 74. Some of the automatic weapons issued to the Home Guard

Within some of the General Service battalions in the county, specialist units were formed to carry out particular functions. These included river patrols at Upton, Worcester and Stourport, although, strangely, no evidence has been found of similar patrols on the River Avon. Two Home Guard transport units were formed: No.2243 Independent MT Platoon, based at the Bransford Road Garage in St John's, Worcester, led by the proprietor of the garage, Lieutenant (later Captain) Reginald W. Holder, and No.2244 Independent MT Platoon, at Dudley. These two transport columns would later be affiliated to the RASC.

One of the difficulties with such a scattered force, particularly in the rural areas where most of the men would not have a telephone, was calling the Home Guard to action. The signal to 'muster', as it was called, would come from Western Command, then filter down through the military hierarchy by wireless and telephone to the Home Guard battalion headquarters. From there it would go out by telephone and Home Guard dispatch riders, in the early days using their own motorcycles, to the company and then platoon commanders. It was the responsibility of each platoon commander to ensure that all his men were informed. This was achieved by the so-called 'snowball' system, whereby the platoon sergeant would tell the next geographically nearest man in his platoon, and then go to the muster point. The man he had informed would then inform his neighbour, who would then inform his next nearest neighbour, each leaving for the muster point as soon as the message was passed on, and so on until everyone was informed and heading to the muster by whatever was the speediest means available. A period of between two and six hours could therefore elapse before a full muster was achieved.

Throughout the summer nights of 1940, the Home Guard of Worcestershire waited and watched; gradually accumulating equipment and weapons, while the air battle of Britain was being fought in the south-east. August saw an increase in air activity by the Luftwaffe in the Midlands and further north and a cranking up of psychological pressure on the defenders by dropping empty parachutes in the county. This caused increased patrolling activity, notably for the Redditch and Bromsgrove battalions.

The air battle was not going well for the RAF during the early part of September and Military Intelligence had concluded that an invasion was imminent. The codeword 'Cromwell' was sent to all the ground forces, including the Home Guard, on the 7th of the month, signifying that an enemy invasion could be expected. The effect was that all defences were manned on a 24-hour basis for a couple of days, before the crisis passed. Some units misinterpreted the meaning of Cromwell and thought that it meant an invasion had actually taken place. There is no evidence that this occurred in Worcestershire, but elsewhere bridges were blown until the misunderstandings were sorted out.

By October 1940, the Territorial Army Association had recorded a total of 19,755 men, a considerable defence force for the county and which appears to have been the peak reached. Nationally the peak was not reached until the end of 1942 at 1,850,757. That was in addition to a Regular Army of 1,500,000 men on home soil.

Members of M (Malvern) Company of the 7th Worcestershire (Malvern) Battalion Home Guard practise with one of their American water-cooled Browning machine guns at the West Malvern range. (Courtesy of Sheila Edmunds)

Large numbers of American-manufactured weapons and large quantities of ammunition came into Britain during July 1940, and were quickly distributed to the LDV. During October 1940, the Territorial Army Association was able to record that the following weapons and quantities had been issued in Worcestershire:

- Rifles .300 (this is the American P17 rifle) - 6,530.
- Rifles Ross (this is a Canadian .303 rifle) - 534.
- Rifles Private (these are likely to have been mainly the .22 sporting rifle) - 128.
- Shot guns (these will have been local weapons collected by the police) - 436.
- Hotchkiss machine guns (these were ex-World War I tank weapons) - 8.
- Browning machine guns (these were American .300 calibre weapons) - 30.
- Browning Automatic Rifles (these were American .300 calibre weapons) - 152.
- Lewis LMG (both .300 and .303, these were largely British World War I stock) - 12.

Missing off this list are 249 SMLEs and 300 P14s, all .303 calibre rifles, noted from a later list, but surely issued in 1940. The miscellany of weapons and ammunition could lead to confusion and the possibility of rifles being jammed as a result of using the wrong ammunition.

Uniforms also appeared and the quality of training improved. As winter approached a programme began of requisitioning village halls and other properties to provide lecture rooms and sleeping accommodation for men on night duty. Most of the Territorial Army drill halls in the county had already been put at the disposal of the Home Guard to provide at least some of the battalion and company headquarters, together with the established rifle ranges, both indoor miniature ranges and the outdoor full-bore ranges, to allow the opportunity for the volunteers to practise their shooting. Other rifle and grenade ranges were created by the individual Home Guard battalions themselves in suitable locations, usually the local quarry backing onto a hillside, where stray shots could be contained.

Stourport Drill Hall before its demolition to make way for new apartments. This was the HQ of the 11th Worcestershire (Stourport) Battalion Home Guard. The former PSI's house and offices, on the right, were retained in the new development

The Army Council had formed a sub-committee to deal with Home Guard affairs and, at their meeting in October 1940, noted that with the longer nights and the fact that both dawn and dusk would occur during the hours of civilian employment, the standard of vigilance maintained up to that time by the Home Guard could not be continued during the winter months. This was seen as an inevitable consequence of the principle that, except in the case of an emergency, a man's civilian employment ranked first and his military duties second.

Despite the Army Council's understanding of the difficulties being experienced by the Home Guard, a memorandum, dated 23 December 1940, was sent out from the Home Guard Zone Headquarters at the Drill Hall in Silver Street, Worcester, to all the Home Guard battalion commanders to keep them on their toes. It reminded commanders to check that sufficient men and equipment was available to mount their road blocks and that defence posts were prepared.

1941 brought further changes in the organisation of the Home Guard. This was another move by the War Office

From the winter of 1940/41, local schools and village halls were pressed into service for Home Guard instruction. Here men of the 9th Worcestershire (Redditch) Battalion appear to be intently studying map reading, judging by the map pinned to the blackboard. Such instruction would become compulsory after 1942. (Courtesy of Mr E.P. Grace via Mike Johnson)

to counteract the German accusation that the Home Guard were *franc tireurs* and not a legitimate military force and so could be shot out of hand if captured. It was decided that from 1 February, Home Guard officers should receive The King's Commission and that the establishment would be based on a conventional military hierarchy with appointments made down to Warrant and NCO ranks. For the moment, the men of the Home Guard still continued to be referred to as volunteers but that would change in due course. Medical officers were also to be appointed to each battalion and company in order to provide casualty treatment in the event of action. Local doctors were recruited to fill these posts and their involvement in the Home Guard provided a ready means of checking the seriousness of ailments put forward by individuals for missing parades. Having doctors on the staff did allow Home Guards to receive training in first aid.

Expansion of the Home Guard role and the consequential increase in administrative and training demands being made on the volunteer staff, led to the appointment of Quartermaster/Adjutants and Permanent Staff Instructors to each battalion. These full-time appointments were made from Regular Army staff, with a Captain taking the first position and a Sergeant the second, although the latter would normally be made up to temporary, unpaid, warrant officer status.

In July 1941, the role of factory Home Guards was reconsidered. It was now thought that the defence for a specific factory was best achieved by cooperation in the general defence of an area. This was well illustrated in St John's, Worcester, where difficulties were being experienced in adequately manning the long outer defence line of Laughern Brook, and where it was decided that the nearby factory units should help man the line in an emergency. Nevertheless, a small anti-sabotage guard was to be maintained in each factory, should the potential for such damage warrant it.

Other tasks of the Home Guard were to guard crashed aircraft, whether British or enemy, and to apprehend and guard prisoners of war. An interesting instruction was sent out to all ranks in May of this year to the effect that German Air Force personnel had been allowed to remain at large, sometimes for several hours and within sight of troops, Home Guard and civilians. In some cases, it was claimed, they had voluntarily surrendered to indifferent bystanders. Once taken, the instruction goes on, they had apparently been treated like benighted guests rather than enemies and had been able to destroy maps and documents that would have been of great value to RAF intelligence. The instruction finishes with, 'This spirit of apathy prior to capture and camaraderie after must not be allowed to continue'. Clearly some people just did not realise that there was a war on!

The complexity of Home Guard duties, should an enemy attack be made, was expanded still further to include helping with the following:

- denial of fuel resources to the enemy,
- denial of railway locomotives and rolling stock,
- immobilisation of vessels on inland waters,
- immobilisation of motor vehicles and vehicle repair shops,
- immobilisation of telephone exchanges and wireless stations and
- destruction of carrier pigeons.

Trained Home Guards could take a Proficiency Test and, on passing, receive a Proficiency Certificate such as that issued to John Rowberry of the 62nd Mobile Company, as illustrated here. (Courtesy of John Rowberry)

As part of the Home Guard system of communications, carrier pigeons had been kept at Norton Barracks since 1940 and subsequently also at the Worcester Sub Area Headquarters in Droitwich, for use as message carriers during an enemy attack on the county. Six birds would be supplied to each Home Guard battalion for use by mobile columns in an exercise involving communications later in the war. Sadly many of the pigeons were to lose their lives or were wounded during practice flights, shot by people wishing to supplement their rations with pigeon pie. An appeal was subsequently made in the local newspapers for carrier pigeons to be spared this fate!

A wider range of weaponry was made available to the Worcestershire Home Guard during

1941, with many more American P17 rifles, making the total issued of all types now 13,647, and with more automatic weapons and machine guns which now totalled 347, including 70 Thompson sub-machine guns. A variety of grenades was also made available to supplement the very basic Molotov Cocktails. Almost 25,000 grenades of all types were issued, including the M36 or Mills Bomb, the Self Igniting Phosphorous Bomb and the Sticky Bomb. Most of these would have been thrown by hand, but two grenade launching systems were also issued to the Worcestershire Home Guard in 1941: 94 Northover Projectors and 550 rifle cup dischargers. A single flame thrower was also supplied to one lucky battalion. Another weapon issued in late 1941 that was less than welcome, was the infamous pike. Crudely formed by welding a World War I 17-inch bayonet into a length of steel tube, most were confined to the battalion stores in disgust. One of these can be seen on display in the Worcester Soldier exhibition in the Victoria Institute, Foregate Street, Worcester. The issue of the

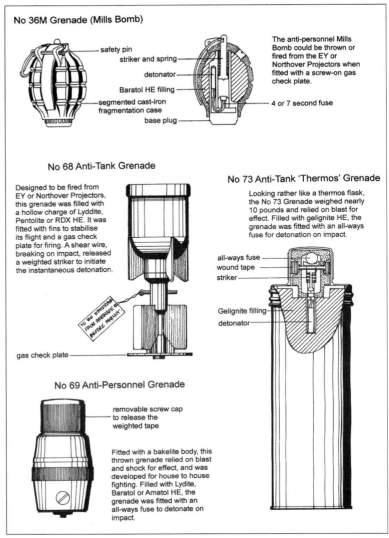

Figure 75. Grenades issued to the Home Guard (1)

Blacker Bombard or Spigot Mortar in 1941, another piece of Home Guard weaponry for tackling enemy tanks, led to the creation of more defence positions overlooking road blocks and the need for additional training. It has been said that as the Home Guard had just finished training on one weapon they were issued with another and would begin the process again. It was also said that when the Home Guard went into battle he would need a hand cart to carry all his equipment! What a contrast to the summer of 1940, when weapons and ammunition were in such short supply.

The supply of more rifle ammunition encouraged shooting competitions between battalions, including both small and full-bore, and did much to stimulate marksmanship within the Home Guard. The availability of live grenades precipitated training in their use and many Home Guards were to be made aware of the dangers of this particular activity. In fact 11 of the Worcestershire Home Guards lost their lives and 291 claims for disability were made as a result of injury, all

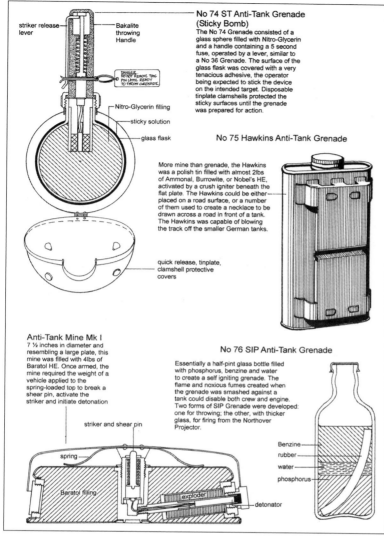

No 74 ST Anti-Tank Grenade (Sticky Bomb)
The No 74 Grenade consisted of a glass sphere filled with Nitro-Glycerin and a handle containing a 5 second fuse, operated by a lever, similar to a No 36 Grenade. The surface of the glass flask was covered with a very tenacious adhesive, the operator being expected to stick the device on the intended target. Disposable tinplate clamshells protected the sticky surfaces until the grenade was prepared for action.

striker release lever — Bakalite throwing Handle

Nitro-Glycerin filling
sticky solution
glass flask

No 75 Hawkins Anti-Tank Grenade

More mine than grenade, the Hawkins was a polish tin filled with almost 2lbs of Ammonal, Burrowite, or Nobel's HE, activated by a crush igniter beneath the flat plate. The Hawkins could be either placed on a road surface, or a number of them used to create a necklace to be drawn across a road in front of a tank. The Hawkins was capable of blowing the track off the smaller German tanks.

quick release, tinplate, clamshell protective covers

Anti-Tank Mine Mk I
7 ½ inches in diameter and resembling a large plate, this mine was filled with 4lbs of Baratol HE. Once armed, the mine required the weight of a vehicle applied to the spring-loaded top to break a shear pin, activate the striker and initiate detonation

striker and shear pin
spring
Baratol filling
exploder
detonator

No 76 SIP Anti-Tank Grenade

Essentially a half-pint glass bottle filled with phosphorus, benzine and water to create a self igniting grenade. The flame and noxious fumes created when the grenade was smashed against a tank could disable both crew and engine. Two forms of SIP Grenade were developed: one for throwing; the other, with thicker glass, for firing from the Northover Projector.

Benzine
rubber
water
phosphorus

Figure 76. Grenades and mines issued to the Home Guard (2)

attributable to Home Guard service during the period May 1940 to December 1944. Not all were caused by grenade training; accidental discharge of rifles, experiments with explosives, road accidents and heart attacks during training all took their toll. 'Easing the spring' of a rifle, to release the five rounds of ammunition from the magazine, after a stint of patrolling, seems to have been a particularly risky time and I have been told of a number of occasions when a bullet has been accidentally fired during this procedure, narrowly missing other members of the patrol. In at least two cases they didn't miss. Other Home Guards lost their lives making their way to or from duty, or while off duty. One unfortunate man of the Bromsgrove Battalion was killed by an anti-aircraft shell, while another lost his life due to enemy action, presumably in an air raid. Death or injury by your own side was a particular hazard in most rural parts of the county, where the air gunners of the RAF crews under training at Pershore and Honeybourne airfields, would be firing live at towed targets. The late Colin Curnock was one amongst several who had the experience of being out ploughing and seeing a line of machine gun bullets stitching their way across the field close by!

On 22 September 1941 shoulder flashes were added to the Home Guard uniform indicating their county allegiance — WOR for Worcestershire — and battalion number.

Up until 16 February 1942, the Home Guard was made up entirely of volunteers and an individual could leave the force by giving two weeks notice without giving any reason for wanting to do so. After that watershed date, the privilege was withdrawn as a result of the Compulsory Enrolment Order 1942. In order to keep up the numbers of Home Guards available for the multifarious roles they now had, compulsory service in the force was required for a strict number of hours of duty per week. With the change in status of the Home Guards came a change of title:

M (Malvern) Company Home Guard at grenade practice at an unknown location. It seems likely, from the nonchalant stance of those in the background, that this is some form of distance competition, with a dummy grenade. (Courtesy of Sheila Edmunds)

One of the most accessible of the former rifle ranges in the county is that on the ham at Upton upon Severn, where the butts wall can still be seen at SO 860 396. This former 1,000 yard 19th-century rifle range was reactivated by the Upton Home Guard during World War II

men were no longer referred to as 'volunteer' but 'private'. A good reason would henceforth have to be given for not serving in or for leaving the force. Before the watershed date a man could also be dismissed for not attending parades and training; after that date such behaviour would result in prosecution, a heavy fine, imprisonment, or in one instance in Worcestershire, 14 days hard labour. Such prosecutions were now regularly reported in the local press. A fine of £5 or £10 was not unusual, then a substantial amount of money.

For those earlier volunteers who did 'stick it out' compensation was payable where a loss of wages was actually incurred. This had been set at the same rate as those volunteers in Civil Defence: a maximum of ten shillings for a working day. A 'tight' administrative procedure was organised to ensure that the money was paid by the War Office, through the Territorial Association, and that there was no opportunity for fiddles!

A total number of approximately 18,500 Home Guards in Worcestershire was maintained until stand down in 1944, albeit the numbers varying from month to month.

1942 brought a further reorganisation of the Home Guard with the creation of sectors, where three or four battalions would be grouped together under a sector commander in order to provide a more coordinated response to an attack. Sector Headquarters were established in Worcester, Redditch and Kidderminster, but for operational purposes four of the county's Black Country battalions were incorporated into either Birmingham or South Staffordshire sectors.

1942 also heralded the arrival of American troops as part of the build-up to the D-Day landings — codenamed Operation Bolero — and marked the end of the period when Germany might have risked a full-scale invasion of Britain. Nevertheless, the possibility of spoiling raids to disrupt the preparations for D-Day and sabotage of key industries were still possible and the Home Guard planned their training activities around that eventuality. Now that the British Regular Army was also turning its thoughts and training towards the eventual invasion of mainland Europe, it was planned that the Home Guard should take on yet more of the home defence tasks, including that of providing some of the counter-attack forces to

The simple breach mechanism and the crude but effective back sight are apparent in this close-up of a Northover Projector designed to fire various grenades and issued to the Home Guard in 1941 as an anti-tank weapon

supplement those of No.23 ITC at Norton Barracks, the Free French OCTU at Ribbesford House and at Malvern, *HMS Duke*.

Five Home Guard counter-attack columns were formed, each to be 120 men strong, armed with one light machine gun, 6 Stens, 80 rifles and grenades. Transport would be in three Midland Red buses (five at Dudley), three lorries as load carriers and two cars. These were earmarked beforehand and for exercises, or an emergency, would be requisitioned from the owners as required. The role of the columns was to be patrolling, ambush and counter-attack within a limited radius.

1942 also saw an expansion of Army Cadet Units. These were affiliated to the Home Guard in order to take advantage of the training facilities now offered by Home Guard battalions and provide youngsters in the age range 14 to 17 with some military training before being called up or joining the Home Guard proper. Twelve new units were formed in Worcestershire with a planned establishment figure of 1,900 officers and cadets, including the pre-existing school OTCs. New units were raised in Alvechurch, Astwood Bank, Bromsgrove, Droitwich, Dudley, Halesowen, Malvern, Pershore, Redditch, Stourbridge, Upton upon Severn and Worcester. Dudley raised the

Members of the 9th Worcestershire (Redditch) Battalion Home Guard receiving a briefing for a weekend exercise from what appears to be a Regular officer. Note that some men are wearing their field service caps, while others are wearing steel helmets. This was a common practice when it was necessary to distinguish between attacking and defending forces during battle simulation. (Courtesy of Mr E.P. Grace via Mike Johnson)

largest contingent, with three companies, while the villages might manage just one platoon. Besides training, the cadets would participate in Home Guard parades and summer camps, as well as provide help, usually as messengers, for the battalion to which they were affiliated.

This year also saw the supply of the Sten machine carbines to the Home Guard but the withdrawal of the heavier, but much loved, Thompson SMG. Automatic weapons would be carried by NCOs, while the Home Guard privates would make do with a rifle. The official line was that Stens would be more appropriate in urban areas than a rifle and so the scale of issue would reflect this.

From the outset, factory Home Guards in Worcestershire had mounted one or more of their automatic weapons on the roof of their factory to form at least some anti-aircraft defence for their firm but, as part of the national policy of moving more and more defence responsibilities onto the shoulders of the Home Guard, a considerable number of members of the force were formally transferred to anti-aircraft batteries to man everything from 3.7 inch and Bofors 40 mm guns to AA rocket launchers. From the Worcestershire battalions, two LAA troops were formed at Redditch and a third in Oldbury.

With the Home Guard command structure described above and greater mobility, large scale battle exercises could now be undertaken involving a number of battalions, and 1943 witnessed a county-wide scheme. This exercise began in the evening of Saturday, 17 April and finished at mid-day on Sunday. It involved Regular troops and the Free French from Ribbesford House. Worcestershire was attacked from three directions, the principal thrusts being made against the towns of Kidderminster, Redditch and Evesham. Heavy fighting was reported around all three towns and while Kidderminster was occupied by 'enemy' troops, 'The Keep' at Evesham was held and Redditch too held the attacks apart from the loss of the outskirts of the town. After the scheme, the officers controlling expressed great satisfaction with the operations and the interest and keenness of the men, as did a number of Army commanders who had watched the battle. Apparently the umpires had been forced at one stage to separate the protagonists to stop them literally coming to blows!

A number of weaknesses in the defences were spotted and improvements identified.

Another feature of Home Guard plans for their response during an enemy attack, or more specifically, after an area had been occupied by the enemy, was for survivors to continue to carry out guerrilla attacks against the occupying forces. This policy had been advocated from 1940 onwards both officially and by former members of the International Brigade, most notably Tom Winteringham and Hugh Slater. Lord Bridgeman, who had been appointed in 1941 as the Director General of the Home Guard, also advocated a guerrilla role for the force. In 1943, however, the War Office had a change of heart and was now advising that Home Guards were not trained or

Sergeant Hill directs the catering arrangements on Malvern Link Common. This was a part of the Home Guard Third Anniversary celebrations by the M (Malvern) Company of the 7th Worcestershire (Malvern) Battalion Home Guard. Note the young man bending over the cooking utensils. He is one of the cadets who were attached to the Home Guard battalions for training and use as messenger boys. (Courtesy of Sheila Edmunds)

equipped for this role; any survivors were expected to engage the enemy and impose maximum delay with every means possible from the immediate vicinity of their defended locality. A roving guerrilla role was thought likely to have an adverse effect on the activities of the mobile field force formations conducting an organised counter-attack. There was a grave risk that if Home Guards believed they could become a guerrilla unit, the obligation to fight to the last in a defended position would not be met. One unit that ignored this advice was C Company of the Stourport Battalion, which intended to carry out guerrilla actions in the Teme valley should the area be attacked. The woodlands overlooking this area would have made at least a temporary safe haven for these men.

1943 also saw the recruitment of women in some numbers to the ranks of the Home Guard. As early as December 1940, a request had been made on behalf of the Womens Defence Corps for the enrolment of their members in the Home Guard as combatants. This had been refused by the War Office for a number of reasons, including the undesirability of competing with other forms of service for which women were more urgently required.

The enrolment of the Womens Defence Corps in the Home Guard continued to be pressed by, among others, Dr Edith Somerskill MP, and discussions continued on the basis of women being employed to carry out duties similar to those serving in the regular forces. Eventually the War Office relented and it was agreed that women could be employed in auxiliary duties of clerking, driving and cooking, a function previously undertaken by the Womens Voluntary Services, but that they should not become signallers or first aiders. No uniform was to be issued but a suitable brooch would be provided. In the event, uniforms were acquired by most of the women, in the case of June Hebden of Malvern, by tailoring her own from a man's uniform. The employment of women in the Home Guard continued to be a vexed question, even the name for them caused much debate. In the end the Director General of the Home Guard found it necessary to write to all commands to explain that the correct term was 'Nominated Women', not Women Auxiliaries or Home Guard Auxiliaries.

Despite the official edict that they should not wear uniforms or have signals or first aid roles, the Platoon Commander of the Clifton on Teme Home Guard contrived to provide his 'nominated women' with dark blue uniforms and have them practise the banned roles. Here the signallers are wearing forage caps complete with light piping and the first-aiders are wearing berets.
This photograph was taken outside the Lion Hotel at Clifton. In the back row from left to right are Mrs Winn (who instructed on first aid), Mrs Thompson, Mrs Mary Mitchell, Mrs Burford and Mrs Mabel Turner (née Millward). In the front row are Nora Sanders, Mrs Joan Warren (née Ennion), Lieutenant Henry R. Winn, Platoon Commander, Josie Thompson and Muriel Kirkman.
(Courtesy of Joan Warren)

With the continuing build-up of armaments and men in readiness for the D-Day landings in early June 1944, the possibility of spoiling attacks by German airborne troops on communications and key installations became ever more likely and the Home Guard were called upon to place a guard on vulnerable points in the county from 4 June, two days before the D-Day landings. The Teme railway bridge, at Bransford and the Colwall Tunnel were considered to be vital points on the railway system to the south-west ports and had a 24-hour guard.

Even greater mobility was now envisaged for the Home Guard and a massive RASC affiliated mobile column of battalion size was organised and based in the Moseley area of Birmingham, commanded by Lieutenant Colonel A.V. Parsons. Called the Warwickshire Home Guard Transport Column, with a compliment of 815 men, 72 of the them had been transferred from transport columns of the 1st Worcester and 12th Dudley Home Guard battalions. Arrangements for how this large, and possibly unwieldy column, was to be assembled and moved into battle have not yet been discovered. In addition to this loss of men, difficulty was experienced in some of the county units of maintaining numbers due to the transfer of men to anti-aircraft units.

The success of the allied armies in France, and an indication that an end to the war was in sight, led to calls in the Press for the Home Guard parades to be wound up. On 6 September, Sir James Grigg, Secretary of State for War, broadcast a statement that compulsory parades would cease after Sunday, 10 September, whilst paying tribute to this unpaid army of almost two millions that had kept the base safe while the allied invasion forces were being assembled.

The Worcestershire Sub District War Diary noted that it was not an exaggeration to say that the actual instructions were received with general consternation by the majority

Camping gave Home Guards an opportunity to leave their work and cares behind for a few days and concentrate on training. The location and date of this camp of M (Malvern) Company Home Guard has not been identified but the landscape suggests that it was close to the West Malvern rifle range. (Courtesy of Sheila Edmunds)

of Home Guards, certainly 75%, and were considered to be premature as well as being promulgated and drafted in a most unfortunate manner. Special exception was taken of the order to return clothing and boots. This parsimonious act was later rescinded and the men were able to keep their boots and uniform, apparently after intervention by Winston Churchill.

The Worcestershire Home Guard ceased operational duties on 11 September and guards were withdrawn from all Vulnerable Points. The Folly Point Aqueduct was considered to need a guard for a further ten days and so the Vulnerable Points Police (CMP) were called upon to take on the task. Telephones at all Sector and Battalion Headquarters ceased to be manned.

Apparently every weekend in September showed strong attendance at rifle competitions, as ammunition so painfully short in the early days, was now blasted away. The classification of signallers and motor cycle trials carried on in one last burst of enthusiasm before instructions were received to hand in all equipment, weapons and ammunition at the end of the month.

The instructions for the Home Guard to stand down were received on 1 November and arrangements made for final parades by each battalion of the Worcestershire Home Guard on Sunday, 3 December, a day that turned out to be a wet and grey, matching the mood of many of the participants; there is one instance recorded in Worcestershire of a man becoming so depressed

as to commit suicide. Many wanted to continue the friendships and camaraderie that had built up in the four years of its existence and associations were formed throughout the county to maintain the spirit of the force.

A history of the Evesham Battalion lists 4,273 men having served in that battalion which had an average strength of over 2,000 men at any one time. If this can be taken as a reasonable measure then it is likely that something over 40,000 men passed through the ranks of the Worcestershire Home Guard during the war. Many fell by the wayside as a result of reaching the upper age limit of 65, while others fell ill, some were deemed unsuitable for soldiering, while others became disillusioned and resigned while they could before the watershed date. A good proportion, 12% in the case of Evesham Battalion, left to serve in the Armed Services.

Left: To qualify for the Defence Medal, a Home Guard had to serve for a minimum of three years, and the medal had to be claimed and proof of the period of service provided before the medal would be issued by the former Army Medal Office. Many Home Guards who qualified simply did not bother to claim the medal at the end of the war. (Courtesy of Bill Preece)

CHAPTER 12

Resistance Organisations

A small, but nevertheless significant, part of the manpower resources for the defence of Worcestershire was the GHQ Auxiliary Units, a name deliberately chosen to disguise the true nature and function of this secret organisation that was recruited during the summer of 1940 to carry out acts of sabotage and resistance against enemy invasion forces. Their call to action would come after the more conventional defences, described earlier, had failed and German forces had occupied at least part of the county.

The Mercian Maquis, published by Logaston Press in 2002, provides a detailed consideration of Auxiliaries in Herefordshire and Worcestershire but this volume gives the opportunity to add the results of subsequent research and bring the story up to date.

To explain the thinking behind this clandestine force it is necessary to go back to the experiences of British officers fighting the Boers in South Africa at the turn of the century, then the use of Arab irregulars by T.E. Lawrence against Turkish forces in the Middle East during World War I, followed by the campaign against the Irish Republican Army between the two wars. General Ironside had had experience of fighting in Russia during the ill-fated allied intervention at the end of World War I and had no doubt become aware of the Bolshevik partisan units used in that particularly vicious civil war. Another of the officers who had had experience in Russia and later in Ireland was Captain Colin McVean Gubbins, who by 1940 was a member of Section GS (R) of Military Intelligence that, together with Section D, had been studying guerrilla and sabotage warfare, the former organisation dealing with the theoretical aspects, the latter with technical matters.

At least a part of the inspiration for forming resistance groups inland of the coastal areas came from General Andrew Thorne, who was responsible for the defence of Kent during the summer of 1940. He thought that if he was pushed back by the enemy to the GHQ Line where he would make a stand with whatever reserves he had available, any delay or interference by irregulars operating against German supply routes and concentration areas would, however limited, improve the chances of repelling the attack.

In July 1940, when an invasion of Britain seemed most imminent, Gubbins was promoted to the rank of Colonel and briefed to recruit, train and supply small groups of civilians in rural areas

Taken on the steps of Coleshill House on 28 January 1942, this photograph shows the Intelligence Officers and Training Staff of the time. Captain Todd, who had recruited most of the Auxiliaries in Worcestershire, had gone by this date, to be replaced by Captain Sanford of Eye Manor in Herefordshire. He can be seen in the back row wearing the Field Service cap. To the left of him is Anthony Quayle. The Commanding Officer is now Colonel Major, in the centre of the front row, who has replaced Colonel Gubbins. The second in command is Colonel Beytes, to his right, and Major Petherick MP, in charge of Special Duties Section, is to his left. The two ATS officers, Barbara Culleton, in the second row, and Beatrice Temple, front row, were both of Special Duties Section. (Mick Wilks collection)

to become a resistance force that would 'stay behind the enemy lines' and carry out acts of sabotage against the enemy forces, gather intelligence on those forces and by various means make the information known to the more conventional forces attempting to hold up and defeat the enemy. After an initial and very short period in London, a secure headquarters and training facility for the new force was established at Coleshill House, near Swindon, in Wiltshire. Here, the spacious grounds provided the opportunity for intensive training and the high wall around them security from prying eyes. Officers of the training staff were accommodated in the big house, while other ranks and Auxiliaries under training were accommodated in the outbuildings.

Colonel Gubbins left Coleshill in late 1940 to take control of the newly formed Special Operations Executive (SOE) and was replaced by Lieutenant Colonel Major. He was to be replaced by Colonel, The Lord Glanusk in February 1942, with Colonel Douglas replacing him a year later and serving until the Auxiliaries were stood down in November 1944.

With the influence by General Thorne and Colonel Gubbins, and the support of Winston Churchill, the GHQ Auxiliary Units seem to have become an integral part of Ironside's defence plans for Britain and it is interesting to analyse their role and location in relation to the more conventional defences being constructed. Given a lengthy coast-line to be defended by a thinly stretched element of the Field Force, Ironside was relying on the inland stop lines to help delay the invading forces, most notably the GHQ Line, sited inland and parallel to the east and south coasts. The majority of Auxiliary patrols were therefore recruited and based in the area between the coast and the GHQ Line where they would have conducted sabotage attacks on German preparations for advancing inland, once a lodgement on British soil had been achieved by the invading troops. The sabotage would have occurred at night using explosives to destroy fuel stores, ammunition dumps, tank laagers and lorry parks to disrupt the preparation for further attacks. At the same time information would be passed to the British command as to the type and disposition of German Forces. It was never intended that the Auxiliary patrols would confront the German forces but would carry out their operations covertly. However, Winston Churchill, who was always an advocate of irregular warfare, was insistent that the Auxiliaries be well-armed should they be caught in the act of sabotage or out in the open.

The possibility of an enemy attack against the South Wales coast and a thrust into the West Midlands, in order to pinch off the supply of armaments to the Home Forces from the factories in that area, led to the recruitment of Auxiliary patrols along, and just inland, of that coastline, along the west side of the Bristol Channel and the Severn Estuary and then into the Wye and Severn valleys. Patrols recruited in the counties of Herefordshire and Worcestershire are the most inland of the GHQ Auxiliary Units and represent further evidence of the importance attached by General Headquarters to the protection of the vital war industries of the West Midlands.

To help Colonel Gubbins recruit, supply and train the Auxiliary patrols, 12 Intelligence Officers were appointed, with Captain John Todd being made responsible for Area 19, incorporating the counties of Worcestershire, Herefordshire, Monmouthshire and Glamorganshire. Evidence suggests that Captain Todd approached the LDV/ Home Guard commanders in the area in order to identify potential patrol leaders who, once recruited, would be given the rank of sergeant and in turn asked to recommend and recruit the remainder of their patrol that would number six or seven men. All the Worcestershire recruits had already enrolled in the LDV/ Home Guard when asked to volunteer for Auxiliary service, and so had already been approved by the police as upright citizens.

Geoff Devereux, formerly of Broadheath, was probably the first patrol sergeant to be recruited in

Geoff Devereux, former sergeant of 'Samson' Patrol, later in World War II as a newly commissioned 'one pip wonder' in an anti-tank regiment of the Regular Army. (Courtesy of Geoff Devereux)

Broadheath Scout Hut prior to World War II being painted by some of the scouts and later members of 'Samson' Patrol. Geoff Devereux is on the ladder, Rob Boaz at the bottom of the flagpole, Ron Seymour standing in front of the window and Arch Clines on the roof. Only the yew tree remains to be seen by Broadheath Common. (Courtesy of Geoff Devereux)

Worcestershire during the late summer of 1940. He was a 17-year-old King's Scout, and working for the Meco Company in St John's, when contact was made with him by Captain Todd. After swearing on a bible that he would abide by the Official Secrets Act, Geoff was asked to recruit and lead the local patrol. He chose young friends who, with one exception, were from the Broadheath Scout Troop. They were duly sworn in and made aware of the seriousness of the undertaking. John Todd had made it very clear that their life expectancy, if the Germans came, was about 15 days! The patrol established their first headquarters in the scout hut at Lower Broadheath where they received their initial training. It was here that John Todd introduced them to the then new Plastic explosive and to demonstrate its relative ease of handling he flung a handful against the hut wall. Without a detonator fitted it was quite inert but the patrol members may not have known this!

John Todd informed Geoff Devereux that he would be provided with an underground Operational Base or OB and was asked to choose a suitable site. Geoff was a little dubious about using an OB which might prove to be something of a trap for the patrol should it be discovered. Nevertheless John Todd insisted and a site was chosen in the centre of Sneyds Coppice, on the north side of the A44 between Cotheridge and Broadwas. Regrettably, most of the coppice was cleared some years ago and the OB destroyed. The location was chosen as it was intended to carry

206

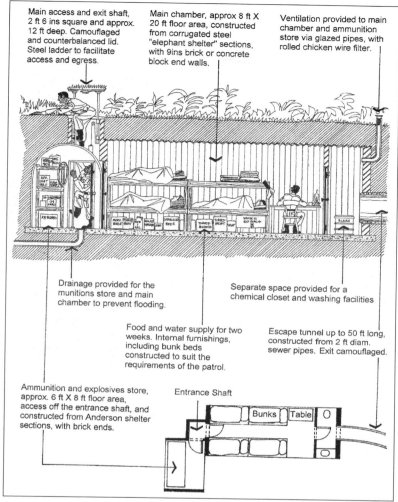

Main access and exit shaft, 2 ft 6 ins square and approx. 12 ft deep. Camouflaged and counterbalanced lid. Steel ladder to facilitate access and egress.

Main chamber, approx 8 ft X 20 ft floor area, constructed from corrugated steel "elephant shelter" sections, with 9ins brick or concrete block end walls.

Ventilation provided to main chamber and ammunition store via glazed pipes, with rolled chicken wire filter.

Drainage provided for the munitions store and main chamber to prevent flooding.

Separate space provided for a chemical closet and washing facilities

Food and water supply for two weeks. Internal furnishings, including bunk beds constructed to suit the requirements of the patrol.

Escape tunnel up to 50 ft long, constructed from 2 ft diam. sewer pipes. Exit camouflaged.

Ammunition and explosives store, approx. 6 ft X 8 ft floor area, access off the entrance shaft, and constructed from Anderson shelter sections, with brick ends.

Entrance Shaft

Bunks   Table

Figure 77. A Worcestershire-style auxiliary patrol operational base

out sabotage operations against German forces using the western approaches to Worcester, primarily along the A4103, A44 and A443, but most importantly along the railway in the Teme valley.

From Geoff's description of his OB and the remains of two others, there are sufficient details to produce Figure 77 showing an OB in use. The Sampson Patrol OB was built very quickly by a platoon of 'sappers' and Pioneers from Scotland, specifically so that they would have no local knowledge or contacts. They were briefed to tell any inquisitive locals that they were examining possible sites for anti-aircraft guns. This was a common cover story used by Royal Engineer squads constructing OBs elsewhere.

A few days after choosing his OB site, Geoff was on his way to Coleshill, near Swindon, for training in the use of explosives, sticky bombs, phosphorous grenades, booby traps and field craft. After returning from his trip to Coleshill, Geoff was taken to his now completed OB and was very impressed with the standard of construction and the efficient camouflage. His earlier misgivings about the OB were now mollified and the six members of his patrol could now live in the OB at weekends, and sometimes during the week, when they would practise night attacks on vehicles and laagers. As a cover, they were dressed in their Home Guard uniforms and

Left: Bernard Lowry climbing down into the entrance shaft of 'Jehu' Patrol's underground OB on a wet day in 1999

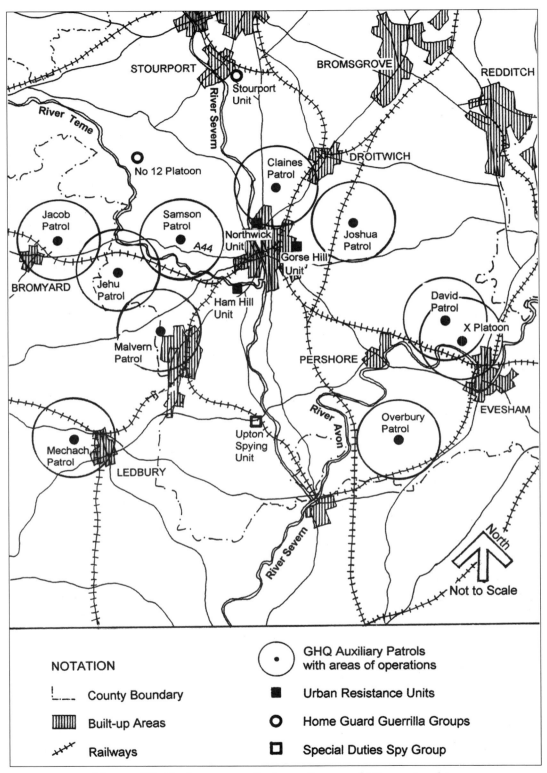

Figure 78. Resistance units in and around Worcestershire

told the locals that they were a Boy Scout unit to be trained along the lines of the original Baden-Powell Army Scouts to carry messages, and this was apparently accepted.

In the event of an invasion, Geoff would receive the simple message that 'the balloon has gone up' and would then gather his patrol together at the OB. There they would stay, carrying out their nocturnal sabotage attacks on enemy forces until they were caught or they ran out of explosives. Their main attacks would be made against enemy tank laagers and vehicle parks and the railway line into Worcester. Potential laagers and parks, including road lay-bys and wide road verges were identified and recce'd in order to work out times needed on the delay fuses to give themselves time to get back to their base before the explosives were detonated.

The above is but a brief description of the establishment of the first of the Auxiliary patrols to be recruited in Worcestershire and its preparations for the invasion. This process was repeated with the patrols established near Alfrick, Claines, Crowle, Evesham, the Lenches, Malvern and Overbury. The majority of the patrols were given a code name based on a biblical character and this theme seems to have been chosen by John Todd to give the patrols a degree of anonymity and avoid using an identifiable geographical location.

With the exception of the Broadheath patrol, the majority of the personnel in the other Worcestershire patrols were mainly recruited from the farming community or were estate workers. Common factors in their recruitment were a keen sense of duty, an intimate knowledge of their locality and, within each patrol, loyalty to one another resulting from long term friendships. During the life of the patrols — 1940 to 1944 — the personnel changed as the regular forces claimed men, or members moved away to work elsewhere.

Since the research was undertaken for *The Mercian Maquis*, evidence of two further patrols in Worcestershire has come to light: one in the Malvern area and another associated with the BBC at Wood Norton. The former patrol was discharged as surplus to establishment in July 1941 and it has not yet been possible to track down any members of the patrol in order to determine their area of operation or role. Similarly, little is known about the BBC Patrol, which appears to have been given the name X Platoon rather than a biblical name and was also short-lived. The location of the patrols is shown on Figure 78 together with the biblical code name where known.

Initially, John Todd coordinated the activities of the patrols and arranged the training and supply of armaments and explosives, although there is some evidence that Thurston Holland-Martin also occupied a more senior position and coordinating role in the Worcestershire Auxiliaries organisation, as well as being the Overbury Patrol Sergeant. Overbury Court and estate certainly became the focus for meetings and training for the Auxiliaries from the early days of their existence until Thurston Holland-Martin moved to South Africa. In 1941, two diamond merchants of Dutch ancestry were recruited to the Auxiliaries by John Todd and were to become Group Commanders tasked with administering the Worcestershire patrols. How the van Moppes brothers, Lewis and Edmund or 'Gug', as he was known to the Auxiliaries, came to be in Worcestershire is intriguing.

A number of sources indicate that the two brothers were instrumental in retrieving the stock of Dutch industrial diamonds before the invading Germans captured Amsterdam in May 1940. Having brought the diamonds from Amsterdam, it made good sense to have the location of the two brothers and their business as far away as possible from the British coastline, where raids and reprisals by enemy agents would be less likely or practical. Having moved from London, they took up residence at Yewtree House, at Ombersley, and re-established their business at Lower Wolverton, near Peopleton. Here, at Wolverton Hall, the diamond processing was carried out in the big house and outbuildings, employing local people on the production work. The location of the business close to the war materials manufacturing industries of the West Midlands must also have been a factor in their coming to Worcestershire. The brothers were given the code names Castor and Pollux — the heavenly twins of mythology — during their Auxiliary service, but it is possible that these code names were the product of their earlier clandestine operation for MI6 to secure the Dutch diamonds.

Officers and NCOs of the Worcestershire Auxiliary Patrols in 1944. (Courtesy of John Fernihough)
Back row, left to right: Sgt John Wythes ('Joshua' Patrol), Sgt Dick Philips (Claines Patrol),
Sgt Alec Fernihough ('David' Patrol)
Middle row, left to right: Cpl Ivor Thomas ('Joshua' Patrol), Sgt Basil Tadman
(Overbury Patrol), Sgt T.C. Dawe (QMS), Cpl Vincent Poland (Claines Patrol),
Cpl Harry Curnock ('David' Patrol)
Front row, left to right: Sgt Val Clines ('Samson' Patrol), Lt Edmund van Moppes (Group
Leader), Capt Lewis van Moppes (Group Leader), Lt Roger Smith (Group Leader),
Sgt George Dalley ('Jehu' Patrol)

Captain Todd left the Auxiliary Units and transferred to the Special Operations Executive in early 1942 to deal with aspects of the invasion of the island of Madagascar, moving to South Africa in order to arrange the surrender of the Vichy French forces on the island. Captain Christopher Sandford of Eye Manor in Herefordshire became the replacement Intelligence Officer until 1943, when Captain Lloyd Bucknall RA took his place. Probably before John Todd had left the area, Lewis van Moppes was promoted to Captain and became the senior Group Commander in the Worcestershire Auxiliaries and took over much of the responsibility of coordinating,

Wolverton Hall, wartime base of the van Moppes diamond processing company and headquarters of the auxiliary patrols in Worcestershire. (Courtesy of Susie Elliot)

supplying and training of the patrols in the county. The venue for much of the local training consequently shifted from Overbury to Wolverton and some of the Auxiliaries recalled staying for weekends there while under training. Edmund van Moppes retained his Lieutenancy and became Group Commander for Group 1(a) comprising the Alfrick, Lenches and Overbury patrols, while Roger Smith, of Commandary Farm, Crowle, was promoted to Lieutenant and Group Commander responsible for Group 1(b) comprising the Broadheath, Claines and Crowle patrols.

All remaining Auxiliary units were stood down at the end of November 1944, just as quietly and secretly as they had been formed. The members of the patrols received a letter of thanks from Colonel Douglas, their last commanding officer at Coleshill, explaining that public recognition for what they had done would not be possible. A small shield-shaped lapel badge was the only other tangible memento that they received for their efforts.

No documentary evidence has yet been traced of the tactical thinking behind the disposition of the Auxiliary patrols in Worcestershire but no doubt Captain Todd would have been liaising with the military defence planners of Western Command at Chester to establish the pattern indicated on Figure 78. It is interesting therefore to compare the location of the patrols with the more conventional ground defences of the county described elsewhere in this account and speculate upon the intention behind John Todd's planning. Most immediately obvious is the relationship of the patrols to the wartime railway system. Destruction of sections of this transportation network by the use of explosives would have seriously disrupted the ability of German forces to move troops and supplies in support of further advances, particularly from the south and west. This strategy was to be successfully used later by SOE and the French Resistance to help disrupt the movement of German reinforcements and supplies to Normandy as a support to the invasion by allied forces on 6 June 1944 and in the subsequent allied advances into France.

Left: 'Samson' Patrol reunion, March 2001. Left to right: Bert Davis, former Special Duties radio mechanic at Coleshill; Geoff Devereux, the first patrol sergeant; Ron Seymour, one of the original members of the patrol; Peter Wright and John Boaz, two later members of the patrol

Junkers Ju 52 aircraft being used to transport fuel during the Balkans campaign. Similar scenes could have been re-enacted in Worcestershire, where both aircraft and the fuel dumps would have been targets for destruction in night operations of the Auxiliary patrols. (Courtesy of the late Howard Inight)

Discernible, too, is a concentration of patrols along the A44 and the Teme valley and then in an arc around Worcester city. One of the Herefordshire patrols, 'Jacob', has been added to Figure 78 to complete the pattern along the A44. All of these patrols appear to be related to the designation of Worcester as an anti-tank island and it can be deduced that the three patrols along the A44 and the railway following the Teme valley would have had the role of disrupting an attack from the west, over the Bromyard Downs and then through the 'Knightwick Gap', where both the road and the railway squeezed through the north-south line of hills that divide the counties of Herefordshire and Worcestershire. The railway has now gone as part of the Beeching cuts but the road illustrates how relatively flat is this approach to Worcester, and the most suitable route for enemy armoured columns to enter the county from the west. All other passes over the hills have both more twisting or steeper road approaches and would be more difficult for armoured vehicles to negotiate. However, it is possible to speculate that the short-lived Malvern Patrol would have had a role in covering one or other of the other approaches to Worcestershire from the west. There are a number of wooded hilltops in the area west of Malvern where their camouflaged OB may have been located, and would have provided observation posts overlooking these approaches. However, there is some hearsay evidence of an underground facility being constructed to the south of the main Worcester to Hereford road, at Storridge, a quite feasible location. The Mechach Patrol, at Ledbury, would have had a role in screening the approaches to Malvern from the southwest and is also shown on Figure 78.

Little is known about the BBC Patrol although there is some hearsay evidence that there was an OB in the woods above and behind the BBC site. It appears to be a quite likely location, but nothing has been found so far, except for a strangely isolated, and crumbling, standard Home Guard explosives store at SP 020 475, that may have some connection with the unit. Again it is possible to speculate that such a patrol would have two functions: firstly, sabotage of the BBC

The former BBC broadcasting station in the centre of the picture used to stand by the canal near Gregory's Bank. It would have had a role in broadcasting to the people of Worcester should the city have been captured by the Germans. It has now been demolished. (Courtesy of Colin Jones)

broadcasting facilities and destruction of the aerial on top of the hill to prevent the enemy using it for their own propaganda broadcasts, as had happened in Norway, and secondly observation and disruption of any German troop movements along the main Evesham to Worcester Road, the parallel railway line, and the River Avon.

Should enemy forces have reached Worcester, and the all round defences have held for even a short time, then the result was likely to be a city besieged. In these circumstances, it is easy to imagine the Auxiliary patrols in the arc around the city coming out of their Operational Bases behind the enemy forces, and helping disrupt further attacks against the city or, if the enemy chose to bypass the 'obstruction', disrupt their attacks northwards towards Birmingham and the Black Country.

In interviews, members of David Patrol, in the Lenches, have said that they had the specific task of watching Tilesford airfield, later expanded to become RAF Pershore, should the facility have been occupied by German aircraft during or after an invasion. Their task would have been to enter the airfield at night and sabotage parked enemy aircraft. It is likely that the Claines Patrol would have had a similar role in connection with Perdiswell airfield. This sort of action could have had a serious delaying effect on the re-supply of German forces preparing for an attack further north towards Birmingham and the Black Country.

Special Duties Section

Another, and perhaps more secretive, organisation was recruited in 1941 and known as Special Duties Section. This was another of those innocuous names chosen to disguise the true function of the force. It was also based in Coleshill and headed by Major Maurice Petherick MP, assisted by a team of Intelligence Officers and Royal Signals men. These Intelligence Officers generally operated separately from the officers attached to the GHQ Auxiliary Units although, exceptionally, it appears that Captain John Todd dealt with both aspects of recruitment and training in the South Wales, Herefordshire and Worcestershire area.

Special Duties Section established a pattern of civilian spies who, like the Auxiliaries, would be activated when an area had been occupied by enemy forces and would operate in generally the same areas as the Auxiliaries, along the south and east coasts, the South Wales coast and up into Herefordshire and Worcestershire. The spies would note down details of German units, their strength and locations on rice paper, a material which could be eaten should an operative be caught by the enemy. These messages would be left in 'dead letter drops' where they would be picked up by a relay of civilian message carriers or couriers and eventually arrive in the hands of a civilian radio operator, who would then transmit the contents to a hidden Control Zero Radio Station, normally manned by ATS radio operators. These girls would, in turn, transmit the information on the more powerful Army No.17 R/T sets to the local Army Command.

Evidence of a spy ring run by the local coal merchant, Edgar Gurney, has been received for the Upton area with a dead letter drop located at Pool House, on the Hanley Road out of the town, while in Worcester half a dozen post office men were recruited as message carriers. Evidence of the complimentary radio stations in south Worcestershire has not so far been discovered. Fortunately, the late George Vater, a retired farmer formerly living in the vicinity of Abergavenny, has provided written testimony of how the Special Duties operatives were organised in that area.

The No.17 radio operated by Special Duties Section ATS operators from their 'Control Zero' underground stations. This set is displayed at the Parham Museum of British Resistance in Suffolk

This provides a model of how the system would have worked elsewhere.

He was secretly recruited, apparently by Captain Todd, as a message carrier responsible for getting messages to the Reverend Sluman, the vicar at Llantiilio Crossenny, who had his radio hidden under the church altar. George was one of a team of half a dozen men who would collect information and deliver it to the vicar. George's dead letter drop was a split tennis ball hidden in nettles at the base of a yew tree, other field post boxes in his area included a loose stone in the wall at Llanddewi Church and a loose board in a barn door at Llanarth. The Reverend Sluman's radio messages were picked up by a Control Zero Station on the nearby Blorenge hill for onward transmission to Western Command.

Miss Edwina Burton, now living in Malvern, but one of the 'Secret Sweeties' as the ATS radio operators were rather disparagingly called, recalls spending a fortnight practising transmitting with her No.17 set from an underground Control Zero Station that apparently still exists on a wooded hillside overlooking the A20, near Harrietsham, in Kent. Here the brick-built structure was accessed via a vertical shaft and appears to have been similar to an Auxiliary Operation Base in its form and construction. Miss Burton had received her training as a radio operator at Coleshill but had, at the time, been billeted at nearby Hannington Hall.

Although no direct evidence of a Control Zero Radio Station has so far been discovered in Worcestershire, it is likely that one or more of the Regular Army radio stations in the county would have had a stay-behind facility. Candidates for one of these might well have been the signals unit operating the Pulley Lane Wireless Station at Droitwich. It is significant that an underground OB-like structure was discovered in the Ladywood area, to the south of Droitwich and about a mile to the west of the Pulley Lane site.

The radio station, provided by the BBC, in a wooden shed beside the canal near Gregory's Bank, was apparently to have had a role in broadcasting to people in the locality after Worcester had been captured by the Germans, and it is possible that another wartime radio station in the back garden of a house in Malvern Road, St Johns, would have had a similar function. Whether these were associated with Special Duties Section has yet to be established.

Since the *Mercian Maquis* was written, another scrap of evidence has been unearthed which may have some significance, when and if further pieces of the jigsaw are discovered. Part II Orders for the 11th Worcestershire (Stourport) Battalion Home Guard indicated that in December 1941, Lieutenant A.L. Thomas was to be made up to Major and posted to Special Duties at Battalion

Headquarters. Later a Private H.J. Lewis was made up to Sergeant and again posted to Special Duties. This may have some connection with hearsay evidence that there was a clandestine unit operating on Hartlebury Common.

Although not part of the Auxiliary Units, and much against the advice of the War Office, No 12 Platoon of C Company of the 11th Worcestershire (Stourport) Home Guard were intending to undertake what is described as a guerrilla role in the Company History, written by the Company Commander, Major Ashton. Since this platoon was responsible for the defence of Ham Bridge, on the River Teme, and would take up their guerrilla activities only after the bridge defences had fallen, it is possible to speculate that their area of operations would be along the Teme valley where the woodlands would have provided the opportunity to hide. This might also explain the presence of an 'air raid shelter' overlooking the point where the Worcester to Leominster road passes through the Abberley Hills. This underground structure has many of the features of an Auxiliary-style OB.

Major Arthur L Thomas was ostensibly the Commander of A Company of the 11th Worcestershire (Stourport) Battalion Home Guard, but was appointed to 'Special Duties' in December 1941. Was he the leader of the clandestine unit said to operate on Hartlebury Common? (Photo: The Worcestershire Regiment Museum)

Sites of Auxiliary-like OBs have been recorded in the area of Worcester although none exist now. These structures had no relationship to the Auxiliary patrols that are known and described above. Recent contact with a former Worcester Royal Grammar School OTC Cadet, who wishes to remain anonymous, has now provided an explanation and identified another OB location on the north-east slopes of Gorse Hill. His account reveals the presence of an entirely separate resistance organisation from the Auxiliary Units, recruited and trained in the Worcester area in readiness for occupation of the city by enemy forces. Our contact was 14 years old when recruited, with three other cadets, to join a resistance organisation to operate in the east of the city, should the area have been occupied by the Germans. They were recruited at the school by three Army officers who had no insignia on their uniforms and could have been either Regulars or Home Guard. For their parents, or anyone else who might ask, they were to say that we were now Home Guard Messengers. (Cadets were recruited for this purpose and it would have been a reasonably good cover for their future activities.) They were ordered to report, after dark, to a certain location in Tolladine on the east side of Worcester, where they were met by two NCOs in battledress but again with no insignia. These men were of mature years, particularly hard characters and not local to Worcester. No proper names were ever used and the boys were trained by these men to carry out acts of sabotage and resistance working alone, or at most in pairs.

The boys were shown their underground OB, located on the north-east side of Gorse Hill. It had one room and was crudely constructed with railway sleepers and only a bucket in the corner for their most basic needs. Grenades and explosives were stored in a cupboard but there was little food since their life expectancy, should the Germans come, was expected to be very short; 72 hours at most. The weapons supplied were very similar to the Auxiliaries but the addition of a Vickers machine gun and later a Bren, suggests that the boys' handlers were Regulars.

Most of the training was conducted at night and would include setting trip wires, arranging ambushes and stalking the enemy. Some of the schemes for despatching the enemy were just too horrific for our contact to relate.

The Gorse Hill patrol was stood down in 1942, when their Sergeant told the boys that it was finished. Our contact considered that the two years of intensive training ruined his education and took away his youth. Subsequently, he joined the Army and served in an airborne unit. He has since been back to Gorse Hill to find his OB but it has gone and the area now developed with housing.

With the known location of OBs at Powick, Old Northwick Farm and now Gorse Hill, it is reasonable to speculate that these patrols would have operated in the suburban areas of the city, between the outer defence line and the inner defences described earlier. But just how much wider did this sort of urban resistance organisation spread in the county and further afield?

The Worcester contact's experience has certain similarities to an account given by a former Birmingham Home Guard corporal. He was introduced to a Lieutenant who asked if he was interested in joining a special unit called 'X Branch', which would require extra training. He was taught how to make up demolition sets using multiple No.73 Grenades, the manufacture of his own explosives, the setting of booby traps and the skills of dirty fighting, including the use of a knife.

Apart from occasional contact with the Lieutenant he was expected to train and operate alone and generally keep a low profile within his more general Home Guard duties. He did not know of anyone else who was recruited by X Branch, although he thought there must have been others in his area. Information was only divulged on a 'need to know' basis.

The reference to X Branch is intriguing, especially since the Auxiliaries at the BBC Wood Norton were X Platoon. It is also significant that the travelling training wing from Onibury Home Guard School was X Wing. This tends to suggest that arrangements for some elements of the resistance in the Midlands may have been organised from within Western Command, despite the War Office attitude towards guerrilla activity by Home Guards, and was therefore a local initiative. It is entirely possible that X Wing was the equivalent of the Regular Army Scout Patrols used elsewhere in Britain to train irregulars.

Another piece of evidence for urban saboteurs and assassins came to light, after the *Mercian Maquis* was written, from a contact in the Black Country. The man involved is no longer alive but he had been enrolled to assassinate collaborators after the area had been occupied by the Germans. His method was to use a slow-acting poison, administered by syringe. The syringe would be hidden in his gloved hand and would be injected while the victim's attention was distracted. All the victim would feel was a slight pin-prick and would die later of an apparent heart attack. Since this sort of method has been used post-war by some East European agents, it is entirely feasible.

The conclusion to be reached from the foregoing is that the web of resistance workers recruited and trained ready for the occupation of Britain by German forces is wider than hitherto thought, and that the urban recruits would be working in an entirely different, more solitary way to the team working of the GHQ Auxiliaries. While the latter force was primarily recruited from the Home Guard and would be initially administered locally by the Territorial Army Association, in Silver Street, Worcester, through the appropriate Home Guard companies, the urban equivalents seem to have been deliberately kept in the dark about the identity of their handlers. This suggests that they may have been organised by British Intelligence, and administered and trained by the Regular Army. The truth will possibly never be known but it does help explain the presence of hidden arms caches and unaccounted for OBs being recorded in the county. Military Intelligence certainly had a hand in establishing arms dumps in south-east England before the Auxiliaries were recruited and it is feasible that similar arrangements were made in the Midlands.

Conclusions

Some say that if the Germans had invaded Britain immediately after Dunkirk, then it would have been a walkover. This is as much as anything a product of German propaganda films portraying their apparent invincibility. It is a common 'what if' scenario and many books have been written about the possibilities; some concluding that an invasion would have been successful, others that it would not! I am sure that the subject will keep writers speculating for evermore, but there are some indisputable facts that more recent academic studies press home.

Firstly, the enemy would need to gain air superiority over the British Isles during the air Battle of Britain before an invasion could be commenced. That was never achieved, although it was close to being so over the south-east of Britain in early September 1940. From that point on, the RAF gained strength and Beaverbrook's Ministry of Aircraft production out-performed the German aircraft industry in the production of new aircraft and the repair of damaged ones. Worcestershire made an indirect contribution to that defence by the widespread involvement of the factories here in aircraft component and armaments manufacturing.

Secondly, the Germans needed to assemble an invasion fleet to carry their tanks, guns, troops and horses across the tricky Straights of Dover, or elsewhere for diversionary attacks, but it was late September before the Kriegsmarine managed to assemble a barely adequate fleet of mainly river barges in the channel ports for the purpose. When loaded, these shallow draught vessels would have very little freeboard and would require the English Channel to have been like a mill-pond to have stood a reasonable chance of making it across. How often does that happen in the channel? Most of the barges would have to be towed in groups of up to three, at a speed as little as three or four knots, and so they would be very unwieldy in the slightest swell. It was said at the time, by some of the German senior staff themselves, that Ceasar's invasion fleet two thousand years before had travelled faster! A surprise landing would therefore have been impossible, since the few knots that the majority of the shipping was capable, would have resulted in them spending all night travelling to the landing beaches to make a dawn landing. The British warship fleet available in the English Channel ports alone far out-numbered the whole of the German surface fleet that had been considerably reduced in the Norwegian campaign. The Royal Navy would not even have had to fire at the barges; a quick dash alongside them, during the night, would have been quite sufficient to have capsized any number of them.

Thirdly, had a landing been achieved, re-supply of the invasion troops using the remnants of the barge fleet would have been difficult, if not impossible, given the vicissitudes of the English Channel in the late summer and early autumn. Using the slow barges for re-supply would probably not have kept up with demand anyway. Re-supply from the air may have worked for a while but we have seen that the Germans lost two-thirds of the Junkers Ju 52 transport aircraft participating in the attack on Holland. With the obstruction of all landing grounds, it is likely that the pilots would have put down their aircraft come what may, as they had in Holland, and the attrition rate would have been considerable. The Auxiliary Units would have added their skills in disabling aircraft to increase the tally, and the German stock of transport aircraft would have been quickly used up. An enemy landing in Britain was in fact the subject of a war game at the Royal Military Academy, Sandhurst, in the early 1970s. Involving former senior military figures from both Britain and Germany, the outcome was just as described above with the loss of the majority of German paratroops and ground troops that had made the initial landing. Only a few would have escaped.

Despite the theories, had a successful landing been achieved in September and armoured columns had indeed found their way inland, they would have met the web of defences organised first under General Ironside's and then under General Sir Alan Brooke's influence. Every settlement of size would have been a strongpoint to be overcome and the generally 'close' countryside of woods and hedgerows in Britain would have delayed any columns attempting to circumvent them. The momentum achieved by the armoured columns in Poland, the Low Countries and France could not have been achieved nor could a supply of fuel be so readily found. A virtual 'scorched earth policy' was going to be conducted by Home Forces, with petrol, food and any usable transport being denied to the Germans. Whilst German propaganda films portrayed German tanks speeding through France and Poland deliberately give an impression of invincibility; the reality was different. The majority of German troops travelled on foot, at marching speed and many of their supplies were carried by horse-drawn vehicles. The failure of the French to recognise the need to interdict the German supplies and so isolate the armoured columns was a major tactical error.

In Britain, the task of interfering with German supplies would have been a function of the Home Guard in the anti-tank islands, defended localities and centres of resistance, and especially by the Auxiliary Units in the countryside. Without fuel and ammunition, the tanks would have quickly ground to a halt and would then have been prey to tank hunting mobile columns, initially of the regular forces and later the Home Guard operating during the day, and the Auxiliary and other resistance units at night. In Worcestershire, regular troops, both of the Field Force and the static troops of the air defences throughout the county and a number of training establishments meant that the Home Guard would not have had by any means the major responsibility for defence of the county. In 1940/41 the Home Guard would have been in partnership with a very considerable body of regular forces that in total probably matched them in sheer numbers.

One of the unique defence arrangements in Worcestershire, as elsewhere in Britain, from 1940 onwards, but an element of defence missing in the rest of Europe until the Germans belatedly recruited the Volksturm in 1944, was indeed the Home Guard. The raising of such a volunteer defence force as a response to the threat of invasion, had a number of parallels throughout British history. Sadly, the *Dad's Army* series has coloured many people's opinion of the Home Guard and so comments do vary about its value: some say that they would not have coped with the German all-arms methods of waging war; others, including the Spanish Civil War veterans, thought that they would have been eminently suitable for dealing with the techniques of Blitzkrieg, especially if trained to use irregular methods of fighting. It is often not realised just what a body of experience there was within its ranks; a good percentage of them had already been 'shot over', had beaten the Germans once before, and had every intention of doing so again.

During many interviews, more than a few Home Guards have said to me that they, and the defence structures put in place, would not have been able to stop the Germans had they invaded Britain. It is likely that they were unaware of the totality of the defence arrangements in Britain, or indeed Worcestershire, and their view will have been coloured by knowledge of probably only their small part in it. Certainly, the numerous traffic control road blocks, manned by many Home Guards who have expressed this view, would not stop an armoured column for one moment, but then they were not meant to. The role of many Home Guards was primarily to deal with any Fifth Column threat and their particular lightly constructed road blocks were primarily for traffic control, but there were many other blocks that would have given the Germans, in their generally light tanks of the time, cause to stop! Any momentum that the enemy had hitherto relied upon to achieve success, would have been lost.

The Home Guard was investigated quite closely, in early 1941, by representatives of the Massachusetts Committee on Public Safety, who subsequently reported their findings to the US War Department in Washington. Their report included the following comments:

For the British, General Sir Alan Brooke had this to say: 'The Germans have developed a strategy of infiltration which results in battlefields not being confined to front lines of the opposing forces. To meet this strategy and its accompanying tactics, there must be a widely dispersed force to take the shock of the enemy's primary attacks. Consequently, the most modern defensive strategy involves just such a force as the Home Guard and its function is just as important to the organisation of the defence of a country as the functions of any of the other forces such as the regular army.'

For the Polish, an interview with Major Dowdrowsky and Colonel Torks, of Polish forces in Britain drew the comments that: 'Fifth Column activities and landing of parachute troops without opposition, which completely disrupted lines of communication and disorganised the rear of the Polish Armies, would have been minimised by the existence of such a force as the Home Guard.'

For the Norwegians, interviews of Mr Trygve Lie, General Fleisher and Major Peterson provided the view that: 'by the surprise of its initial attack on Norway, Germany was able, by the employment of very few troops, to obtain an advantage Norwegians, and the British acting with them, were never able to overcome. They seized all the aerodromes in southern and central Norway, every port, where heavy material could be landed, the termini of Oslo to Trondheim, Oslo to Bergen and Oslo to Kristiansand highroads and railways, the chief cities and most of the magazines and depots of the Norwegian Army. They seized control of the communications system of the country, including the telephone and radio. This situation created such confusion throughout the country that the Norwegian effort was paralysed. All this resulted from the effort of small numbers of German troops who could have been met successfully, particularly in the initial stages by such an organisation as the British Home Guard.' General Fliesher was part of the Norwegian Military Commission and Commander in Chief of the Norwegian forces in Britain, but before the occupation of Norway, the Commander of the Norwegian Northern Army. He was of the view that, 'had Norway had a force similar to the British Home Guard, there would have been an entirely different picture'. He believed that the Germans could not have successfully taken Norway.

For the Dutch, Captain Schoonenburg, said that: 'the German campaign in Holland was characterised by extensive Fifth Column activities, combined with such an extensive use of parachute troops and airborne forces as had never before been witnessed in warfare. The Germans were able to accomplish certain very definite military missions through the employment of these methods. In the first place they were able to seize and hold certain strategically important points, such as the Moerdyke Bridge, the Waalhaven Aerodrome at Rotterdam, etc. In the second place, they were able to create all over Holland, in the rear of the front line, so many small engagements that they prevented the Dutch reserve troops from being used as previously planned. Most of the Fifth Columnists, parachute troops and airborne detachments were ultimately wiped out by the Dutch, but the effort of one whole army corps in accomplishing this was such that it was exhausted, dispersed and could not be used as planned. Properly organised and equipped, local military units such as the British Home Guard would have prevented the Germans from accomplishing both of the above results.'

For the French viewpoint, the Committee representatives interviewed General Eastwood, General Sir Robert Bridgeman, Colonel Shortt, Lieutenant Colonel Elias-Morgan, Lieutenant Colonel Wouters and a French officer of the Division Legere Motorise (DLM), whose name was not given because his family were still in occupied France. It was recorded that 'The Panzer division, after the breakthrough, proceeded at will and without resistance all over the rear of the armies, creating a confusion and disorganisation which contributed largely to the ultimate German success. The civilian population fled in great disorder and blocked all the roads so that the defending armies were tremendously handicapped. Such a static force as the Home Guard, completely covering the rear areas would have served to eliminate these two factors which contributed greatly to the success of the German Blitzkrieg.'

As a result of their interviews, the Committee representatives reported that an analysis by the High Commands of the British and those of the invaded countries came to two conclusions: that the only way to meet the German offensive tactics of penetrating the defence with their Panzer divisions and air forces, was by the use of like forces in the 'counter-offence', and secondly, the corollary that to give the 'counter-offence' opportunity to go into action effectively, a complimentary strategically static, local defence force should be organised. In order not to disrupt production, this force must be raised locally from the producers of the country volunteering part of their free time for this service. A local force, through the use of its peculiar knowledge of the terrain, if properly instructed could be effective against the most modern German equipment. A force organised in a similar way to that of the British Home Guard was, therefore, indicated as a strategic necessity in modern warfare.

One of the significant conclusions reached by the Americans was that *they* themselves were not immune to the German weapons of sabotage and espionage — the Fifth Columnists. How better could a country be protected against these weapons than to have a force whose primary purpose is the protection of its country, and reaches into every city, town and village, into every home, office and plant? It seems that they were impressed by the Home Guard and so perhaps should we be!

What can be concluded about the Auxiliary Units and other resistance organisations in Worcestershire and elsewhere? Would they have given a good account of themselves had there been a German invasion of Britain? Winston Churchill certainly thought so, holding the view that 'these units in the event of an invasion, should prove a useful addition to Britain's regular forces …' and wished to be kept informed of progress in their formation. General Andrew Thorne, one

Some of the men of the re-constituted 1950s Home Guard. There has always been a strong shooting tradition in the county and these men of the 5th Battalion (Worcester and Malvern) were particularly successful at a Western Command competition at Altcar.
The team members from left to right are:
Back row: Major W.F. Taylor, Captain W.C. Allington, Lt C.J. Holloway and Lt R. Lunn.
Front row: Lt S.M. Guinan, Sgt H.W. Bramwell, Sgt J.L. Morgan and Sgt J.A. Rowberry.
Both Bill Allington and John Rowberry had also served in the wartime Home Guard.
(Courtesy of Bill Allington)

of the progenitors of the Auxiliaries, thought that if he was pushed back to the GHQ Line, any delay or interference by irregulars operating against German supply routes and concentration areas would, even to a negligible degree, improve the chances of repelling an attack.

Peter Fleming was one of the first intelligence officers appointed by GHQ with the task of forming Auxiliary patrols, in his case in perhaps the most critical area of XII Corps in Kent and East Sussex. He was of the opinion that they would have struck some useful blows before 'melting away in the white heat of German ruthlessness'. However, he found it difficult to find fault with Churchill's estimate of Auxiliaries being a useful addition to the regular forces.

The recruitment of other forms of resistance groups is puzzling in view of the War Office stance that they did not advocate Home Guard guerrilla activity. Nevertheless, there is good evidence that such groups and individuals did exist in Worcestershire and, it has to be assumed, elsewhere in Britain. Who recruited them is still a mystery, but their existence was, perhaps, indicative of the high morale that existed in some quarters at the time, with many people considering that they were going to, at least: 'Take one with them', as Churchill had advocated, and it seems, by whatever means available.

It is now generally forgotten that the Home Guard were re-activated in 1952 as a result of the perceived Eastern Block Communist threat to Western Europe, intensified by the war in Korea. Five battalions were raised in Worcestershire, of cadre strength, which it was expected could be enlarged if the threat became more intense. The possibility of guerrilla warfare was again considered and Bill Allington, who served as a company commander in this later force, recalls being approached to consider forming such a unit. This later manifestation of the Home Guard was stood down in 1956, but the fact that it was reactivated by the government of the day, and that a resistance organisation within it was being considered again, is a clear reflection of the value put on such forces for home defence in time of threat and possibly a cause of the long-lasting secrecy surrounding the Auxiliary Units.

Appendix

War production facilities in Worcestershire, operating under the auspices of the Ministry of Aircraft Production or Ministry of Supply, and Vulnerable Points (VPs) listed by the LDV/Home Guard as being of local importance. All would require protection in the period 1940 to 1944 both as individual sites and in many cases within anti-tank island defences.

Ministry of Aircraft Production

Abbey Garage, Pershore.
Accles and Pollock Ltd, Broadwell Works, Oldbury.
Accles and Pollock Ltd, Paddock Works, Oldbury.
James Archdale & Company Ltd, Blackpole Road, Worcester.
Auto Exchange Ltd, Sidbury, Worcester.
Barnes Garage, Old Swinford.
Birmetals, Amblecote.
Birmingham Omnibus Company Depot, Bromsgrove.
Boycott Garage, Bromsgrove.
Bowman and Acock's Garage, Malvern Link.
Britannia Batteries Ltd, Lodge Road, Redditch.
British Hard Rubber Company Ltd (Morris & Yeomans), Astwood Bank, Redditch.
British Wire Products Ltd, Tenbury.
Brook Tool Company Ltd (Carpet Manufacturing Co), New Street, Kidderminster.
BSA Guns Ltd (Paragon Works), St John Street, Bromsgrove.
BSA Guns Ltd, Hurst Green, Halesowen.
BSA Guns Ltd, (W.&R.R.Adams Ltd), Birmingham Road, Kidderminster.
BSA Guns Ltd (G.K.Davies & Co Ltd), Hayes Lane, Lye.
BSA Guns Ltd, Ipsley, Redditch.
BSA Guns Ltd (Bond Worth), Severn Road, Stourport.
Central Motor Works, Farrier Street, Worcester.
Clifford Aero and Auto Ltd, Hoobrook Mill, Kidderminster.
Cross-Keys Garage, Bromsgrove.
Dyson Filling Station, Bransford.
T.A.Everton, Haulage Contractors, Worcester Road, Witton, Droitwich.
Flight Refuelling Ltd (Morgan Motor Company), Pickersleigh Road, Malvern.
George Burnham's Garage, Clifton upon Teme.
George Elt and Company, Bromyard Road, St John's, Worcester.
H.A.Saunders, Castle Street, Worcester.
Heenan and Froude, Shrub Hill, Worcester.

High Duty Alloys, Windsor Road, Redditch.
W.A.Holloway & Sons, Sidbury, Worcester.
Hull and Westwood Park Garage, Haden Hill, Halesowen.
Hurry Aero Ltd, St George's Hall, Abberley.
J.B.Brookes & Company Ltd, Barbourne Works, Worcester.
J&R Fleming Ltd, Optical Works, Littleton and Badsey Station, Blackminster.
Laughton Goodwin Garage, George Street, Kidderminster.
Lewis Spring Company, Resilient Works, Redditch.
Metal Castings Ltd, Droitwich Road, Worcester.
Midland Motors, Newtown Road, Worcester.
Modern Seamless Tube Company Ltd, No 11, Bromyard Terrace, St John's, Worcester.
Morganite Crucible Company Ltd, Norton.
Mount Pleasant Garage, Redditch.
Muller & Company (England) Ltd, Alton Works, Long Bank, Bewdley.
Myring Bros and Burton Ltd, Hewell Road, Bromsgrove.
Nife Batteries, Hunt End Works, Redditch.
Reynolds Tube Company Ltd, Studley Road, Redditch.
Rotol Airscrews Ltd, Worcester Garages, St Martins Gate, Worcester.
Semape Ltd, Red Mill House, Stourbridge.
Short Brothers Ltd (Victoria Carpets), Green Street, Kidderminster.
Stanford Court Garage, Stanford on Teme.
Steatite and Porcelain Products Ltd, Bewdley Road, Stourport.
Steatite and Porcelain Products Ltd (Worcester Porcelain), Severn Street, Worcester.
Stewarts and Lloyds Ltd, Coombe Wood Tube Factory, Halesowen.
H.W.Ward & Company Ltd, Blackpole Road, Worcester.
Webley & Scott (No 1 Factory), Hewitts Garage, High Street, Amblecote.
Webley & Scott (No 2 Factory), Vauxhall Garage, Perkfield Road, Stourbridge.
Worcester Sheet Metal Company Ltd, St John's, Worcester.
Worcester Sheet Metal Company Ltd (Ebenezer Bayliss), Redhill, Worcester.
Worcester Windshields Company Ltd, Gregory Mill Street, Worcester.
Wyatt's Garage, Rectory Road, Redditch.

Ministry of Supply
Albright and Wilson Ltd (Bond Worth Carpets), Severnside, Stourport.
Albright and Wilson Ltd (Tomkinsons Carpets), Duke Street, Kidderminster.
Baldwins Ltd, Stourvale Works, Kidderminster.
Enfield Cycle Company, Windsor Road, Redditch.
Norman Engineering Company, Millers Road, Worcester.
H.W.Ward & Company Ltd, Blackpole Road, Worcester.
ICI (Metals) Ltd (Tomkinsons Carpets), Churchfields, Kidderminster.
ICI (Metals) Ltd (Brintons Carpets), Exchange Street, Kidderminster.
ICI (Metals) Ltd (Carpet Trades), Mill Street, Kidderminster.
ICI (Metals) Ltd, Summerfield, Kidderminster.
Parsons Chain Company, Worcester Road, Stourport.
Smethwick Drop Forgings Ltd, Stourport Road, Kidderminster.
Steel Stampings, Cookley.

VPs of local importance listed by the LDV/Home Guard

Communications
BBC Transmitter, Gregory's Bank, Worcester.
Telephone Exchange, Foregate Street, Worcester.
Worcester Evening News, The Trinity, Worcester.

Public Utilities
British Camp Reservoir, Malvern.
Bromsberrow water pumping station.
Cookley water pumping station.
Elan Aqueduct, Cookley.
Elan Aqueduct, Folly Point, Bewdley.
Elbury Mount Reservoir, Worcester.
Electricity Switching Gear, Headless Cross, Redditch.
Electricity Transformer, Worcester Road, Stourport
Electricity Works, Malvern.
Electricity Works, Hylton Road, Worcester.
Foregate Street Station, Worcester.
Gas Works, Malvern.
Gas Works, Worcester.
Sewage Works, Bromwich Road, Worcester.
Waterworks, Barbourne, Worcester.

Rail Transport Infrastructure
Avon Railway Bridge, Eckington
Avon Railway Bridge, Fladbury.
Avon Railway Bridges (east and west), Evesham.
Blackminster Railway Bridge.
Fernhill Heath Railway Bridge.
Henwick Road Station, St John's, Worcester.
Hoobrook Viaduct, Kidderminster.
Lowesmoor Railway Bridges.
Railway Tunnel, between Stourport and Bewdley.
Railway Tunnel, Kidderminster.
Railway Tunnel (operational), Malvern.
Railway Tunnel, Tunnel Hill, Worcester.
Severn Railway Bridge, Dowles, near Bewdley.
Severn Railway Bridge, Worcester.
Severn Railway Bridge, Ripple.
Shrub Hill Station and Control Centre, Worcester.
Teme Railway Bridge, Bransford.

Road Transport Infrastructure

Abbey Road Bridge, Evesham.
Avon Bridge, Pershore.
Hawford Bridge, north of Worcester.
Holt Fleet Bridge.
Knightsford Bridge, Knightwick.
Teme Bridge, Powick.
Severn Bridge, Stourport.
Severn Bridge, Upton upon Severn.
Severn Bridge, Worcester.
Workman Bridge, Evesham.

Storage Facilities

Timberdine Petrol Depot, Worcester.

War Production

British Slug and Annealing Company, Brickfields Road, Worcester.
Meco Works, Bromyard Road, Worcester.
Metal Box Company, Perry Wood, Worcester.
Royal Ordnance Factory, Blackpole, Worcester.

Select Bibliography

A large number of historical documents, books, pamphlets and articles have been used as source material for this account: some to provide a context for what was happening in Worcestershire during the period 1940 to 1944, others actually identified individual sites that have been recorded by the Defence of Worcestershire Project. The list of documents was far too long to incorporate here, but the following are recommended for further reading.

Alanbrooke, Field Marshal Lord. *War Diaries 1939-1945*. (Weidenfeld and Nicolson, London, 2001)

Alexander, Colin. *Ironside's Line*. (Historic Military Press, West Sussex, 1999)

Becker, Cajus. *Luftwaffe War Diaries*. (MacDonald & Co, London, 1966)

Birt, David. *The Battle of Bewdley*. (Peter Huxtable Designs Ltd, Great Witley, 1988).

Campbell, Duncan. *War Plan UK - The Secret Truth About Britain's Civil Defence*. (Barnet Books Ltd, London, 1982)

Carpenter, J. *Wartime Worcestershire*. (Brewin, Warwickshire, 1995)

Carpenter, J. and Owen, B. *Worcester at War*. (Worcester City Leisure Services Committee and Worcester Museums, Arts and Leisure, Undated)

Chamberlain, P and Doyle, H. *Encyclopedia of German Tanks of World War Two*. (Cassell, London, 2004)

Collier, Basil. *The Defence of the United Kingdom*. (The Imperial War Museum, London, 1995)

Ellis, Major L F. CVO CBE DSO MC. *The War in France and Flanders*. (HMSO, London, 1953)

Fleming, P. *Invasion 1940 - An account of the German Preparation and the British Countermeasures*. (Rupert Hart and Davies, London, 1957)

Gaunt, H.C.A. *Two Exiles - A School in Wartime*. (Samson Low, Marston Co Ltd, London, 1946)

Graves, Charles. *The Home Guard of Britain*. (Hutchinson, London, 1943)

Hogg, Ian. *Anti-Aircraft. A History of Defence*. (Macdonald & Janes, London, 1978)

Jong, Louis de. *The German Fifth Column in the Second World War*. (Routledge and Keegan Paul, London, 1956)

Kedward, Brian. *Angry Skies Across the Vale*. (Privately published, Evesham, Undated)

Kersaudy, Francois. *Norway 1940*. (Collins, London, 1990)

Lampe, David. *The Last Ditch - The secrets of the nationwide British Resistance Organisation and the Nazi plans for the occupation of Britain 1940-1941*. (Cassel and Co Ltd, London, 1968)

Lefevre, Eric. *Brandenburg Division. Commandos of the Reich*. (Histoire and Collections, Paris, 2000)

Lowry, Bernard. *British Home Defences 1940-45*. (Osprey Publishing, Oxford, 2004)

Lowry, B and Wilks, M. *The Mercian Maquis - The Secret Resistance Organisation in Herefordshire and Worcestershire during World War Two*. (Logaston Press, Herefordshire, 2002)

Mackenzie, S P. *The Home Guard. A Military and Political History*. (Oxford University Press, 1995)

Macleod and Kelly (Editors). *The Ironside Diaries 1937-1940*. (Constable, London, 1962)

Mason, Francis K. *Battle over Britain*. (McWhirter Twins, London, 1969)

Miller. Howard. *Tenbury and District in Wartime*. (Howard Miller, Tenbury Wells, Undated but 1990s)

Osborne, Dr Mike. *Defending Britain - Twentieth Century Military Structures in the Landscape*. (Tempus, Stroud, 2004)

Oxenden, Major N.V.O. MC. *Auxiliary Units - History and Achievement. 1940-1944*. (1944, reprinted by the British Resistance Museum, Paraham)

Renier, O. and Rubenstein, V. *Assigned to Listen. The Evesham Experience. 1939-43*. (BBC External Services, 1986)

Seebag-Montefiore, Hugh. *Dunkirk - Fight to the Last Man*. (Viking, London, 2006)

Smith, David J. *Britain's Military Airfields 1939-45*. (Patrick Stephens Ltd, Northamptonshire, 1989)

Smith, J R. and Kay, Anthony. *German Aircraft of the Second World War*. (Putnam and Co Ltd, London, 1972)

Stokes, Paul. *Drakelow Unearthed*. (Self Published, Kinver, 1996)

Thomas, Hugh. *The Spanish Civil War*. (Eyre and Spottiswood, London, 1961)

Tomkinson, K and Hall, G. *Kidderminster Since 1800*. (Self published, Kidderminster, 1975)

Thompson, Melvyn. *Woven in Kidderminster*. (David Voice Associates Ltd, Kidderminster, 2002)

Trevor-Roper, H.R. *Hitler's War Directives*. (Sedgewick and Jackson. London, 1964)

Warren, Glyn. *RAF Pershore - A History*. (Enthusiasts Publications, Newport Pagnell, 1982)

Warwicker, J. *With Britain in Mortal Danger. Britain's Most Secret Army of WW II*. (Cerberus. Bristol, 2002)

Wheatley, Ronald. *Operation Sealion - The German Plan for the Invasion of Britain 1939-1942*. (Oxford University Press, 1958)

Whittaker, LB. *Stand Down. Orders of Battle for the units of the Home Guard of the United Kingdom. November 1944*. (Ray Westlake Military Books, Gwent, 1990).

Wilkinson, P. and Astley, J.B. *Gubbins and SOE*. (London, 1993)

Wilkes, Nils. *A History of Eckington*. (Self Published. Eckington, 1996)

Wills, Henry. *Pillboxes*. (Leo Cooper, 1985)

Winteringham, Tom. *New Ways of War*. (Penguin Books. Harmondsworth, 1940)

Index

(Page numbers nn italics relate to illustrations)

The Folklore of Worcestershire
by Roy Palmer

Roy Palmer presents the folklore of the county as a series of themes that embrace landscape, buildings, beliefs, work, seasons, people, sport, dance, drama and music. In so doing, ten chapters are crafted that can stand alone or be read as a whole, each full of snippets of insight into the county's past in a way that adds to anyone's enjoyment of Worcestershire. After a reading of the book, features of the landscape, for example, will appear as landmarks associated with certain folk beliefs adding to their interest and to one's own sense of 'belonging' to the county.

The volume contains a great deal of information on the various customs of the county, on its music, drama and dance, together with the cryptic and not so cryptic tales of life recorded on gravestones, as well as various spectral apparitions. In addition some 'customs' have been revived or even created, whilst others, not long re-established have once again gone out of fashion.

Roy Palmer has written on the folklore of many counties in the west midlands and along the Welsh border as well as a number of anthologies of traditional songs, and a study of songs of social comment, *The Sound of History*.

Paperback, 368 pages with over 200 black and white illustrations
ISBN 1 904396 40 2   Retail Price: £12.95

Churches of Worcestershire
by Tim Bridges

Introductory chapters tell of the spread of Christianity across Worcestershire and detail the early development of churches. The major events that affected church building in the county — from new architectural fashions to political upheavals — are detailed to provide a background to the gazetteer that follows. Likewise a history of the changes in internal layout, and in the furnishing, design, carving and stained glass is given.

The core of the book is a gazetteer to the Anglican churches of Worcestershire — some 270 in total — allowing this book to be used as a guide when exploring the county. Each entry places the church in its setting, describes the church, gives its building history and details the main decorations, monuments, glass and any notable external features such as lychgates and crosses. As such it is an invaluable aid to exploring what you are seeing — and for ensuring that you don't miss anything on your visit.

Paperback, 288 pages with over 200 black and white illustrations
ISBN 1 904396 39 9   Retail Price £14.95

Also from Logaston Press

The Mercian Maquis
The Secret Resistance Organization in Herefordshire and Worcestershire during World War II
by Bernard Lowry & Mick Wilks

For decades after the end of the Second World War little was known about the secretive organisation known as the Auxiliary Units. Formed in 1940, at the same time as the Home Guard, its members were recruited from amongst a tightly-knit farming community and from those in other reserved occupations. Organised into patrols of about half a dozen men and knowing their locality intimately, their role would have been to carry out acts of sabotage and terror behind the German invader's lines whilst the Regular Army regrouped for counter offensives.

Whilst the bulk of the patrols covered the coastal areas, this book details the Units' most inland operational area. The establishment, operation and function of the 12 patrols formed in Herefordshire and Worcestershire are fully explained, together with information on the even more shadowy world of the Special Duties spies and urban saboteurs.

From carefully camouflaged underground Operational Bases liberally supplied with explosives and arms and constructed in woodland on high ground, patrol members would have set out at night to harry the invader. This was to be done in the knowledge that they and their families risked summary execution if captured.

This book covers a period of little known local history now revealed through research of the few remaining documents and by interviewing surviving patrol members. Over a period of several years the authors have found or identified Operational Bases near Dinmore, Dinedor, Credenhill, Ross, Ledbury and Bromyard Downs in Herefordshire, and near Alfrick, Broadheath, Claines, Crowle, The Lenches and Overbury in Worcestershire.

Paperback, 160 pages, 70 drawings, plans and photographs
ISBN 1 873827 97 0   Price £7.95